THE HISTORY OF
THE SALVATION ARMY

THE HISTORY OF
THE SALVATION ARMY

Volume I
1865–1878

by

Robert Sandall

Foreword by General Orsborn

Thomas Nelson and Sons Ltd
London Edinburgh Paris Melbourne
Toronto and New York

First published 1947

DEDICATION

This first volume of the History of
The Salvation Army is dedicated
to the Glory of God
and
the memory of the company of
saints who, notwithstanding the
limitations of their humanity and
the difficulties of their circumstances, put into effect
His purposes

FOREWORD

SHORTLY after the close of the first Great War, General Bramwell Booth initiated the gathering of detailed records of the rise and development of The Salvation Army. Later his successor, General Higgins, commissioned COLONEL ROBERT SANDALL, an officer of wide experience, to write this official History.

I welcome the publication of this the first volume of *The History of The Salvation Army*. This publication we owe very largely to the personal interest of my predecessor in office, General George Carpenter, to whom I would express the deep appreciation of myself and all Salvationists.

After reading the manuscript of this volume, I wish to pay tribute to the persistent care with which the author has given himself to his task.

Much in this first volume may be surprising to many of our friends and even to Salvationists. Some of the facts revealed, and adequately verified, conflict with ideas long and widely held. For example, the History discloses that William Booth's decision, in 1865, to "give myself" to East London, was supported by a preparation stretching back many years, to which numerous persons and organizations contributed. The Salvation Army, established as a result of William Booth's historic dedication, is thus shown to be in an authentic succession of Divinely inspired efforts toward the salvation of the masses.

The Salvation Army was not planned in advance by any man or body of men. William Booth never claimed to have invented or created it ; indeed, no hint can be found that he, his devoted wife, or his zealous and undauntable followers dreamed to what they were proceeding—until they found established an Army of which they were Soldiers.

On the other hand, The Salvation Army must not be regarded as a product of eccentricity. Its establishment was not planned, but its development and organization were the subject of careful planning. In all they did, its originators had the set purpose of finding and using the best methods of reaching the people with the Gospel. They soon saw that converts must be set to work to save others, and that to do this effectively required organization. The application of this principle resulted in the survival of The East London Christian Revival Association—from among many similar missions in London's East End which have disappeared—and its eventual emergence into world-wide service to God and man as The Salvation Army.

When William Booth took the initiative, or when he and his eager followers—inspired opportunists indeed !— broke the bonds of convention, they took the new departure in their stride and marched on, recognizing in the progress made and the souls won all the proof they needed that they were being marshalled for the battle by the Captain of the Hosts of the Lord.

More than eighty years after the small beginnings of what has become a world-wide movement, may the study of its History bring to many readers a new stimulus to holy enterprise. I pray that it may serve to maintain the spirit of Salvationism : by reminding us how graciously God uses humble people; by impressing upon Salvationists in particular the need at all times for complete devotion to Christ ; and by emphasizing those principles in practical service which invariably succeed in securing the triumph of the Cross.

LONDON, *December* 1946   ALBERT ORSBORN
                                                             General

CONTENTS

APPENDICES

LIST OF PLATES

CHAPTER ONE

THE BIRTH OF THE SALVATION ARMY

ONE fine evening of June 1865 a tall, strong-featured man in ministerial garb strode along the northern side of Whitechapel Road, East London. Though a stranger to the district, and not going anywhere in particular, he nevertheless moved purposefully.

Neither the shops on the one hand, nor the motley collection of stalls and gaudy sideshows, nor even the raucous cries of the shouting cheapjacks on the other, held his attention more than momentarily. He had eyes only for the people. He saw them crowding into the beer shops and gin palaces, multitudes of them ; saw them besotted, poverty-stricken, and perishing. Yearning pity and deep concern filled his heart to overflowing. Could he not do something for these lost sheep ?

When he had got as far as the " Blind Beggar " he halted. In front of this noted Bethnal Green public house on Mile End Waste [1] a group of Gospel missioners were concluding a meeting. Their leader, as was customary, before pronouncing the benediction was asking whether any converted bystander would like to " have a word." The Rev. William Booth, for the passing stranger was none other, responded at once. Nothing in the world could, at that moment, have pleased him better.

His commanding figure and forceful words immediately challenged attention. Passers-by stopped to listen. They drew nearer. Soon a crowd had gathered. Not before had these people heard sin denounced, the love of God extolled

[1] Appendix A, Scene of the Beginning

and Salvation offered so plainly. The language used was the simple speech of their everyday life. Every point of importance, too, was aptly and clearly illustrated. They not only heard ; they understood !

One of the missioners, Alfred Agar,[1] throughout the seventy-four years between that day and his passing at the age of ninety-five, delighted to tell his friends how profound was the impression William Booth made—not least on the missioners, who whispered earnestly one to another, " This is the leader we want at the Tent ! "

Most of these missioners were members of The Christian Community, an association formed by Huguenot refugees in the seventeenth century ; others were linked with one of the many small missions established by the East London Special Services Committee, an outcome of the 1859 revival. A few belonged to other denominations. Seeking to save the lost in the seemingly godless and God-forsaken districts of Whitechapel and Bethnal Green, they were for the time being unitedly taking part in a special mission, the head-quarters of which was a tent erected on a disused burial ground belonging to the Society of Friends.

A few days after that open-air meeting, a deputation—composed of Samuel Chase and John Stabb, both members of the East London Special Services Committee—waited on William Booth to ask whether he would take charge, temporarily, of the Tent Mission. An evangelist who had been engaged had been taken ill and could not come.

William Booth decided to accept the invitation.

Twenty-four years later, when from that apparently insignificant decision had sprung the movement that already encircled the earth, William Booth declared : " While in the Metropolis, my heart grew interested in the East End. Then came the birth of The Salvation Army in the old Tent ! "

[1] Appendix B, Early Witnesses

Chapter Two

PREPARATION OF WILLIAM AND CATHERINE BOOTH

I

THE movements of God are to be seen clearly in those events in the life of William Booth which prepared him for his destiny. By these, and by his response to them, three main ends were secured : his conversion in boyhood ; his training and equipment for service by the experiences of early manhood ; in maturity, fulfilment of the Divine purpose for his life.

Catherine Mumford, who was to become William Booth's beloved partner and later to be known as " the Army Mother," likewise was providentially fitted for her life-work.

Both were born in 1829 : Catherine Mumford at Ashbourne, Derbyshire ; William Booth at Nottingham.

First in his preparation came the moment when in his youth William Booth, completing a soul-transaction that had progressed from conviction of sin through repentance, restitution, and faith, was instantly converted by the operation of the Holy Spirit. The reality and the definite nature of this experience are beyond question, and they formed the groundwork of his preaching.

The deprivations of his early life, the misery that in his boyhood he had seen around him, his memories of children crying for bread in the streets—all helped to set up in his mind the purposes that later came to such fruitful issue.

When the Rev. James Caughey visited Nottingham in 1846, his red-hot revival oratory set aflame the fire ready laid in the boy's heart, and William Booth determined that " God should have all there was " of him. With companions as youthful and as eager as himself, of whom he quickly became leader, William Booth organized street preaching, cottage meetings, and other activities. It was at this time that he marched a tatterdemalion contingent from the Nottingham slums into Wesley Chapel.

At the age of seventeen he was appointed a local preacher and on Sundays walked long distances to fulfil country engagements.

In 1848 William Booth had completed apprenticeship to a business he thoroughly disliked—pawnbroking. For a year he sought in Nottingham more congenial employment ; failing to find it, he went to London, but was still unable to obtain other work. Weak in body, engaged daily for long hours in exhausting and distasteful toil, he nevertheless gave all his Sundays and his one free week-night to his Church. He was put " on the plan," but as there were twenty preachers in the circuit, and only a trifling amount of pulpit work to be divided among them, he became impatient at having so little opportunity to preach. Single-handed, he began open-air work in the streets and on the greens of Kennington. To be free for this he tendered his resignation as a local preacher, but asked that his name should be continued on the list of members of the Church.

At this time (1851) the Reform Movement in the Methodist Church was causing acrimonious controversy. The minister of William Booth's circuit, an over-zealous anti-Reformer, jumped to the conclusion that the youth was a rebel, curtly refused his request and withheld his ticket of membership. William Booth's later comment (1889) was that the agitation had in the main concerned ecclesiastical questions for which he did not care a penny.

2

By 1844 the Mumford family had moved to London, and Catherine had joined the Brixton Wesleyan Church. Always serious-minded, she had delighted from her earliest days in religious meetings and studies. When twelve years old she was secretary of a juvenile temperance society ; she also took keen interest in foreign missions. But not until in her eighteenth year (1846) did she believe herself to have been truly converted.

The quiet routine of Miss Mumford's life was disturbed by the growing intensity of the Reform agitation. In her desire to see a revival of old-time Methodism, she had hailed this movement as making towards that end and warmly espoused the cause of the Reformers—and was likewise expelled.

No sooner had the Reformers heard of William Booth's expulsion than they invited him to join them. Prominent among them was Edward Harris Rabbits, a prosperous business man who had been greatly stirred by William Booth's preaching at the Walworth Road Chapel.

Some months after he had joined the Reformers William Booth preached at their chapel in Binfield Road, Clapham, where Mrs. Mumford and her daughter were members. Miss Mumford was greatly impressed by the sermon and by the preacher. Shortly afterwards they met at the house of Mr. Rabbits, and on several other occasions, and regard quickly ripened into affection.

William Booth's standing with the Reformers progressed until on 10th April 1852, his twenty-third birthday, he left pawnbroking to become preacher at the Binfield Chapel at a salary of £50 per year, provided by Rabbits.

A letter from William Booth to Rabbits, concerned

mainly with the negotiation of this change—found among papers left by Rabbits—reveals more clearly than does anything else extant the workings of William Booth's mind at this time. The key-note is struck in his opening passage :

In my present position I am unsettled—unhappy—my occupation is so contrary to my views that I am continually desiring something different—I feel it in my heart—on my soul from day to day that I would be a missionary of God.

But William Booth's experience with the Reformers was not satisfactory to him. Power had become vested in men who had neither spirit nor capacity to use it rightly. Before long he came to the conclusion that existing conditions were not likely to lead to the establishment of stable organization. His life would be wasted if he continued to work in such circumstances ; moreover, if he were to marry he must have an assured and sufficient income.

Then Miss Mumford suggested that William Booth might become a Congregational minister. Negotiations followed and appeared to have reached a satisfactory conclusion, indeed arrangements had been made for him to enter a training institution, when difficulty regarding the doctrine of election brought all to a full stop.

In November William Booth accepted the charge of another Reform circuit—Spalding, Lincolnshire—but he continued to feel that unless the Reform Movement became organized and set up a central authority he would have to leave it and attach himself to some Church that possessed these essentials of stability. This he found in the Methodist New Connexion, which he entered early in 1854.

His first appointment was as assistant pastor to the London circuit, Rabbits, who had followed him into the New Connexion, paying the salary of a second minister for the circuit, on condition that William Booth should be appointed to it. One of the stations of this was a small chapel in Watney

Street, Wapping. His sympathy was aroused by what he saw of the wretchedness and wickedness of the neighbourhood, but no trace can be found of any connection between his ministry here and his later being called to take charge of the Quaker Burial Ground Tent Mission.

William Booth quickly showed that he was able to stir up revival fervour and direct it to the winning of souls. When the New Connexion Conference next met (Sheffield, 1855) it was resolved that " the Rev. William Booth whose labours have been so abundantly blessed in the conversion of sinners be appointed to the work of an evangelist."

On 16th June of that year William Booth and Catherine Mumford were married. During the next two years they together conducted revivals at many places, the results proving beyond all question that they were in their right sphere. Then clouds gathered. Some of the older ministers, it is said, felt that William Booth was but young, and wondered whether so much success with its attendant popularity was good for him at the beginning of his career. Jealousy also showed its ugly head. Conference (Nottingham, 1857) decided by 44 votes to 40 that he should be withdrawn from evangelistic work and appointed to a circuit. William Booth received the decision calmly :

My concern [he wrote] is for the Connexion—my deep regret is for the spirit this makes manifest, and the base ingratitude it displays. However, I leave the matter with the Lord. My work and reputation are in His hands. I wait the manifestation of His will, and wherever He points there will I try to go.

Many of his friends urged him to break loose from the Connexion, and Mrs. Booth was inclined to favour his taking this course.

The appointment was to Brighouse, and to Brighouse they went. At Sheffield, in February, they met the Rev. James Caughey, who had passed through a similar experience with the American Wesleyan Church and had resigned rather than be confined to a circuit. But when William Booth asked his advice he counselled that he should wait patiently at least until after his ordination.

At the next Conference (Hull, 1858) William Booth was ordained. It was proposed that he should go to a circuit for another year, and that at the end of this he should be recalled to revival work by a unanimous vote of Conference ; but later it was found that the resolution that had been adopted made no mention of the stipulated restoration to evangelistic work. William Booth, not yet being a superintendent minister, was not a member of Conference and consequently was not present when the resolution was discussed.

Appointment to Gateshead followed. In the three years of his ministry there (1858-1861) William Booth was successful in lifting the circuit out of a condition of depression and waning interest to a high state of spiritual prosperity. So many sinners were brought to God that the Bethesda Chapel earned the name of " The Converting Shop."

At Gateshead Mrs. Booth began systematic house-to-house visitation in the poorer districts, devoting two evenings a week to it. She wrote a trenchant pamphlet maintaining the right of women to preach, called forth by criticisms levelled at the part taken by Mrs. Phoebe Palmer in revival services conducted by her in conjunction with her husband, Dr. Palmer.

Up to this time Mrs. Booth had not spoken in public, though she had led in prayer. Receiving an inward urge to apply the reasonings of her pamphlet to herself, she determined she would conquer her natural timidity. On the morning of Sunday, 8th January 1860, to the astonishment of the congregation, and not least of her husband, she walked up the aisle as he was concluding his sermon and told him that she desired to speak.

8

Later, when her husband was absent through illness, Mrs. Booth clinched her arguments and action by filling his appointments throughout the circuit.

At Gateshead, too, William and Catherine Booth decided that it was incumbent upon them to set forth definitely and regularly the doctrine of Full Salvation. With John Wesley they had come to the conclusion that the very object of the Atonement was the conquest and removal of indwelling evil, and that the heart could be purified from its evil tendencies which would otherwise prove too strong for it and render it the helpless prey of every passing temptation.

3

The year 1861 was critical. It brought to a definite and final head the question whether the Booths were justified in any longer allowing the prejudices of perverse persons, some of them obviously moved by unworthy motives, to deny to them the field of usefulness to which they were convinced they had been called by God and in which their work had so greatly prospered. No longer could they postpone action without disobeying the Divine will as revealed to them. Nevertheless, William Booth acted with every deference due to Conference and took pains to make it clear that he was influenced only by conviction that he must obey God.

When the question came before Conference (Liverpool, 20th May 1861) a long and vehement discussion followed. Some members argued that it was an insult to a pastor to introduce any outside agency ; others roundly denounced revivalism. It is true that some had the grace to qualify their objections by admitting that William Booth possessed exceptional gifts, though they still argued that he could best serve by labouring in a regular circuit.

William Booth was invited to read a letter that he had addressed in March to the Annual Committee. This made a good impression, and the debate was drawing to a close seemingly with every prospect of a satisfactory result, when suddenly it was proposed that as a compromise he should be appointed to a circuit with liberty to make arrangements to spend a portion of his time in carrying on revival services elsewhere. That such a course was impracticable he had proved at Gateshead, and he refused to accept the proposal. But a vote was taken before his supporters had time to recover from their surprise, and the amendment was carried by a large majority.

Mrs. Booth had been seated in the gallery at a point where she and her husband, on the floor of the chamber, could see each other. When the result of the voting was announced she rose. With determination of look and voice she exclaimed, " Never ! " At the foot of the gallery stairs they embraced and left together, their minds made up to follow their convictions regardless of the consequences.

To those who later made efforts to persuade him to accept the compromise, William Booth replied that it was in fact no compromise at all. The condition of the Newcastle circuit to which it was proposed he should be appointed was such, he knew, that its needs would require his undivided attention.

William Booth, still reluctant to take action that would finally sever him from the New Connexion, endeavoured to reach a workable compromise. He offered to forgo his salary and house in order that the circuit might be able to arrange for a supply minister and thus set him free to engage in evangelistic work as opportunity might offer. The Annual Committee, through Dr. Crofts, expressed dissatisfaction with this arrangement and pressed William Booth to take his circuit " according to the rules and usages of the

body " and " according to the resolution of Mr. Cooke."
Thus, William Booth found himself forced to resign in
order that he might be free to act in accordance with his
convictions.

When his resignation was presented to the next Conference (Dudley, June 1862) it was accepted by 56 votes
to 15. Nothing more was recorded than this bare fact.

4

The story merges into that of the attitude of the Churches
to the Revival of 1859 and the evangelistic efforts springing
from it, which brought about William Booth's call to East
London, with its astounding justification of these tedious
preparatory years and seeming frustration.

Within the intervening period (1862–1865), William and
Catherine Booth had outstanding success as revivalists in
connection with Churches in Cornwall and the provinces,
thus playing no small part in the localised awakenings Great
Britain experienced, until action taken by the Methodist
Conferences shut them out of their buildings.

Of this period, and the part it played in preparing William
Booth for his future, General Bramwell Booth was later to
write :

For two years after the Churches were thus closed against him,
he (William Booth) wandered about the country without a
religious domicile. . . . Those two years were probably the
darkest in his whole life, at least from the time of his ordination
onwards. Small buildings only were available for his services—
he who had been accustomed to great congregations. . . . Yet
this period, dark and perplexing as it was, was a period in which,
I consider, he was being most marvellously fitted for the work
which, unknown to him, was awaiting his hand in the East End
of London.

William Booth's own verdict was given when he spoke at the celebration of his sixtieth birthday at the Congress Hall, Clapton :

I see in all the unpleasant experiences of my early days the hand of God Himself, leading me by a way that I knew not—that I could scarcely believe at the time to be His way.

To which, on the same occasion, the last on which she spoke to an audience, Mrs. Booth added :

The prevailing feelings of my heart are gratitude and thanksgiving to God who has done it all—who has done it without our ever contemplating, or fore-seeing, or fore-ordering its doing, but who took hold of us, presenting ourselves as we did, at least honestly and thoroughly, for the carrying out of His purposes of which we then saw so little, and led us by a way we knew not.

CHAPTER THREE

REVIVAL—AND ANTI-REVIVAL

I

THE period following the great spiritual awakening of 1859 has been described as one of the most fruitful in the annals of Christianity in the United Kingdom. For one thing it brought into being the Home Mission Movement, one of the products of which was the East London Special Services Committee,[1] the agency that called William Booth to East London.

Contemporary records confirm much of what is thus claimed, notably in respect to Northern Ireland ; but they also make it clear that in England the revival was very seriously hampered—it might even be said it was quenched— by the unsympathetic attitude of the Churches. In many quarters opposition was open and undisguised. The least that can be said is that the opportunity was allowed to pass without adequate effort being made to improve it.

Opposition to the holding of revival services was even carried into Parliament. In February 1860 a resolution was moved in the House of Lords condemnatory of the performance of divine worship at Sadler's Wells and other theatres by Church of England clergymen. Never in the memory of the earliest member of their Lordships' House, declaimed the mover, Viscount Dungannon, or of the oldest living person, had the fact of a clergyman appearing upon the boards of a playhouse been paralleled or even heard of, nor had he found any record of such event !

The Archbishop of Canterbury (John Bird Sumner) said

[1] Appendix C, Membership of Committees

that while he would not have sanctioned these services he could not intervene to put them down. He could not be induced to take upon himself responsibility for discouraging those who had thus provided the outcast and the poor with means of hearing the word of God.

Lord Shaftesbury, prime mover in providing the services in question, asserted that not two per cent. of the working men of London attended any place of worship; the incumbent of St. Thomas's, Lambeth, had said that he could testify that the moral and religious tone of that district would not bear comparison with that of Sierra Leone; indeed the native congregations of that land had contributed towards a new church for Lambeth !

The Bishop of London (Archibald Campbell Tait), though not gladly approving of the services, asked, supposing an inhibition were made legal, if the mover would find it his duty to drag before a court of law any clergyman who from conscientious motives took part in these meetings.

The resolution was reluctantly abandoned.

In the same year a committee that had arranged a series of Sunday revival meetings in Exeter Hall, London, had to move to a theatre after the first such meeting because the managers would not permit a second service of the same description to be held. Reginald Radcliffe, Richard Weaver, and William Carter were the revivalists concerned.

As late as 1864, the *Church Review* attacked the holding of religious services in theatres, lamenting that " the evil of these will remain in the lowered estimate of the dignity and solemnity of the Most High " !

A few courageous clergy and laymen of the Established Church persisted with these and other efforts, but they did so in face of condemnation that failed of effect only from apologetic refusal on the part of Church authorities to accept the onus of taking action to stop them.

2

It is impossible to avoid the conclusion that those in power at that time in the governing bodies of the principal Methodist Churches also were opposed to revivalism. This opposition had begun to show itself before 1859 ; indeed, by 1857 it had gathered sufficient force to bring about the withdrawal of William Booth from evangelistic work. The proceedings of the New Connexion Conference of 1861 which concerned William Booth's final request for reappointment as an evangelist, and the resolutions concerning revivals adopted by this and later Conferences, indicate how persistent this opposition was and how purposeful it became.

These resolutions, commented W. T. Stead, were " undoubtedly directed at keeping William Booth out of the pulpits." But they had a much wider effect. They shut out other revivalists of repute and generally damped down revival enthusiasm and effort.

The resolution adopted by the New Connexion (Liverpool, May 1861) stated :

The subject of employing evangelists to visit our churches for the purpose of reviving the work of God having been brought before the Conference, Conference declares that any circuit with the consent of the Superintendent Preacher is at liberty to make such arrangements with any of our ministers and their respective circuits for the holding of revival services.

The full implication of this resolution is not easily seen, but in effect it not only restricted the choice of evangelists to those who were " our ministers," but limited that choice to ministers who were in circuits. It was in application of this stipulation that William Booth was appointed to the Newcastle circuit.

The Primitive Methodists (Sheffield, June 1862) did not waste words, but bluntly declared :

That Conference urges all station authorities to avoid the employing of revivalists so-called.

The Wesleyan Methodists (Camborne, July 1862) dealt with the matter at greater length, and seemingly with more sympathy, though with equally prohibitory effect :

Special services. In accordance with suggestions from certain large district committees the Conference deems it expedient to direct Superintendents not to sanction the occupation of any of our chapels for continuous services by persons who are not amenable to our regular discipline. The ministers of the body are specially referred to Minutes for 1847, question 39, vol. 10, pages 551 and 553. The object of this record is not to discourage efforts to promote revivals of religion (for these we have ever sought to encourage by such means as consist with sound doctrine and godly order) but to prevent irregularities which tend to impair the true and lasting prosperity of the Church.

Within a year or two the prohibitions were made effective. One result of this was to bring about developments in the methods employed by the Booths which more and more approximated to those that later on were to have full deployment in The Salvation Army. Among these was the use of secular buildings, notably a circus building at Cardiff in 1863, and the holding of mass open-air meetings.

Perhaps the most significant development of all had its rise at Walsall (1863). Here "trophies" of startling character—ex-gamblers, pugilists, drunkards and such like—were announced to take part in the proceedings as " The Hallelujah Band " and their testimonies were made a feature of the services. Here, too, William Booth reached a conclusion that was to have great effect upon his future work, especially in the establishment of The Salvation Army, namely, that the working classes were most effectually influenced by their own flesh and blood.[1]

[1] Appendix D, William Booth's Call to the East End and his Plan of Work

3

But the most important result of the closing of the orthodox Methodist Churches to William and Catherine Booth was that they were thereby compelled to seek openings elsewhere. At length, early in 1865, the exceptional success of meetings conducted by Mrs. Booth in a Methodist Free Church chapel at Rotherhithe presented the prospect of obtaining engagements in and around London. In consequence they decided to move from Leeds, where they were then living, to London ; and they made their home in Shaftesbury Road, Hammersmith.

In deciding upon this move the Booths were also influenced by the fact that they were securing but brief evangelistic engagements, at places usually distant from where, at the time, they had established a home. These engagements provided only a precarious income ; for instance, in a letter to her mother after they had left Walsall, Mrs. Booth stated that they had not " at present received as much as our travelling expenses and house rent." It was also hoped that, with their home in London, William Booth might be able, at last, to find a field in which he could put into effect his slowly growing conviction that " the best way to reach the masses was by an outside agency, specially adapted to their needs and independent of Church usages and conventionalities."

4

The attitude of the Churches to revivalism was not allowed to pass without at least one strong protest. In " A Call to the People of God " (*Baptist Almanac*, 1863), the Rev. Charles Spurgeon wrote :

The present state of our Churches fills me with alarm. The gracious revivals of the last few years were indications of the

Lord's readiness to work in the midst of our land. . . . I fear that we have slighted a golden opportunity which may not return while any of this generation are alive. . . . Communities which despised the revival are confirmed in their sin by its manifest subsidence. . . .

Long ago the Methodist Church revised its attitude to revivalism. The wrath of man is made to praise God ; likewise are mistakes and misjudgments made to contribute to the fulfilment of His purposes. That the revival should have been quenched was a calamity, so far as human wisdom can compass eternal issues. By the same token, however, it would have been little short of calamity had William Booth not been forced out of the Church to become the Founder of The Salvation Army.

A Methodist leader of later days, the Rev. John Telford, B.A., Connexional editor, well expressed the view (1908) now generally accepted :

General Booth, one of its zealous local preachers, was lost to Wesleyan Methodism, as at a later date he was lost to the New Connexion. There also we trace the Providence that guides the Church's service. The worker needed a wider field, a freer hand than Methodism was then ready to offer him, and the result is one over which Christian men rejoice . . . it seems a legitimate conclusion from the facts we have passed in review that special forms of Church life are developed to meet the varying needs of succeeding generations.

CHAPTER FOUR

CONTRIBUTORY MOVEMENTS

I

ANOTHER remarkable phase of providential preparation attendant upon the founding of The Salvation
Army was the number and variety of organizations and
agencies that made substantial contributions to its establishment.

The coldness of the Churches toward the revival was,
in many places, offset by the establishment of undenominational missions. Moreover, " free-lances " of evangelism
who had no connection even with these missions, ardent
knights-errant of the proclamation of the Gospel on the
streets, became numerous. They were ready to assist any
other preacher, or to hold forth single-handed whenever
opportunity offered. In particular, the East of London—
untouched by the revival in any other way and neglected
till its people had sunk to appalling depths of irreligion and
physical misery—attracted fervent lovers of souls who could
find no outlet for their ardour within the Churches ; it
became their special field.

By 1866 the number of persons preaching in the open
air in London every Sunday *during the season*—some in
groups, but many singly—amounted to hundreds. Yet over
and over again it was stated that the need remained greater
than the attempt to meet it. And there was always an
underlying lament of a lack of permanency in the results,
seen especially in oft-repeated public discussion of the ques-

tion, "What can we do to keep our converts ?" To which none among the preachers was able to give a satisfactory answer.

In his later years William Booth sometimes spoke of having stood alone on Mile End Waste. In view of his previous ministry as a lone speaker in Kennington, as well as of the custom prevailing in the East End at the time he was seeking a sphere of work, it can be taken that, when visiting Whitechapel, in addition to joining with others in preaching the Gospel—as on the occasion when he spoke in the Tent Mission open-air meeting—he would not hesitate to do so when alone. But this would be before his engagement as a " supply " evangelist at the Tent.

This view is further supported by the picture forming the frontispiece of *Heathen England* (first published in 1878), in connection with which it was recorded in the *War Cry* (24th April 1884) that William Booth took Railton, who wanted the information for the purpose of having this picture prepared, to show him the exact spot where he had first spoken to the East Enders. In the picture William Booth is shown, Bible in hand, addressing a few bystanders, in front of the " Vine," a public house then standing in the middle of the waste to the east of Cambridge Road, but later demolished. That the first open-air meetings conducted by William Booth in connection with the Tent campaign were held in front of the " Blind Beggar " (west of Cambridge Road) was not only attested in comparatively recent years by several persons who stood there with him, but in a *War Cry* report of a visit to the Whitechapel Corps, as early as 2nd March 1882, it was stated :

One who has stood by Mr. Booth from the first pointed out to me the little meeting-place, the nucleus of this now grand army of liberation . . . close to the sign of the " Blind Beggar " of Bethnal Green.

William Booth

Catherine Booth

The photograph of William Booth was taken at Penzance
within three years of his beginning work in East London ;
that of Mrs. Booth a little later

Mile End Toll Gate (from Cambridge Road to Sidney Street)
Removed 31st October 1866.   (*See* pp. 1 and 239)

And again, in July 1890, some Salvationists from South Shields were taken to Whitechapel to see the " very spot " on Mile End Waste, " opposite the ' Blind Beggar.' "

2

Out of this ferment of religious awakening—the Home Mission Movement—there came, as already noted, the East London Special Services Committee. Reginald Radcliffe, a Liverpool lawyer who had become prominent " by his evangelistic zeal and the skill with which he set Christians to work," came to London in 1861 and called a meeting of " representatives and friends of all the agencies carrying on the Lord's work in the East End."

William Booth and Reginald Radcliffe had met at Chester in 1857. Radcliffe's planning of an " attack "—with tract-distributors and preachers—on the crowds attending a public execution there had greatly interested William Booth, who about that time had also received, through one of Radcliffe's preachers, an invitation to conduct meetings in a theatre at Liverpool. " But," he had said in a letter to Mrs. Booth regarding this invitation, " I cannot at present entertain anything of this character."

The meeting called by Radcliffe was held in the Sussex Hall, Leadenhall Street, 23rd January 1861, and was attended by about two hundred persons. The Hon. and Rev. Baptist W. Noel (St. John's Baptist Chapel, John Street, Bedford Row), speaking at this gathering, prophetically declared, " I believe we are on the eve of a greater work than England ever saw ; and the East of London is the place to begin."

It was decided to form an organization to be known as the East London Special Services Committee [1] to encourage

[1] Appendix C, Membership of Committees ; Appendix D, William Booth's Call to the East End and his Plan of Work

and extend mission work in East London. By May it was in operation.

In 1864, 34 Sclater Street, Shoreditch, was the headquarters of the Committee. Gloucester Hall, Philpott Street, Commercial Road, was another of its prominent stations. For a time a second body, known as the Additional Services Committee, appears to have been concerned with the financing of the services. Some members served on both committees.

The last meeting of the East London Special Services Committee of which record has been found was held in Bedford Hall, Commercial Street, Whitechapel, 3rd October 1865. At this it was stated that thirty mission rooms and other halls had been opened by the Committee since it had been constituted. Among those present at this meeting was William Booth.

In June or July 1861, William Booth visited London to make inquiries regarding employment in Home Mission work. He called upon certain well-known evangelists and others interested in undenominational efforts to reach the masses with the Gospel ; among these were E. P. Hammond, William Carter, and George Pearse, the last-named a member of the East London Special Services Committee.

He was told by Pearse that his name had been mentioned at a meeting of the Committee, under whose direction services were then being held in the Garrick Theatre, Leman Street, Whitechapel ; in these Pearse invited William Booth to take part. Pearse went on to explain that the Committee were but humble people and the work at the theatre was likewise humble. They thought that if William Booth offered himself he should do so in dependence upon God alone, but they would, as far as they were able, open halls for him and give him pecuniary assistance. Evidently the Committee—composed for the most part of business men of some standing—was not wanting in worldly wisdom !

Describing his experience at the theatre, William Booth wrote to Mrs. Booth :

Yesterday, accompanied by father [Mr. Mumford], I went over to the Garrick Theatre. We arrived there at half-past three and found about forty " workers " who were receiving an address. Then prayer was offered . . . and they went off to the surrounding neighbourhood. Some went to the lodging-houses, where about sixty persons were found in one room, others from door to door, and others to the open-air for meetings at the corners of the streets. I joined the last, and gave two short addresses. At five all came back to the theatre for tea. Then there was more prayer, and all went forth again to bring people up for the service at seven. The attendance was not large. I preached ; had a little liberty in talking to the people. I found that a sermonic address is but of little service. A random talk is the most effective. A meeting for conversation with anxious persons was held afterwards. Several were much concerned, and with some of the cases I was pleased. But it was a very different affair altogether to what I have ever taken part in.

Nevertheless William Booth added :

I feel much easier in my mind. In fact, I have a measure of trust and confidence that all things are working for a desired end, to a degree that I have never had before.

While in London, William Booth tried to see John Stabb, also a member of the Committee, but he was not at home. Later he wrote to him :

I am still undecided how the Lord would have me act. I fear to imitate Peter in his walk upon the water lest I should prove like him—wanting in the needed faith. I must for the present moment at least watch and pray. More light is wanted to do His will, and I feel certain He will intimate by His Providence or Spirit more distinctly what He would have me do : and when I hear His voice I think I shall be found responding, " Behold the servant of the Lord, be it unto me even as Thou wilt."

These explorations of openings for evangelistic work came to nothing—or seemed to have done—for William

Booth returned to the North to make his final effort to reconcile the demands of the New Connexion Conference with the line of duty to which his convictions directed him, and thenceforth proceeded with the holding of revival services elsewhere. Later the Committee did become the agency through which William Booth was called to East London, but obviously his first contact with its members did not create in him any desire to work with them. Neither, perhaps, was he then ready to accept joyfully the destiny that later came to him with all the glory of realization that it was a royal gift from Heaven.

3

When the revocation of the Edict of Nantes (1685) deprived the Huguenots of protection, they suffered such cruel persecution that thousands fled from France to England, and large numbers, the majority highly-skilled weavers, settled in Spitalfields and Bethnal Green, to the great benefit of those districts.

The energetic and practical religion of these immigrants quickly found an outlet for the constraint laid upon them to preach the Gospel. Before the first year of their exile had closed, those who had come to East London had set up there an organization for this purpose known as " La Communauté," now anglicised as " The Christian Community."

By about the middle of the eighteenth century fervour had so declined that the Community almost ceased to exist. In 1772, however, it attracted the attention of John Wesley, and was re-organized under his patronage. Though still independently administered, its members became Methodists. Rules dated 1811 describe it as " A mission to workhouse paupers and vagabonds."

In consequence of the Community's having taken sides

with the Reformers in the movement that in 1849 rent the Methodist Church, at one stroke all its preachers were expelled from membership at Wesley Chapel, City Road, and the vestry room in which the Community had held meetings for more than seventy years was closed to it.

Cut off from the Methodists, the Community became undenominational. Its membership increased and its activities were extended to take in, among other additions to its work, visitation of common lodging-houses. A link with the Booths was forged when Mrs. Booth addressed meetings arranged by the Community for " fallen and other women inmates of low lodging-houses in Spitalfields " and held in the George Yard Ragged School.

By July 1865 The Christian Community had developed a large force subject to no outside control. Had it remained in official relationship with the Methodist Church its members would hardly have been free to work, as a number did, under William Booth's leadership at the Whitechapel Tent.

It is one of the treasured traditions of the Community that it was thus well represented among those who helped to bring about the establishment of The Salvation Army. Some became missioners and, later, Salvationists, prominent among them John Eason and James Jermy.[1]

A well-organized institution of a different type from many small missions of the Sixties which have disappeared, The Christian Community is still doing good work.

4

The Society of Friends, though not coming into the picture as directly as The Christian Community, was another old-world organization that was helpful to the Tent Mission.

[1] Appendix B, Early Witnesses

In the first place the Society permitted the now historic tent to be put up on ground belonging to it. Frequently, after The Christian Mission had been established, Friends and missioners united in efforts to help the poor. Broad-brimmed hats and Quaker bonnets were often seen at the meetings. The position eventually taken up by The Salvation Army in regard to the sacraments constitutes another link.

Of more recent establishment was The Open-air Mission, founded in 1853 by John MacGregor (Rob Roy). In 1860 Gawin Kirkham became its secretary, and his writings included more than one appreciative sketch of the earlier efforts of The East London Christian Mission. These sketches, printed in the *Revival*, were full of graphic detail and unequivocally approving. The first described an experience meeting held in the East London Theatre on Sunday, 31st January 1869. Kirkham, too, became one of the referees of the Mission.

The Evangelisation Society was founded still later—in 1864—with the object of sending out evangelists " to preach the Lord Jesus to the unconverted." The Society gave generous financial aid to the Mission when it was in that stage of its development which brought it within range of the provisions of the Society's constitution.

The Midnight Meeting Movement—founded in the autumn of 1859—was associated with The Christian Community in holding the meetings for outcast women in East London which were addressed by Mrs. Booth. John Stabb was one of the promoters of the Movement, which from time to time, especially in later years at Portsmouth, co-operated with the women's social work of The Salvation Army. It has been absorbed by the London Female Preventive and Reformatory Institution (re-named, in January 1946, London Haven for Women and Girls).

5

A section of the religious press of the Sixties gave much space to sympathetic reports of the doings of William Booth and The Christian Mission in its early days. The *Wesleyan Times*, the *Christian World*, the *Christian Times*, and the *Nonconformist* were notable examples. The first-named alone of leading Methodist journals reported at length the revival meetings of the Booths and, later, the work of the Mission. The *Christian Year Book* of 1868, under the heading "Irregular Agencies," gave a detailed description of "the evangelistic work" that "in the East of London the Rev. William Booth is carrying on on a large scale."

But the *Revival* might well be termed the *War Cry* of those days, so detailed were the reports it printed of the doings of the Mission, and so constant its solicitude for the Mission's financial support and general welfare.

In 1859 Samuel Chase and Richard Cope Morgan, both keenly interested in evangelistic work, had entered into partnership as printers and publishers (the firm has now become Messrs. Marshall, Morgan and Scott, Limited). When need arose for a weekly record of the happenings of the revival, they brought out the paper which took its name from its purpose. The first number, eight pages in size, was dated 30th July 1859. By September its circulation had increased from 8,000 to 80,000. In 1870 it was renamed *The Christian*.

"When we entered into business," said Morgan when Chase died in 1871, "we asked our Heavenly Father that He would occupy us very directly in His service . . . these prayers were answered." Truly they were.

CHAPTER FIVE

EAST LONDON IN THE SIXTIES

I

THE East of London, as the capital's east end was usually designated at the time of the birth of The Salvation Army—in 1865—was almost incredibly squalid, filthy, and crowded. The contrast between conditions then and now, the courage of those who faced them as they were, and the betterment they helped to bring about, alike provide ground for grateful acknowledgment and hopeful reflection.

It would be incorrect to conclude that the whole of East London was in the same deplorable condition. The main thoroughfares and their immediate vicinity carried a fringe of shops and better houses occupied by tradesmen and work-people who were in comparatively good employment. Probably the majority of William Booth's first helpers belonged to the "fringe." They were in a very real sense missionaries who took the Gospel to the truly heathen inhabitants of the "jungles" of East London's back streets. Converts made from among those born into the miseries of the "jungle," or who had found their way there as a result of misfortune or sin, were later added to The Christian Mission's fighting force, and together they formed the "organization of converted working people" which was gradually brought into being, and which was so described by the Mission's reports.

The disturbance of trade consequent upon the American Civil War caused a great increase in unemployment. Even dwellers in the "fringe" were adversely affected, while distress and starvation settled on the back streets seemingly without possibility of remedy. In 1867 not only were the workhouses of East London filled, but nearly 25,000 persons were receiving outdoor relief. In Poplar and Bromley unemployed men numbered 9,000 more than the year before. Five thousand of them, it was stated, would never be employed again there ! Frequently men starved to death, their dead bodies being found in the streets.

A representative of the *Pall Mall Gazette* in the winter of 1865–66 paid a visit to a casual ward :

Provided with a lump of bread he was made to strip, and then with only a check shirt and a rug for his shoulders, after a dip in a bath described as " disconcertingly like weak mutton broth," was compelled to walk through the open air and on bare stones and on a frosty night to the half-open shed where thirty casuals were lying each on a thinly stuffed hay bag.

A *Lancet* commissioner, reporting on Metropolitan workhouses, stigmatized them as being nurseries of disease :

In almost every case the management was found to be " utterly abominable and the guardians cruelly negligent, incompetent, and impudent beyond all palliation." The privations and sufferings of the inmates were declared to be a disgrace to civilization, even milk provided for children being stolen and sold by nurses.

In Ratcliffe Workhouse, Stepney, in men's and women's wards alike, inmates had to sleep stark naked and herded together on the floor !

A Church of England clergyman wrote of the East of London that it was a locality

where men and women live in such a state that they seem to have lost everything but the mere outside appearance of humanity. The whole moral being is laid truly waste and the degradation is something unspeakable.

The writer of a contemporary pamphlet on Whitechapel— George Goodwin, F.R.S., F.S.A.—stated :

For an hour or more we traverse narrow lanes and places which do not deserve the name of streets. Some of the courts are in decent condition, but, although in most instances the places within the liberties of the City are provided with main drains, many of them, owing to bad pavement and the dirty habits of the people, are partly strewed with decaying matter and dirty water. Near Rag Fair (Petticoat Lane) there is a piece of land in a closed neighbourhood covered with the refuse of fish, vegetables, broken baskets, dead cats and dogs, piled up enough to create a fever in any neighbourhood. . . . In most of the small courts in this neighbourhood the landlord obtains a rent of from 3s. to 3s. 6d. and often 4s. for two very small rooms, and surely ought to attend to the provision of proper drainage and paving. It seems difficult to discover the climax of London poverty and destitution. In every depth there seems a deeper still. The prices of various kinds of provisions in these neighbourhoods give a forcible notion of the condition of their swarming population. In most of these neighbourhoods you can purchase a half-pennyworth of soup or other matter in proportion. The luxuries are singular in their price and character. A farthing's worth of damaged oranges, for example, being hawked about the streets and sold in shops. Rag Fair, that well-known mart for every description of second-hand clothing, will supply good habits at any price.

Another writer, Henry B. Wheatley, thus described the conditions that prevailed :

Till within memory the district north of High Street, extending from Petticoat Lane to Osborne Street, and stretching back to and including Wentworth Street, was one of the very worst localities in London ; a region of narrow and filthy streets, yards, and alas ! many of them occupied by thieves' dens, the receptacles of stolen property, gin-spinning dog-holes, low brothels, and putrescent lodging-houses, a district unwholesome to approach and unsafe for a decent person to traverse even in the daytime. In George Yard, one of the worst of these dark ways, was Cadgers' Hall, notorious as a haunt where mendicants who lived on assumed sores met and regaled.

In this yard were the lodging-houses whose inmates Mrs. Booth addressed at meetings arranged by The Christian

Community and the Midnight Meeting Movement, as was the schoolroom in which the meetings were held.

2

The Coroner for Middlesex was moved to call public attention to the dreadful state of things which had been brought to his notice at his court :

The sickness and destitution prevailing [he said] were scarcely to be believed except by eye-witnesses. In round terms he denounced the shameful neglect of sanitary boards, and the criminal conduct of water companies which had brought about the disgusting condition and arrangement of water supply, drainage, and closets which prevailed. There were houses without water-butts or dustbins, cellars full of putrid rubbish, rooms that had not been whitewashed for thirty years. In one house where forty-one persons were living the water supply of only eighteen gallons was kept in a cask alongside a dustbin ; over fifty people were in another instance dependent upon one small pipe turned on for only an hour or two daily.

At an inquiry into the death of a child who had been living in Gun Square, Houndsditch, evidence was given which showed :

That the wooden houses round the Square, ten in number, had each three rooms all with floors on the earth and damp and decayed. They were covered by leaky lean-to roofs of a height to begin with of only six feet nine inches. By the time the roof reached the third room it was so low as to make it unfit to live in. The top sashes of the windows were fixed ; in hundreds of houses this was so.

That in the house where the child died seven persons were living. In cold weather they crowded into one room because in the other the chimney would not carry away smoke from what little fire they were able to have. In the room in which they lived, slept, and ate there was a maximum air space of 125 cubic feet per head.

That the only water supply was through a tank placed on top of a dirty building which contained closets.

That the Square was unpaved and rain quickly turned it into a filthy, muddy swamp.

This instance of the absence of the most primitive provisions for sanitation was by no means singular. A local newspaper, the *Eastern Post*, recorded :

Five structures in Edward Street, Mile End Old Town, were homes of pestilence. In one of these in one room a man, his wife, and five children slept. The water supply came from a rotten butt with filth at the bottom. Other abominations were an untrapped and filthy closet, a broken pavement with pools of stagnant water and soapsuds, and an untrapped gully down which night-soil and the refuse from a nearby gipsy encampment were thrown and from which sewer gas escaped unchecked.

Up to 1865 sewage was emptied directly into the Thames. The 1866 cholera epidemic was caused by contaminated water having been turned into the mains from reservoirs at Old Ford. In one week 573 children under five died ; during the summer there were more than 8,000 deaths in East London from cholera and kindred complaints. Next year Parliament compelled the closing of these reservoirs and granted powers for the establishment of waterworks on the upper Thames to supply East London.

Smallpox was rife. In 1876, George Scott Railton, secretary of The Christian Mission and first commissioner of The Salvation Army, nearly lost his life when attacked by it. The "jungle" was not only as heathen as that of any distant tiger-infested land ; to venture into it was as dangerous.

Another illuminating glimpse of the miseries of the fearful struggle for what meagre living the people were able to obtain is given by contemporary records of the sorry plight of matchbox makers of Bethnal Green :

In one house children from four to sixteen years of age were at work ; one, a boy, with a broken spine, was putting sandpaper on the boxes—he could only work kneeling.

In other houses were a mother pasting boxes with a consumptive child on her knees, and a dying mother watching three children at work.

Three hundred match-workers attended a free tea. Among them was found a child of 3½ who worked five hours a day till her mother could get 2d. to send her to school ; a child of 5½ who worked from before dinner till 7 p.m. every day ; a little girl (age not given) who worked from 10 a.m. till 9 p.m. A mother and three children earned together 1s. 3d. when they could get a full day's work, but sometimes could make only 4s. 6d. or 5s. per week. The mother was allowed 1s. relief and 1s. worth of groceries per week. Rent was 2s. per week.

3

The prevailing drinking habits of the people formed a wretched background to every other misery, and were indeed the cause of a very great deal of it. A mistaken notion that making beer easy to obtain would lessen the consumption of spirits—which had reached proportions and was having effects that alarmed even Parliament—had led to legislation (1830) which provided a cheap licence (£2, 2s. per year) for the sale of beer, cider, and perry. This licence could be issued by any two or more commissioners of excise without reference to a magistrate, to any householder who could produce bonds (in one surety of £20, or two of £10 each) to meet penalties, and a certificate signed by six ratepayers that he was of good character. Simultaneously the tax was taken off beer.

Within less than six months 24,342 such licences had been issued ; in 1869, beershops so licensed numbered 49,130. Brewers' agents toured the country, ready to advance the fee and supply beer on credit !

Only a fortnight after the Act had come into effect, Sydney Smith wrote :

The Beer Bill has begun its operations. Everybody is drunk. Those who are not singing are sprawling. The sovereign people are in a beastly state.

The beer-shops could be open legally from four in the morning till ten at night on all ordinary week-days. Thirty years of this orgy of beer-drinking—and after a slight fall the drinking of spirits also increased—had produced the generation of drunkards with which William Booth and The Christian Mission were surrounded. A representative of the *Nonconformist* (4th November 1868) who had gone to East London to describe the work of the Mission wrote :

In the Whitechapel Road within a distance of half a mile, nearly 19,000 persons may be seen to enter the public houses on the Sabbath Day while on Saturday evenings the number is even larger. This place is surrounded by the most hideous vice, the most dreadful crime, and the most abject misery. The scenes of drunkenness and debauchery to be witnessed here almost exceed belief. The crowded gin shops and public house concert rooms go far to explain why poverty and misery reign supreme.

4

But bad as conditions were, and though, twenty-five years later, William Booth's impeachment of civilisation in *In Darkest England and the Way Out* was well founded, nevertheless a new spirit was already astir. Progress towards better things quickened as the Victorian era advanced. Imprisonment until debt was paid was abolished ; education, public health, and housing began to receive attention ; nursing was elevated by Florence Nightingale to the dignity of a skilled and honourable profession ; the duty on corn was removed ;

amendment of the Licensing Act came in 1869 and again in 1872.

A good beginning had been made with legislation having for its purpose the betterment of conditions in factories and mines and of employment generally. For the greater part of this Lord Shaftesbury was responsible. The first results were that an end was put to such inhuman and revolting practices as the harnessing of children three and four years old, like animals, to trucks that they were forced to drag along dark underground passages in mines; the use of "climbing boys" to sweep chimneys; and the shameful treatment and exploitation to which many apprentices were subjected. The hours of employment were regulated, though it was not until 1874 that the Ten Hours Act was passed.

But nothing more plainly indicates that progress was being made than the change in the public attitude towards crime and criminals which brought about the cessation of public executions, though not until 1868. Up till then, these horrible occasions were among the "great shows" of the times. At Exeter, in 1866, when the drop given to a *woman* had been insufficient to break her neck, the hangman dragged on her legs until she strangled! In the same year 50,000 persons assembled to witness an execution at Manchester. Occasions for these unholy holidays had been provided in plenty by the criminal law. Till well into the first half of the nineteenth century thirty-one crimes were accounted capital; revision then had left the number still at ten!

A better day had begun to dawn, though the East of London was shadowed long after the sun had risen elsewhere. Bad as things were in 1865–67, a score of years earlier they had been—though it seems difficult to imagine it possible—very much worse.

From time to time tribute has been paid to what The

Salvation Army, born of the period, has done to quicken the pace of social progress, none more generous—nor more to be valued, because the speaker drew upon his personal knowledge of his subject—than that offered by John Scurr, a Roman Catholic, when Socialist Member of Parliament for Mile End. In December 1927, unveiling the memorial bust of William Booth in Mile End Road, he said of the Army's founder :

He was one of those men who set out to serve his fellows, and he built even better than he knew. He lived a life of great sacrifice. The young people here cannot have any idea of what Mile End was like sixty years ago. To-day it is a place of which we can be proud, and William Booth's sacrifice has been largely responsible for this. He saw that in every person there is always that divine spark that may be kindled into a glowing flame. Many members of my own denomination who had fallen away came back as a result of the life-work of General William Booth. In the name of every Catholic, every Protestant, every Jew and every Gentile, I take this memorial into the care of the people of this Division.

Much as has resulted from the efforts of The Salvation Army to provide employment, housing, feeding, and generally to bring about the betterment of the poor and the redemption of those outcast, its greatest contribution to the world's advancement in this direction has surely been its insistence upon the principle that the salvation of the soul is the key to the salvation of the body. Under the inspiration of this idea, and by virtue of its incontestable truth, miracles have been wrought by the grace of God which have been, and will be, much more far-reaching in their effect upon world conditions than maybe has yet been accepted as possible.

Early Witnesses

1-5 the Agar family : Alfred, Elizabeth (Mrs. Sinclair), Rachel (Mrs. Ebdon), Louise (Mrs. Davis), and John B. (Rachel and Louise were the first two women evangelists to be named " Hallelujah Lasses," *see* page 214), 6 Joseph Fells, 7 Mrs. Carrie Reynolds, 8 Honor Fells (Mrs. Salthouse), 9 George Leedham, 10 Harriett E. Jermy (Mrs. Payne), 11 George T. White, 12 Frederick Coxhead, 13 James Jermy, 14 Mrs. de Noe Walker, 15 John Allen, 16 Elizabeth Jackson (Mrs. Colonel Kyle). (*See* Appendix B)

William Booth at the Tent in the Quaker Burial Ground, Whitechapel, 1865

CHAPTER SIX

THE CHRISTIAN REVIVAL ASSOCIATION—
FOUNDED IN A TENT

I

A DILAPIDATED tent in a one-time graveyard off a
Whitechapel by-street ! It was not large ; its rough
wooden forms provided seating accommodation for 350
persons ! In it, at the close of one sultry July day, were
gathered some two or three hundred unkempt, sweating,
poorly-clad denizens of the lost land of East London. The
breath of many reeked with the fumes of gin or beer which
drove from the already heavy air within those canvas walls the
last vestige of wholesomeness. When dusk fell, the only lights
available were smoking, evil-smelling, and noisy naphtha
flares—hung on wires stretched from pole to pole—abominable even in the open street over a costermonger's barrow ;
but in a tent— ! No wonder the first report of the proceedings stated that the " want of gas " was very much felt !

It was to this that William Booth's acceptance of the
proposal of that deputation had brought him. Could anything have looked more unpromising ? Or could anything
have seemed less likely to be the opening before him of the
door of wider opportunity for evangelistic service, for which
he had sought so long and sacrificed so much ?

At the opening of the great Strand Hall erected for the
International Congress of The Salvation Army held in 1904,
William Booth said :

Thirty-nine years ago, on a hot sultry July Sunday afternoon, I
walked past [the site of] this building on my way to the east end

of this great metropolis, in order that I might go to what was expected to be a very short salvation campaign.

My field of labour was the Mile End ; my tabernacle, an old tent in a disused burying-ground ; my audience, a crowd of poor Whitechapellers ; and the result—blessed be God !—was a few desolate souls at the mercy seat.

A tent, belonging to the East London Special Services Committee, had been used for mission purposes in Victoria Park, Hackney, in the summer of 1862, when Gloucester Hall and another mission (Sclater Street) were associated with it. In July 1863 it was being used in the Park " every Lord's Day, afternoon and evening."

Early in 1864 the holding of meetings in parks was prohibited. *The Times* (2nd July 1864) reported a " meeting of metropolitan members and electors held at the House of Commons " to protest against an order to this effect issued by the commissioner of police.

In the minutes of the trustees who hold for the Society of Friends their Whitechapel burial ground [1] is recorded that on 18th July 1864, permission was granted for a tent to be placed there for " the purpose of religious services amongst the poorer classes not in the habit of attending any place of worship." This was no doubt the same tent. Three months was the term first agreed on, but this was extended from time to time until September 1865. The persons to whom this permission was granted were set down in the minutes as " Four Friends, namely Smith Harrison, Henry Thompson, Samuel Hanson and John Stabb," but only the name of the first is to be found on the rolls of the London District of the Society of Friends for 1864. He, Smith Harrison, was noted in the Society as having " a concern " for the poor of East London and was associated with what is known as the Bedford Institute. Probably he stood sponsor to the Society

[1] Appendix A, Scene of the Beginning

for the other applicants. Henry Thompson and John Stabb were members of the East London Special Services Committee, the latter an office-bearer. Samuel Hanson was a member of the Committee of the Evangelisation Society and associated with other East London religious enterprises.[1]

2

The first public record of the opening of William Booth's campaign in the East of London was in a letter addressed by W. Jones Hayden to John Stabb ; the latter forwarded it to the *Revival*, which printed it in its issue of 13th July 1865. Hayden was a member of the East London Special Services Committee and for two years had been connected with the Gloucester Hall and Sclater Street missions. He wrote :

I am very happy to inform you that the Lord has been with us at the Tent this week, and has blessed the labours of our dear Brother Booth. On Sunday, 2nd July, after our brother's address many stayed behind to be spoken to about Jesus. Four professed to find peace in believing and two backsliders were restored.

Up to the present about four or five hundred persons have attended the services.

The next report was initialled S.C. ; the writer no doubt was Samuel Chase. After stating that Mr. Booth had been preaching in the Tent for about three weeks, "having been before altogether unknown in the neighbourhood," the report concluded :

We shall be glad to know that Mr. Booth saw his way to give himself to the perishing thousands of the East of London ; but this cannot be accomplished without increased funds for these East End services.

This was the first public reference to any possibility of William Booth's remaining in the East of London. Neither

[1] Appendix C, Membership of Committees

the deputation nor he seems, at first, to have had the remotest thought of anything other than his taking charge of the Tent meetings for a brief period.

A statement in the *Christian Mission Magazine* (January 1877), under the heading " Origin of The Mission," put it thus :

Mr. Booth was then (1865) a perfect stranger in the neighbourhood and had no intention of remaining in London ; but so evidently was the seal of the Divine approval impressed on these services and so immensely important did it seem to him that something should be done to reach with the Gospel the teeming thousands who seemed to be outside the pale of all ordinary religious agencies that, after much deliberation and prayer, he gave himself up to this department of labour.

But for William Booth's seemingly chance encounter with the missioners at their open-air meeting, it is doubtful whether the Special Services Committee would have ventured to invite him to go to the Tent. Knowing him as they did, they would need no assurance that he was well fitted to lead the Tent Mission. In view, however, of what had happened when previously they had been in touch with him, but for this incident—doubtless reported by the missioners—they might well have hesitated to approach him lest they should be again rebuffed. Upon what fine points turns the providence of God !

A brief but definite testimony to the success of these early meetings at the Tent was given in a report in the *Wesleyan Times* (20th August 1865) :

The Rev. William Booth has been engaged for the past seven weeks holding a series of special meetings in the East End of London near the London Hospital and in the Mile End Road. Hundreds of working men and numbers of persons who never enter any place of worship have listened night after night to appeals of this devoted servant of God, and many conversions have taken place. The work is assuming a permanent character and a large hall in the neighbourhood is about to be engaged for the winter. . . . In no part of the Metropolis is there greater need for an evangelistic effort.

3

What might be termed the registration of the birth of The Salvation Army was made by William Booth in a letter to the *Revival* at a very early date (17th August 1865). It is true that this was not in the present name of the organization ; but neither in continuity of purpose, nor in that of being, has there been any break between the mission in the Tent, with its Christian Revival Association, and the world-wide Salvation Army of to-day.

Introduced with "William Booth writes . . . ," the letter set out the deplorable spiritual condition of the population of East London, and continued :

As announced by one or two correspondents to your valuable paper, I have been engaged in an effort in this direction (the employment of extraordinary means to make known to the people of East London the love of God) the last six weeks. Invited by Messrs. Stabb and Chase [1] I held a week's services in a large tent erected in the Quakers' Burial Ground, Thomas (Vallance) Street, Whitechapel ; and so evident was the Divine approval that the services have been continued until now.

Nearly every night two meetings are held, first in the Mile End Road, and afterwards in the tent ; and on the last two Sabbaths we have conducted four services each day. We have held two very successful tea meetings, charging 3d. each for admission.

There have been but two or three meetings of the whole course at which sinners have not professed to find mercy, and sometimes thirteen or fourteen have done so in the one evening.

After giving particulars of a number of conversions that had taken place, William Booth stated that, in response to the

[1] See Appendix C, Membership of Committees. Harold Begbie, in *General William Booth*, chapter 22, erroneously terms them " a firm of publishers "

pressing invitation he had received to continue the work in East London, he had consented to do so, and set out his proposals :

We have no very definite plans. We shall be guided by the Holy Spirit. At present we desire to be able to hold consecutive services for the purpose of bringing souls to Christ in different localities of the East of London every night all the year round.

We propose holding these meetings in halls, theatres, chapels, tents, the open-air and elsewhere as the way may be opened or we seem likely to attain the end we have in view. We purpose to watch over and visit personally those brought to Christ, either guiding them to communion with adjacent and sympathetic churches or ourselves nursing them and training them to active labour.

In order to carry on this work we propose to establish a Christian Revival Association in which we think a hundred persons will enrol themselves at once. We shall also require some central building in which to hold our more private meetings, and in which to preach the Gospel when not engaged in special work elsewhere.

There is another side to the story. Returning home to Hammersmith between eleven and twelve o'clock one night after a meeting at the Tent, William Booth, unable to restrain his enthusiastic recognition that the full purpose of his life was unfolding before him, startled Mrs. Booth with his historic declaration, " Darling, I have found my destiny."

At first Mrs. Booth looked askance at this further " departure," but after prayerful consideration she consented to take the new road. " If you feel you ought to stay," she said, " stay ! We have trusted the Lord once for our support, and we can trust Him again."

In the kitchen in her Hackney home some two years later, Mrs. Booth one day told the maid [1] that she had hesitated when her husband had sprung upon her this declar-

---

[1] Mrs. Salthouse, late of Manchester ; *née* Honor Fells. Appendix B, Early Witnesses

ation of his conviction that he was called to give himself to East London, and had argued against it. For him to do this, she had at first maintained, would be likely to estrange the friends who had been helping them, and who were expecting something different. It was not thought possible that an East London mission could be self-supporting, and they might be left with their young and growing family without support.

" But," Mrs. Booth went on to say, " I got the victory."

A further human touch was added when William Booth, having come into the kitchen in time to catch what was being said, took Mrs. Booth to task for having told the maid so much. But in making known the struggle that preceded the consummation of her consecration, has not the Mother of The Salvation Army left to all Salvationist mothers a priceless legacy of kinship in any sacrifice they may be called upon to make ?

At the public celebration of the thirtieth anniversary of their wedding, in the Great Western Hall, Marylebone (16th June 1885), William Booth said :

We have never taken any step of importance without being thoroughly agreed upon it. On two separate occasions since our married life, and once before we had married, I have literally gone out, for conscience' sake, into the darkness so far as earthly support has been concerned, leaving all the friends that we had made. When these steps have been premeditated, which have had such bearing upon home and earthly comforts, my beloved wife has stood by me and said, " William, never you consider me. I can trust in God and go out with Him, and I can live on bread and water ; go out and do your duty ! "

It was not long before Mrs. Booth's faith was honoured. Within a few days a letter was received from Mr. Samuel Morley, a wealthy manufacturer and philanthropist of Nottingham,[1] whose interest had been aroused by what he had heard of William Booth's efforts at the Tent and the likelihood

---

[1] Appendix E, Early Supporters

of his continuing in East London. He was then in Scotland, but promised that on his return he would look further into what was being done. A month later he invited William Booth to come to see him. At the interview Mr. Morley brought up the question of the support of the Booth family, naming a sum which he thought would be sufficient. He suggested that other friends would be pleased to join in making up this amount, and gave William Booth then and there a cheque for £100 as the first of his own annual contributions towards it.

In the first official report of The East London Christian Mission, published September 1867, William Booth again stated how urgently he had been pressed to continue to work in East London. In the first number of the Mission's own magazine—the *East London Evangelist* (October 1868)— in the course of a full account of his beginnings in the Tent, he further stated that he had been about to leave for Derby on an evangelistic tour, when requested to conduct a week's services in the Tent.

These meetings [he added] were largely attended, gracious influences were vouchsafed, many sinners were awakened, and a very general desire was expressed by Christian friends interested in the East of London that I should devote the whole of my time to the Metropolis.

This reference goes further than those previously quoted in that it makes a strong suggestion that William Booth was pressed to continue working in East London by others than the workers at the Tent. When, in his report to the *Revival*, Mr. Chase intimated that there was a desire that William Booth should give himself to East London, he doubtless spoke for the East London Special Services Committee.

The more personal reaction of William Booth to these events is revealed in a statement by him published a score of years later in Railton's *Twenty-one Years Salvation Army* :

Here was the open door for which I had longed for years, and yet I knew it not, and moreover was unwilling to enter it. The main reason for this was that I feared my ability to deal with people of this class ; I had made several efforts, but apparently failed, and the thought saddened and oppressed me beyond measure. I would have given worlds had they been mine to have been qualified to attract and interest and lead to Salvation the masses I saw around me, as completely outside the Christian circle as the untaught heathen of foreign lands, but I despaired of accomplishing it. This I thought was not my vocation. I had forgotten Nottingham Meadow Platts and the work in it when a boy of sixteen, twenty years before.

However, as was my usage, no squeamish difficulties were allowed to interfere with duty. I accepted the invitation, and the hour and the day found me at my post.

On the Mile End Waste [Bethnal Green [1]] the first open-air meeting was held, from whence we processioned to the Tent. From the first the meetings were fairly good ; we had souls at almost every service, and before the fortnight had passed I felt at home ; and more than this, I found my heart being strongly and strangely drawn out . . . I was continually haunted with a desire to offer myself to Jesus Christ as an apostle for the heathen of East London. The idea, or heavenly vision, or whatever you may call it, overcame me. I yielded to it, and what has happened since is I think not only a justification but an evidence that my offer was accepted.

The twenty-one strenuous years that had intervened would seem to have merged in William Booth's mind the calls from without with the impulse that was stirred within in those days of decision. But what matters is that the heat of his desire to save souls—to save the worst—fused calls and impulse into a demand that he met by giving his life to the purpose they represented.

[1] Appendix A, Scene of the Beginning

CHAPTER SEVEN

FIGHTING FOR A FOOTING: 1865–66

I

NOT many who could speak from their own knowledge of the earliest days of the movement lived till the details of its beginnings had ceased to be commonplace and their historical value was recognized. The fingers of one hand are more than enough to count those still living.[1] They were simple people of limited ability. The giants of forceful Salvationism who later shared the burdens of leadership with William Booth were not among them ; they were to come from the converts whom the faithful if humble service of the first missioners helped to make, or from outside the Mission. In those early days William Booth was alone at the head of the Army he was making !

William Booth's first hopes of large enlistment in the Christian Revival Union were not realized. After a year—in 1866—the membership was only sixty. In the meantime there had been a considerable change in the personnel of the Mission. In the eyes of William Booth it had amounted to desertion ; undoubtedly with some who left him it was so. Objection was taken to his teaching the truth of sanctification. Some considered he laid too much stress upon repentance and good works. To others his way of conducting prayer meetings gave offence ; they did not like the penitent form. The mocking and mobbing by the crowds in the streets imposed

[1] Appendix B, Early Witnesses, gives the names and other information with regard to those from whom particulars of this chapter's incidents have been gathered

a stern test that was too much for the endurance of the less zealous.

But some left merely because they had intended to serve at the Tent only until sufficient converts had been made to take their places when they returned to the organizations that had " lent " them for this special campaign.

Whenever the re-alignment took place, and whatever the exact cause, one of its effects was to free the Mission from the incubus of preconceived notions and procedure that had outlived effect. Certainly, had the Mission continued on the old lines, it would never have become The Salvation Army. William Booth's insistence upon definite decision for Christ and out-and-out consecration to His service, as being essential, was happily so strong that no-one could be comfortable under his leadership who was not prepared to go all the way with him in applying these principles to the work in which they were together engaged.

This sifting out of the objectors and faint-hearted provides a significant indication of what would have been likely to have happened had William Booth begun his work under the auspices of the East London Special Services Committee, when opposition to his procedure could have been made effective.

The records show no sign that William Booth was dismayed at the turn events had now taken ; rather they indicate that he went to work more vigorously. From those who remained with him, and from converts, he strove, and strove successfully, to build up a fighting force.

And at the heart of the Mission there were earnest and consecrated workers, though for a time maybe few in number, who stood by William Booth through thick and thin. Those who joined the Mission later did so with full knowledge of its standards and methods ; indeed, were attracted by them.

Of the original Tent workers who remained with William

Booth the most outstanding was James Flawn, though even his gifts were those of a " server of tables " rather than of a public leader. Until the Booth family moved to Hackney in November 1865, William Booth lunched on Sundays with Flawn at the refreshment room that the latter owned in Pudding Lane (where the Great Fire of 1666 began), which ran from Eastcheap to Lower Thames Street on the eastern side of the Monument. William Booth took his own food ; Flawn would make him a cup of cocoa. After lunch he would rest on a sofa in a back room until it was time for him to return to the Mission. Later Flawn served on various committees set up to manage the affairs of the Mission ; he was also active in connection with the soup-kitchens and other relief work. With regard to the first days Flawn told an interviewer in 1897 that

the fortnight's campaign at the Tent was so marvellous in its results that it was by special request extended indefinitely, and crowds—godless, heedless crowds—packed the Tent till one stormy night it was blown to ribbons.

Among the first converts made at the Tent after William Booth took charge was an Irish pugilist, Peter Monk. Meeting William Booth in Whitechapel Road, he was so greatly impressed by his appearance and the few words he spoke to him that he made up his mind to go and hear him preach. Monk was booked for a prize-fight that night, which he won. The next day, though " the boys " were making a hero of him, he would not listen to their suggestions that he should fight again ; as soon as the time arrived when William Booth would be preaching on Mile End Waste, he went off to hear him.

There he was [Monk used to say] holding forth surrounded by the blackguards of Whitechapel, who in them days were the greatest vagabonds you could meet anywhere on God's earth. Some were mocking, some were laughing ; but Mr. Booth he

shouted at them finely, and then gave out a hymn, and led the
singing till he just drowned their noises, or nearly so. Then I
threw off my coat and walked round the ring instead of joining
in the revelry, and in two minutes all those blackguards were as
quiet as lambs.
And not very long after that he had me down at the penitent
form after one of his sermons in the Tent.

Monk constituted himself William Booth's bodyguard, being
known later as " the General's boxer." By January 1866 he
had become registrar of " The East London Christian Revival Union Temperance Society," the designation borne by
a pledge card (signed by Elizabeth Chapman) which he had
countersigned.

2

The first open-air meetings led by William Booth on
Mile End Waste were held opposite the " Blind Beggar "
public house, and from the first at least twenty members of
The Christian Community were included in the band of
workers which supported him.

After 2nd July, meetings were held in the Tent, on week-
nights and Sundays, without any break, until Sunday 20th
August, when William Booth was ill. On every Sunday
but this—until in November he moved to Hackney—he
walked the eight miles from Hammersmith and the eight
miles back. By the next week-end he was able to resume
full duty and the story was continued by him in diary form
in the *Revival* (21st September 1865) :

Sabbath, August 27. After a week's illness, once more by the
mercy of God permitted to go forth to the blessed employ of
proclaiming the love of Christ to a perishing world.
In the morning held an open-air service in the Mile End Road.
Afternoon. Had not strength for a meeting.
Evening. From six to seven open-air and singing procession to

the tent, which we grieved to find sadly rent again after having
been thoroughly repaired at considerable outlay. The attendance
not so large. Suffered from being closed the preceding week.
. . . The following week but little was done. Congregations
greatly declined, and no wonder ; the ground was damp, and
through the rents in the tent the wind blew cold and chilly on
the people. Still, some good was effected.

What a picture of triumph over depressing and difficult
circumstances ! Few people—cold and damp—a clammy
atmosphere laden with odours of an East End insanitary to
a degree beggaring modern imagination—the dancing
shadows thrown by those unsteady naphtha lamps emphasizing the gathering darkness rather than lightening it !

Then came announcement of a move underlining William
Booth's declaration that he had given himself to East London
for good, and that he had followers who accepted his
leadership !

Sunday, September 3. The change in the weather having
rendered the tent unsuitable, we commenced Sabbath services
in a large dancing room, 23 New Road, Whitechapel. The most
eligible place *we can secure for the present.* . . .

This was known as Professor Orson's Dancing Academy,
also as the Assembly Rooms. It has been remodelled and is
now used as a day nursery under the auspices of a committee
of Jewish ladies. The top rooms were occupied by a photographer (Foggity) who did considerable Sunday business ;
his customers passed through a " parlour " opening on to
the preaching room. His wife did colouring and retouching
there and often listened to the preaching, but, William
Booth lamented, could not be brought to decide for
Christ.

Not until the dancers had finished their Saturday-Sunday,
night-till-morning, occupation of the room could the
missioners bring in the forms which had been used at the

Tent, and which provided seats for 350 persons. Early on Sunday mornings these indomitables, clad in working clothes —Sunday clothes were scarce and precious indeed in the East End in those days !—got to work, while William Booth footed it from Hammersmith to reach Whitechapel in time to lead them—now in their best attire—in an open-air meeting that preceded " an address with breaking of bread " in the morning.

Open-air meetings were held in the morning at the Whitechapel end of New Road ; in the afternoon at the Commercial Road end, in the evening on the Mile End Road. To the proceedings at the last " hundreds appeared to listen with undivided attention."

Then, past the brilliantly lit gin-palaces, the missioners marched to New Road. William Booth wrote of this :

We had an efficient company of singers, and as we passed along this spacious and crowded thoroughfare, singing,

> We're bound for the land of the pure and the holy,

the people ran from every direction. Drunkards came forth to hear and to see ; some in mockery joined our ranks ; some laughed and sneered ; some were angry ; the great majority looked on in wonder ; some turned and accompanied us as on we went, changing our song to,

> With a turning from sin let repentance begin,
> Then conversion itself will draw nigh ;
> But till washed in the blood of a crucified Lord,
> We shall never be ready to die.

The hall was filled, the audience was of the right kind, many were awakened, and several professed to find Jesus.

The rent of the Assembly Rooms—the only financial obligation resting on the infant Mission—had been regarded fearfully. A statement, in William Booth's handwriting, of income and expenditure for the last quarter of 1865 shows this to have been £1, 1s. per Sabbath. The thirteen weeks' offerings in the hall totalled £10, 8s. 9d. Private offerings from members added £9, 9s. 7d. to this.[1]

"No-one in the audience," said James Flawn in after years, "seemed worth sixpence, but we had a box at the door that people might give what they could when they were going out—and almost every Sunday we found in it a golden sovereign ! We never discovered how it got there ! We used to say that the Lord Himself put it in ! "

Courageous efforts were made by the missioners to continue to use the Tent for week-night meetings. On Monday a tea, on Tuesday a young lads' prayer meeting, on Wednesday a public service—they got no further ; the weather-worn tent was beyond repair. The epitaph of the tabernacle in which was born The Salvation Army was written in the Friends' minute book—its remains must be removed and damage to the ground upon which it had stood must be made good. William Booth recorded that he paid " Bro. Pye 2s. 6d. and the carman 7s. 6d. for the removal of the tent."

More than once the roof of the tent had been brought down, flapping in the wind, upon the heads of the people within its canvas walls. On one occasion during a storm it had collapsed while between thirty and forty persons were kneeling, seeking Salvation—and the meeting was continued. At another time, when the ropes had given way (Peter Monk declared the roughs had cut them), from the platform William Booth directed, " Go along, my brothers ; go outside and pull the tent up while I carry on with the preaching ! "

3

The Mission had entered on the second phase of its campaign. It must consolidate its hold on the ground won,

[1] Appendix I, Balance Sheets of The Christian Mission

or lose the battle. Neither the missioners nor their leader had had experience of the kind of warfare which they now commenced. Nor could they obtain guidance in the process of consolidation from the small and independent missions carrying on precariously round them. The East London Special Services Committee could not help them ; these other missions, so many of which have vanished, were the sum of all that that body could devise.

" In the meantime," said William Booth in a survey of the position at that time, written three years later :

our efforts were largely directed to the open-air work. This we regarded at the outset, and consider still, our special sphere. . . . We found that though the aversion of the working classes to churches and chapels was as strong as could readily be conceived, yet they eagerly listened to speakers who, with ordinary ability, in an earnest and loving manner, could set before them the truths of the Bible in the open-air. At any season of the year, in nearly all kinds of weather, at any hour of the day, and almost any hour of the night, we could obtain congregations.

Nevertheless it was William Booth's conviction that :

every outdoor service should, if possible, be connected with an indoor meeting, where, free from those dissipating influences which more or less always accompany outdoor preaching, especially in the streets of London, the Gospel could with greater clearness be set forth, further appeals could be made in favour of an immediate closing with Christ, prayer could be offered, and an opportunity secured for personal conversation with the people. . . . In this actual closing with Christ consists the only or chief ground of hope we have for sinners ; without it, all mere resolutions and head knowledge will avail but little ; therefore we attach but little importance to instructing men's minds or arousing their feelings, *unless* they can be led to that belief in Christ which results in the new creation.

The Mission was now sure of its Sunday citadel. Occupancy of the New Road Dancing Academy was continued until February 1867, when meetings were begun in the

Effingham Theatre. But the inclement weather—which had finished off the Tent—and the nearness of winter, in addition to the considerations already set forth, made it imperative that shelter should be obtained for week-night meetings. It was, however, some time before a place was found of which the Mission could have uninterrupted use.

The first week-night indoor meeting was held in an old wool store, Satchwell Street, Bethnal Green. This was packed with people for the first meeting, but for some reason was occupied only for a fortnight, at the end of which time William Booth had to report that, not being able to secure a suitable place for week-night meetings, he had arranged for a series in the open-air.

A spell of exceptionally mild weather followed, during which outdoor meetings were held from seven to nine in the evenings. At the close of these, missioners went among the bystanders and spoke to them personally, with the result that some were converted.

During the meetings in that old wool store a convert was made whose name was Fells. His son and daughter—Joseph, aged 12, though he looked much older, and Honor, 15—were amongst the earliest converts at the Dancing Academy. Joseph received his ticket of membership within the first month (September 1865) that the Academy was occupied ; on it the name of the Mission was given as The East London Christian Revival Union.

At the time of the forty-third anniversary (1908) of the founding of The Salvation Army, Fells described the procedure of those early days :

The central figure in the Mission was of course the General. Tall and dark, with one corner of his Inverness cape flung back over his shoulder, he presented a striking picture. I never knew him to fail in gathering and holding an East End crowd.
One night on Mile End Waste an infidel lecturer made several

attempts to break up the meeting. Finally he agreed to wait his turn until the close. The crowd, however, followed the little procession to the hall, and the infidel, at first very much exasperated, followed too. The result was that he got converted.

For the first two months we used to march along the footpath from the Waste to the Dancing Academy, passing on our way a number of public-houses whose custom it was to serve drinks outside to men sitting at little tables.

As the procession swept by, these places were invariably deserted by the customers, which naturally annoyed the publicans. They complained to the police, and on the Sunday following an inspector tapped the General on the shoulder and told him that the procession would not be allowed to traverse the pavement any more. So we marched in the road through the Mile End Toll Gate. And the crowds still followed.

Although the Dancing Academy was often uncomfortably crowded, all sorts of plans were used to attract fresh people. One of these was the carrying in the procession of half-a-dozen boards on which were printed in bold letters such warnings as " Prepare to meet thy God."

The exact sequence of tenancy and the location of some of the buildings used by the Mission immediately after this are obscure ; use of some was very brief. William Booth, the resourceful leader, and his devoted and undauntable followers, were driven from one rallying point after another, as they sought to establish themselves on the ground they had overrun. This dogged advance across a no-man's-land of lost souls, and occupation of vantage points beyond, can however be reconstructed in outline.

The record for brief occupancy of a meeting-place was surely established by " a stable up a court leading off the Whitechapel Road " :

We had it cleaned and whitewashed, and fitted up [wrote William Booth], and from its situation we were full of hope of seeing a lot done in it. But alas ! " we counted our chickens before they were hatched," as others have done before us. After the first meeting or two we were summarily ejected, the room next to us being occupied by a gymnastic and sparring club ; and our exercises disturbed theirs. They were old tenants, and their work being more in sympathy with the publican to whom the place belonged there was nothing for us but to go.

A contemporary statement, the source of which has been lost, has it that this room was " above a stable in Hosiery Place, next door to Bones, Cheesemonger." No court in Whitechapel has ever been officially known by this name, but directories of the period show that the cheesemonger's shop mentioned was between Great Garden and St. Mary streets, at the corner of an unusually large entry to what within recent years was still a stocking factory. In addition to the " dock " for the factory's use, it contained stables. Corroboration is provided by Mrs. de Noe Walker [1] whose first knowledge of The Christian Mission was when, in 1866, it was, she stated, " in a stable up a court leading off White-chapel Road."

What may have been yet another such meeting-place was described by a Biblewoman (Mrs. Oram) of the Mission :

After an open-air meeting on the Waste we walked across the road to an old place something like a hayloft. We had to go up some old wooden stairs to the room. It was very small ; still, many followed us. This hayloft was up a narrow turning just opposite the Waste. The ceiling was so low that if the General stood in the place upright with his hat on, it would nearly reach the ceiling.

Mrs. Salthouse also spoke of a loft, the entrance to which, she said, was up a wide ladder in a court leading to Redman's Row. From it, she added, they were turned out after only a week's tenancy.

Redman's Row (now Road) began at Jubilee Street and so a court leading to it could not be said to be " off White-chapel Road." An old inhabitant of the neighbourhood (Mr. Ady, Editor of the *East London Advertiser*) declared that

[1] Appendix E, Early Supporters

the first building used by The Christian Mission was " three doors west from the ' Old Red Cow,' the third shop from the corner of Cleveland Street, next to Wickham's." The shop thus indicated is shown by the London Directory (1865) as occupied by Henry Johnstone, milliner. A room there may have been one of the smaller places used for brief periods after the destruction of the Tent.

Buildings lent to the Mission for occasional week-night meetings during this period were : the Free Church, Mile End New Town, a mission-room fronting on to the present Kingward Street, attached to the Rev. W. Tyler's Church (Congregational) in Church (now Hanbury) Street, and the Alfred Street and Watney Street chapels, Stepney. A fort-night's meetings were also held in " a large mission room in Bethnal Green Road."

4

The first building the Mission was able to call its own in the sense that it was completely at its disposal, and in which week-night meetings were continued for any length of time, was reported in the *Revival* by William Booth as being in use in June 1866. This was an old wool store, situated in Three Colts Lane, off Cambridge Road, Bethnal Green, in which it was just possible to seat 120 people. It still stands and is now a carpenter's shop. A small oblong building with a loft above a low-ceilinged ground floor, it has windows on one side only—and these are small and low, opening on to a footpath. If they were opened roughs threw mud, stones, and occasionally fireworks through them. As the place was usually crowded, and ventilation was possible only when no roughs were about, it is no wonder the air often became so bad that none but the strongest could remain inside. Tricks played by the roughs included the laying of trains of gunpowder, the dress of one devoted sister (Mrs. Totman) being thus set on fire ; Honor Fells helped to put the flames out. Another (Mary A. Jones) had her shawl badly burnt, but neither she nor Mrs. Totman suffered serious injury. Closed doors and shutters were often vigorously hammered. Remains of wire-netting are still to be seen on the window frames.

Open-air meetings held nearby were harassed by the police and disturbed by the landlords and frequenters of neighbouring public houses. On one occasion men were given drink and sent, in a half-intoxicated condition, to create a disturbance while a missioner was speaking outside the building. Next a policeman was called, who ordered the preacher to desist and threatened him with arrest. All crowded into the little hall, and before the meeting ended the ringleader of the attack had been converted !

Of the doings here William Booth put on record :

The Lord was with us and numbers of sinners were awakened in this humble place, some of whom are now labouring for the salvation of their fellow-men.

It is no wonder the publicans desired to get rid of the missioners ; according to the *East London Evangelist*, anti-drink activities began with the children :

In connection with the Sabbath School, Sister Jermy, single-handed, commenced a Band of Hope on October 6, 1868, with about six children. The meeting has increased in interest until the attendance ranges from sixty to seventy. About fifty have signed the pledge. I wish all the moderation people in the Mission could hear these young abstainers sing :

> We'll throw down the bottle,
> And never drink again—

to the annoyance of the publican and the beershop-keeper in the vicinity.

Joseph Jermy, brother to Sister Jermy the Band of Hope leader, was the missioner in charge at the opening of this

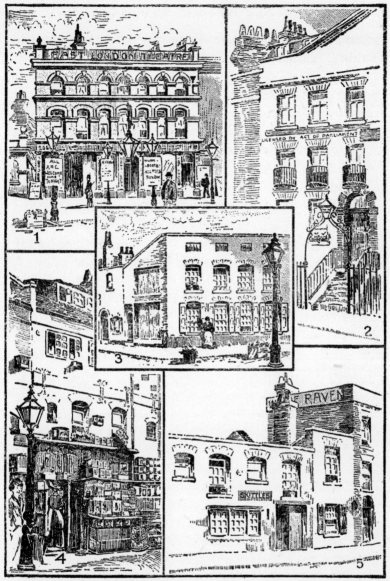

First buildings used by The Christian Mission in East London

1 The East London Theatre, Whitechapel Road 2 The Assembly Rooms, 23 New Road, Whitechapel 3 The "Dingy Cradle," Three Colts Lane, Bethnal Green 4 The "Pigeon Shop," Sclater Street, Shoreditch 5 The Alexandra Hall, "Skittle Alley," Bedford Street, Whitechapel

station. It was in the recollection of one of the band of workers (Elizabeth Chapman) that

hosts of people attended our open-air meetings. There was much horse-play, but we stood our ground and many of the roughest characters followed us to the hall, where some got soundly converted and became out-and-out warriors. A love-feast followed each indoor meeting, and was attended by many earnest souls.

" We were so constantly singing of the Blood, and the Bleeding Lamb," once said James Flawn, " that I recollect a man saying in jest to us one day at Three Colts Lane: ' You fellows ought to have red coats and have done with it ! ' "

The Mission's first All Night of Prayer was held in connection with this station, Mr. Tyler's mission room being lent for the occasion. Flawn's comment on this was :

An eight hours' prayer meeting was a new idea, but it seemed only natural that people ablaze with love for God and sinners should pray all night when their work and duties forbade them doing so all day. Beside, Christ set them the example Himself. Anyway, at this first " All Night," so desperate, so unceasing, and so tremendous was the uproar that towards dawn the Irish living around, finding sleep impossible, gathered round the door. " Sure, they're killing themselves," they whispered with awe-struck looks !

Three years later the publicans got their way. The owner of the hall, yielding after long persuasion and, he said, much against his will, turned the Mission out.

Years afterwards (1886), when passing through Bethnal Green by train, the Founder pointed to this building—it is in full view from the railway—and said to his travelling companions :

That is the old wool-shed where we used to meet after the loss of the famous tent. There is the public-house where the man used to oppose us so much. One day he said to me, " You know it is not pleasant when you are shaving on a Sunday morning to hear somebody thundering in the street that the publican is going to hell ! "

When giving instructions with regard to conducting open-air meetings (1880) William Booth again referred to this incident and commented : " What could I reply [to the publican] but that it was very unwise and improper ! "

On this occasion the wool-shed was designated in the *War Cry* a " dingy cradle " for The Salvation Army. It may have been, but the child throve ! Earlier, Railton had written of it as being " a dismal little crannie."

At this time contact was established with Mr. and Mrs. Henry Reed,[1] of Dunorlan, a mansion with extensive grounds situated near Tunbridge Wells, at which place Mrs. Booth was recuperating from the effects of a severe illness. With William Booth she attended a meeting held on the lawn at Dunorlan. This was addressed by the Rev. W. Haslam, who afterwards introduced them to Mr. and Mrs. Reed. Mr. Reed cordially invited them to conduct on the following Sunday a service in a mission hall which he had erected for his tenantry and neighbours. William Booth was unable to accept the invitation, but Mrs. Booth did and laid the foundation of a lifelong friendship, which proved of no little importance in the early days of The Christian Mission.

5

In Scrutton Street, Shoreditch, stood the hundred-years-old Holywell Mount Chapel (Methodist New Connexion). Once it had had a good congregation, but the neighbourhood was changing ; railways and factories were ousting dwellings, and attendances had so dwindled that to see thirty persons at

[1] Appendix E, Early Supporters

the Sunday night service was exceptional. One day in July 1866 the trustees, meeting to consider what should be done, came to the conclusion that the situation was hopeless. As they were leaving, William Booth was passing on the other side of the road. Their chairman (Mr. J. C. Moore) pointed him out to another trustee (Mr. George White, who became a leading member of The Christian Mission), and said, "*He* would fill the chapel ! " They accosted him, negotiations were entered into, and in the end the chapel was handed over to the Mission—at a rental of £60 per annum for the eighteen months the lease had still to run.

The chairman was right ; crowds were attracted ; hundreds of seekers were registered. Of the first Sunday evening of the Mission's occupation of the chapel George T. White has written :

I remember we started out about 5.40. Mr. Booth, father, mother, my brother, father's apprentice and I. The apprentice was older than we boys. We had a quantity of handbills ; they were a novelty to us ! On the way we distributed them. When we got to the chapel four young men were there with boards on sticks showing texts. Mr. Booth stood in the middle of the road outside the chapel. He said, " We will pray," laid down his umbrella, knelt on it, and prayed aloud. The young men responded with " Amen," " Thank God," etc. All this was new to us boys. It was not many Sundays before the chapel was crowded.

White has described a Sunday School outing at this time :

Holywell Mount had a good Sunday School ; also Three Colts Lane had a fair one. They amalgamated for a day at the forest. We started from the Eastern Counties station at Bishopsgate [then the terminus]. The third-class carriages had no windows— just open spaces without glass. We stopped at Mile End station, Cambridge Road—there was no Bethnal Green Junction—and there took on the Three Colts Lane members. They were a rowdy lot. When they got settled they began to sing :

> In Three Colts Lane in an old wool-shed,
> Glory, Hallelujah !
> We frighten the living and raise the dead,
> Sing Glory, Hallelujah,
> Shout Glory, Hallelujah !
> And while the rats were running round,
> The boys and girls Salvation found.

At this station, too, Mr. Booth, with the smaller children of the family, also Mr. and Mrs. Mumford, Mrs. Booth's parents, joined the party. Mrs. Booth was not able to go.

Though the Mission was still fighting for a footing, when the end of 1866 was reached there were gleams of hope in the clouded sky. And this notwithstanding that as yet the Mission had no other meeting-places than the old Holywell Mount Chapel, the Dancing Academy (Sundays only) and the " dingy cradle " ! Nevertheless, in September William Booth was able to report :

The Lord is continuing His blessing to the work in Whitechapel where, while the people have been weak in the presence of a dreadful pestilence, we have been endeavouring to meet them out in the great thoroughfares with the glad message of love and mercy contained in the Gospel. There has seemed to be a spirit of hearing abroad.

The Assembly Hall (Dancing Academy), New Road, and the little Gospel Hall, Three Colts Lane, have been crowded on Sunday evenings. On two successive nights as many as 12 and 15 souls have sought the Saviour.

At our three places we hold 17 open-airs per week and 20 indoor meetings.

The Lord is raising up among us men who delight in evangelistic labour, and sisters also, several of the latter speaking in the open-air with much expedience, never failing to secure and keep the attention of the congregation. We are glad to secure the co-operation of young, loving, earnest labourers who have received power from on high to speak to the people of Jesus and Eternity. I believe that God will abundantly increase our labourers and open for us wider doors of usefulness and that we shall yet see a mighty work in the East of London. The cost of one place alone is £3 per week, and we have others in view. Another large chapel with a frontage eligible for open-air work can be obtained in a very short time. I intend to take it trusting to God for means. We want funds for free teas, tracts, etc., but most of all we need a Pentecostal baptism of the Holy Ghost.

CHAPTER EIGHT

SAVED TO SAVE !

I

IT was not long before William Booth found himself face to face with what, from its beginning, had been the major problem of the Home Mission Movement—how to keep converts from falling away before they became " established in the faith."

In his first reference to those brought to Christ in the Mission, William Booth stated that it was his purpose to watch over and visit converts.

Very early, also, William Booth made it clear that he held very definite views with regard to the duty incumbent upon all who became Christians " personally to give themselves to the work of enlightening and saving their fellow men." Before the end of 1865 he wrote :

They need to be brought to see that they are not only called to the adoption of sons, but to the work of servants—not only to feel the privileges of the Kingdom but to be actual co-workers for God in bringing others to share these blessings. Even when Christians are brought to discern this duty they require to be taught how to discharge it. . . .

Convinced of these needs, we meet on Friday evenings to urge upon our members this duty and that of personally dealing with sinners.

William Booth had not yet reached the conclusion that it would be necessary to establish any new body. He regarded the purpose of the Mission as being, in the main, to form a link between the unchurched masses and the Churches. His first intentions were summed up in a survey of the position he made twenty years later. At the same time he gave the reasons why he had changed his policy :

All this time we had no regular definite plan for the future. From the first I was strongly opposed to forming any separate organization. It is true that again and again the thought did come to me as to what could be accomplished for God and man by a people who were all actuated by one simple purpose, and that the immediate salvation of the masses and the entire devotion of those thus saved to the work of saving their fellows. The chief sorrow to me in connection with the sects in the past has ever been their divisions on the subject of practical godliness and immediate results, and with this in mind, I constantly put from me the thought of attempting the formation of such a people.

My first idea was simply to get the people saved and send them to the Churches. This proved at the outset impracticable.

First, they would not go when sent.

Second, they were not wanted.

And third, we wanted some of them at least ourselves to help us in the business of saving others.

We were thus driven to providing for the converts ourselves.

On no point were William and Catherine Booth more in agreement than that if converts were to be kept they must be set to work. A letter from Mrs. Booth on " How to Train New Converts " was printed in the *Methodist New Connexion Magazine* (June 1855). Having been written before her marriage, it was signed " C. M." Apart from some letters on total abstinence, written to temperance papers when she was much younger, this was her first appearance in print.

The babe in Christ [wrote Mrs. Booth] must be made to feel his individual, untransferable responsibility. He must be taught that labour is the law of life, spiritual as well as natural, and that, to increase in wisdom and stature and in favour with God, he " must be about his Father's business."

The practice in the Mission was in accord with this principle. An early-day convert (Mrs. Caroline Reynolds) stated of her own experience :

They put me to work right away. We had open-airs, and I remember how I used to have to stand in my own street with them. . . . They also gave me some sick-visiting to do.

Questions characteristic of the attitude of Church members to revival converts were put to William Booth at meetings for professing Christians conducted at this time by Mrs. Booth. It was alleged (a report of one such occasion stated) that only uneducated people were converted at revivals, and that revival converts were not stable. William Booth in turn asked, was not the Gospel for the poor ? He also cited many instances of outstanding and continued change of life among converts of The East London Christian Mission.

Subsequently to this, but in the same year, William Booth wrote :

Great numbers of converts who can be traced give proof of genuineness . . . hundreds. . . . Some have gone to distant lands. Some to other Churches. Many in fellowship with us are earnestly striving to bring others to Jesus.

A year later a representative of the *Nonconformist* commented :

Commencing . . . wherever he could find a spot on which to preach the glorious Gospel of God, Mr. Booth soon collected around him a chosen band of persevering labourers whose numbers gradually increased until they now muster nearly 300, all sincerely pledged to the work of evangelisation among their friends and neighbours.

The " pledge " referred to was contained in what was probably the first printed document of the Mission, headed " East London Christian Revival Society," which dates it within two years of its founding. It had twin sub-headings : " Articles of Faith " and " Bond of Agreement."

Not at any time has the organization (from its beginnings

as The East London Revival Society until its present existence as The Salvation Army) been without a definite creed to which members have been and are required to subscribe. The doctrines were revised by the 1870 Conference and subsequently, but by 1875 had assumed the form in which they were incorporated in that and the 1878 deeds-poll.[1]

Though the problem how to keep converts had baffled the leaders of the Home Mission Movement, they had nevertheless striven earnestly to find a solution. In 1861 a meeting had been called by Reginald Radcliffe to consider " the lamentable loss of converts and what could be done in regard to it." Nobody, however, had been able to suggest anything that went beyond making efforts to link them up with Churches. In the end the conclusions that the conference arrived at were :

1. That young converts must be diligently, prayerfully, and wisely cared for.
2. That a certain amount of system and arrangement is necessary to this being efficiently done.
3. But that it is inexpedient to attempt, and impossible to carry into effect, any extensive organization to this end.

It remained for William Booth and his followers to put into effect the plan which it was agreed was "inexpedient and impossible," namely, the " extensive organization."

2

Early in 1862 a glimmer of light had appeared in a statement that the Special Services Committee had a band of workers formed from converts ; but within a month the old question was brought up again at a meeting of " friends

[1] Appendices F, Doctrines ; G, Pledges ; and R, Foundation Deed (1878) of The Salvation Army

and promoters of certain special services in the East of London." The report of this meeting stated :

The subject [the keeping of converts] was found to be surrounded with difficulties, especially as regarded existing religious bodies ;

and the lament was made :

Even those who had taken the most active part from the commencement confined themselves to evangelising and nothing else, and had never persisted beyond the query which has not yet been answered, " What to do with the converts ? "

There were exceptions. Individuals here and there in East London, as elsewhere, were so moved by what God had done for them that no difficulty or lack of encouragement prevented their persevering in their new-found faith, or restrained them from preaching the Gospel.

The London Congregational Union, which had four evangelists working in East London under local superintendence, issued a statement characteristic of the period :

The increasing number of conversions in Bethnal Green has become a subject of anxiety to the Committee. To form the converts into a church in so early a stage of their Christian life seemed to be inexpedient ; but the Rev. W. Tyler, who had taken the superintendence of the Mission, being applied to, cheerfully undertook to affiliate them with his own Church as a branch fellowship, and they are now thus associated, about forty.

Even Mr. Tyler, a man of the widest sympathies, and later a warm friend to William Booth and The Christian Mission, did not go further than to undertake to affiliate revival converts with his Church as a branch fellowship. For " respectable " congregations to accept them as full fellow-members was another matter.

Complementary to the establishment of The Christian Mission as a separate organization, and of at least equal importance in the solution of this problem, was the innovation that its programme provided for the holding of meetings in and out of doors, *all the year round*. Other missions, with very few exceptions, had divided the efforts of the year between open-air work without indoor meetings in the summer, and indoor meetings without open-air work in the winter. William Booth had insisted from the first that The Christian Mission must have for all-the-year-round use " some central building in which to hold our more private meetings and in which to preach the Gospel." At first the places available were poor, but poor as they might be they were " home " to the converts.

William Booth's point of view in regard to open-air meetings was well put by him in a letter that he wrote to the Rev. Charles H. Spurgeon when some ten years later that great preacher was about to give a special address to open-air workers. William Booth wrote :

At the risk of appearing somewhat officious I want to ask from you in your address a much-needed condemnation of the " open-air season " theory so generally received.
That the many thousands of poor people who attend no place of worship should be left to wander about half the year without hearing the Gospel, on the plea that wind and weather do not permit of open-air preaching, seems to me to reflect upon the manhood, let alone the charity, of Christian men.

From the time William Booth took charge of the Mission till the present day, the proclamation of salvation in the open-air, summer or winter, has been continued without break by its members and, except in a few countries where at times the authorities have not permitted open-air meetings to be held, their successors the Soldiers of The Salvation Army.

Practical application of the underlying purpose of the penitent-form (" the mourners' bench " of Methodist camp meetings) had also a great deal to do with the Mission's success in keeping so large a proportion of its converts. When William Booth began, as a lad, to hold cottage meetings in

Nottingham he required that penitents should make a definite public confession of Christ. When he conducted revival services in churches he invited seekers to kneel at the communion rail. He put the penitent-form into use in the earliest days of The East London Christian Mission. Peter Monk knelt at a penitent-form at one of the first Tent meetings.

In his own accounts of the first meetings held in the Dancing Academy, William Booth wrote of having led seekers " up the room " and " to the other end of the room." At meetings held in the Effingham and other theatres seekers were required to kneel at a penitent-form provided on the stage.

One of the reasons given why some of William Booth's first helpers left him was that they did not like seekers being directed to kneel at a penitent-form instead of being taken into an inquiry room. Further, William Booth deprecated any such use of the Bible in counselling penitents as led to their being told, as was often done, that if they only believed the words of some text, all would be well.

The method eventually adopted by The Salvation Army provides for exhortation to public declaration of the decision to serve God by kneeling at a penitent-form—with subsequent counsel and registration, especially in larger meetings, in the quiet of an ante-room.

In this three-fold manner—by insisting upon a definite confession of Christ, by watching over and instructing converts, and by training them and setting them to work to save others—the problem was solved and the Mission's future as an aggressive organization assured.

Chapter Nine

THE TURNING POINT : 1867

I

Oh, for trust that brings the triumph
When defeat seems strangely near :
Oh, for faith that changes fighting
Into victory's ringing cheer :
    Faith triumphant,
Knowing not defeat or fear !

HERBERT BOOTH'S immortal song of faith was not written till some years later; but may it not have echoed impressions made upon him in childhood by discussion in his home of the Mission's early struggles—when more than once, especially towards the close of 1866, it must have appeared likely that defeat was indeed " strangely near " —and the cheers that hailed the triumph of faith ? The position of the Mission at the opening of 1867 must have seemed precarious indeed, yet before the year had ended proportionately greater advance had been made than in any other of the Mission's existence.

In that year The East London Christian Mission had been so named, and established on a permanent basis ; it had acquired its first headquarters ; paid workers had been added to its staff ; the great venture of hiring a theatre for Sunday meetings had been made—and succeeded ; William Booth's answer to the despairing question of the past, " What shall we do to keep our converts ? " had been put into operation and proved right ; Mrs. Booth had visited a Mission station for the first time ; The Evangelisation Society had come to the aid of the Mission in such generous degree as to be one of the decisive factors in its struggle to gain a footing ; James Dowdle, earliest of those who became prominent leaders at a later date, had begun his career in the Mission ; social relief work had been organized ; the financing of the Mission had been systematized, its funds divided under specific headings and its first financial statement issued ; the Mission had come triumphantly through its first " outside " inquiry ; remarkable publicity had been given to it in the religious press.

The year opened dismally. The cholera epidemic of 1866, together with continued unemployment, had intensified distress. Newspapers were full of appeals for help ; in these William Booth joined. The Mission distributed food and clothing, opened soup-kitchens and provided free teas. " Maternal societies," which found " poor mothers with scarcely a rag of clothing for either themselves or their babies," were put into operation. Also a Biblewoman was engaged, " who is most useful visiting the distressed by day, and assisting in religious meetings in the evening." But William Booth and his workers kept their heads and did not allow themselves to be stampeded either into distributing food, clothing, blankets, etc., indiscriminately or into losing sight of the Mission's first objective.

Notwithstanding these distractions and difficulties, very early in the year William Booth reported :

We have not passed a week, nay scarcely a day, without marked tokens of the Lord's blessing. Twelve months ago we had only one preaching place and that was available for Sabbath only. Now we have six, and are conducting fifty services indoors and out regularly each week.

With the New Year had come occupation of two new preaching stations :

1. The Union Temperance Hall, High Street, Poplar.
" In an equally crowded and perhaps more destitute neighbour-

hood than Whitechapel. Between the Temperance Hall and stables and pigsties is only a wooden partition. The stench which oozes through the cracks in this is enough to poison us all." The site of the pigsties is now part of the Poplar recreation ground.

2. A small shop on a corner of Hackney Road near Cambridge Heath Station, with a fine space in front for open-air meetings. "During this summer this will be a most important place, being close to one of the most frequented exits from Victoria Park."

There was also the first mention of "a Bible carriage." To sustain this agency, to pay rents and meet incidental expenses, £6 per week was needed.

2

The Evangelisation Society now came to the aid of the Mission. A young man whose brother had been converted, and who had himself been powerfully stirred by meetings conducted at St. John's Wood by Mrs. Booth, had visited the Mission. Amazed and delighted, he reported to The Evangelisation Society what he had seen. William Booth had already invited the Society to investigate the work, but without success. Now, however, the committee was induced to look into it.

The minute book of the Society bears eloquent witness to the extent of the help that was at once given and which was continued throughout two years. The earliest records are :

February 13, 1867. Grant of £3 to each of Mr. Booth's five stations where no Church formed.

March 6. Resolved that the following additional grants be made to Mr. Booth :

> Rent of Easton Hall, £12 for a month.
> Evangelist's salary, £4.
> Printing, £1.

In the meantime, as is reflected in the next entry, services had been started in the Effingham Theatre, the first being held on Sunday 24th February :

March 13. Resolved that as Mr. Booth can obtain the Easton Hall for £10 per month, the balance of £2 allowed last week together with an additional £1 be allowed for printing expenses for the month.

Resolved that £10 extra be granted to William Booth towards rent of Effingham Theatre, and the 30s. allowed for the services of six men to be applied towards the printing expenses together with an additional £1 for the two months. Mr. Knott, Mr. Booth's man, 8s. per week for a month with a reasonable supply of tracts.

Grant of 5,000 tracts per week for a month to Mr. Booth.

In March also Mr. Frederick Whittaker, of Gray's Inn, honorary legal adviser to The Christian Mission, announced that a committee of which he was secretary was being formed to relieve William Booth of the heavy responsibility of the pecuniary support of the work. In addition to confirming that meetings were then being held in the Effingham Theatre, Mr. Whittaker stated that it had been feared, because of past experience—in 1862 the Effingham Theatre and the New Road Assembly Rooms (Dancing Academy) had been used by the East London Special Services Committee—that it would be difficult to fill the building. But the venture was proving so successful that it became the turning point in the Mission's struggle for existence.

Frederick Whittaker also announced that the Oriental Hall, Poplar, which was to be opened on Sunday 7th March, would be the Mission's ninth preaching station. Of this building it was later written :

The Oriental Theatre . . . was a dirty, draughty, and comfortless place of the lowest description. The floor used to be strewn with nutshells and orange peel, and there was open communication with cellars from which grievous stenches came up. Just the sort of place they say " decent people won't come to." Just

75

the sort of place in which to catch drunken navvies and train them to be martyrs.

By 1872 the Oriental Theatre had been given up, and the Poplar station fell back on the Union Temperance Hall.

Nearly seventy services, outdoor and in, were being held every week, throughout the Mission, though, with the exception of a Bibleman and a Biblewoman, all labour was unpaid. The £4 per week granted by The Evangelisation Society for the salary of an evangelist—at Poplar Easton Hall—was no doubt at first applied to the general expenses of the Mission. At the time of the opening no evangelist was being paid. Later in the year the Mission had nine workers " wholly occupied " and, presumably, paid.

Frederick Whittaker wound up with a complaint that, although the expenses were comparatively small, " so little support does this work receive that our brother (William Booth) is sorrowing at the thought of having to give up his Bible carriage for want of funds." The Bible carriage was not given up !

3

What was probably the first newspaper report of the Mission's doings covered one of the meetings held in the theatre. It was frankly cynical, and its references to William Booth were the reverse of complimentary, but it confirmed that from the standpoint of the size and character of the audience the venture was fully successful. It also gave some particulars of the methods used to attract the people. Under the heading " The Rev. William Booth at the Effingham Theatre," this report in the *East London Observer* (6th April 1867) began :

This gentleman has for some time past occupied the above named theatre on Sunday evenings as a preaching place, and enormous

audiences have been drawn to listen to his exordiums by the
somewhat plagiaristic announcement of " Change of Performance " and " Wanted ! 3,000 men to fill the Effingham Theatre.
The Rev. William Booth will preach in this theatre on Sunday
evening next ! "
The result of so novel a promise as a change of performance,
coupled with a formidable body of people marching down the
Whitechapel Road singing, we are bound to say with not the
most melodious of harmonies, no doubt drew many persons who
might even now be ignorant of the exact kind of " performance "
so vaguely shadowed forth by the bills. The boxes and stalls
were filled with as idle and dissolute a set of characters as ever
crossed a place of public resort.

Very different was another report under a similar heading.
A series of articles in the *Nonconformist* dealing with " Irregular Religious Agencies " and conditions existing in the
East End featured the work of the Mission. A Sunday
evening at the Effingham was described at length. To the
reporter, who found people waiting for admission half an
hour before the time for the opening of the doors, the
building was

. . . one of the dingiest and gloomiest places of amusement to
be found perhaps in all London. The walls were black with dirt,
the gaudy, tinselled ornaments half hidden by layers of dust, and
the gaslights so few in number as to give an extremely cheerless
and dispiriting look to the whole place.

No wonder that shortly after this the proprietor, Morris
Abrahams, had it pulled down and a much finer theatre
built in its place.
The audience and the effect of the proceedings upon its
members provided material for a vivid word-picture :
The labouring people and the roughs have it—much to their
satisfaction—all to themselves. It is astonishing how quiet they
are.
There is no one except a stray official to maintain order ; yet
there are nearly two thousand persons belonging to the lowest

and least educated classes behaving in a manner which would
reflect the highest credit upon the most respectable congregation
that ever attended a regular place of worship.

" There is a better world, they say " was sung with intensity and
vigour . . . everybody seemed to be joining in the singing.
The lines

> " We may be cleansed from every stain,
> We may be crowned with bliss again,
> And in that land of pleasure reign ! "

were reached with a vigour almost pathetic in the emphasis
bestowed upon them. As they reluctantly resumed their seats a
happier expression seemed to light up the broad area of pale and
careworn features, which were turned with urgent, longing gaze
towards the preacher.

Mr. Booth employed very simple language in his comments . . .
frequently repeated the same sentence several times as if he was
afraid his hearers would forget. It was curious to note the intense,
almost painful degree of eagerness with which every sentence of
the speaker was listened to. The crowd seemed fearful of losing
even a word.

It was a wonderful influence, that possessed by the preacher over
his hearers. Very unconventional in style, no doubt . . . but it
did enable him to reach the hearts of hundreds of those for whom
prison and the convicts' settlement have no terrors, of whom
even the police stand in fear. . . . The preacher has to do with
rough and ready minds upon which subtleties and refined discourse would be lost. . . . He implored them, first, to leave
their sins, second, to leave them at once, that night, and third, to
come to Christ. Not a word was uttered by him that could be
misconstrued ; not a doctrine was propounded that was beyond
the comprehension of those to whom it was addressed.

There was no sign of impatience during the sermon. There was
too much dramatic action, too much anecdotal matter to admit of
its being considered dull, and when it terminated scarcely a person
left his seat, indeed some appeared to consider it too short,
although the discourse had occupied fully an hour in its delivery.

And William Booth had earlier feared that he was not fitted
to deal with such audiences !

Then came the prayer meeting. Not a few, it is recorded, went on to the stage and knelt there.

All the time distress was increasing, especially in the Poplar district. William Booth in the course of a further urgent appeal for help wrote :

It has been a week of great sorrow, indeed I am almost worn out. The people are starving at Poplar. My visitors say that visiting is almost impossible without the means of relieving the people. Late last night one of my helpers at Poplar was here with a most harrowing account. I had thought of giving up the soup kitchen, but I am assured that the soup and the bread given with it are all many poor creatures have to eat the day through. In White-chapel too we have similar cases of destitution.

A second article in the *Nonconformist* " Irregular Religious Agencies " series produced further evidence that the Mission was now making rapid progress. Preaching places occupied since the beginning of the year in addition to those already recorded, were, it was stated :

1. The Alexandra Hall.

This was a covered skittle-alley attached to the White Raven public house, Raven (renamed Bedford) Street, Whitechapel, now a printing-works. It seated about 250 persons. A few boards, placed over the frame where the ninepins were fixed on weekdays, served as a platform. When the " Eastern Star " hall came into use it would seem to have been given up.

2 and 3. Gospel Halls on Bow Common and in Whitechapel Road. The latter was used for week-night meetings when the Effing-ham Theatre was first used on Sundays.

4. The Cambridge Music Hall.

" A more interesting or more beautiful chapter of home missionary enterprise is not perhaps to be found in the annals of Christian work," commented the writer, who added :

Dean Stanley not long since earnestly inquired in what manner he might draw working men to Westminster Abbey. If he would allow such men as Mr. Booth and his colleagues the use of the consecrated edifice for a Sunday or two he would have no need to repeat the question.

In conclusion came the first reference to efforts towards self-support by the Mission :

Although in the humblest circumstances, the helpers themselves contribute about £3 per week, while for the remainder (it was stated in addition to the help given by The Evangelisation Society £20 per week was required for the expenses of the Mission) the Mission is entirely dependent upon voluntary offerings.

The story of this vital year is continued in the minutes of The Evangelisation Society.

April 17. Resolved that a further grant be made to Mr. Booth for the Oriental Music Hall, Poplar, on the same terms as before for another month. See minutes, 6th March. Namely to £17.

This is the Society's first mention of the Poplar Hall by this name. The minute of 6th March had " Easton Hall."

4

The minute book of The Evangelisation Society recorded the first approach to the acquisition of the " Eastern Star," the one-time beer-shop that became the Mission's first headquarters.

June 12. Secretary read a letter from Mr. Booth inquiring if the committee would assist him in taking the Pavilion Theatre [for the holding of Sunday services while the Effingham Theatre was being rebuilt], the Wilton Music Hall [situated in Grace Alley, Well Close Square, Wapping, but not again mentioned], and a shop in Whitechapel Road [the " Eastern Star," 188 (now 220) Whitechapel Road ; identified by Mrs. Salthouse (1934), who lived there for four years (1872–76)], when same was referred to Mr. Pearse to inspect and report on.

In a letter to the *Nonconformist*, dated 12th June, William Booth stated that he had in view the securing of a central place for private and week-end meetings. The last place so occupied, he wrote, was over a stable and latterly they had been without any place at all for these purposes. This "central place" again was the "Eastern Star." It had been agreed to pay £120 for the lease, which had eighteen years to run, and £10 deposit had been paid. To fit it up £40 more was required. The "Star" had been burnt down, but rebuilt. Before its destruction it had been "notorious for immorality and other vices."

June 26. Resolved that the Pavilion Theatre, Whitechapel, be taken for Mr. Booth for 8 weeks at £6 per Sunday night. Also that Mr. Booth be requested to take up the work at Sclater Street with the arrangement that a Biblewoman be engaged at 5s. per week, and all expenses of cleaning.

The East London Special Services Committee had had its headquarters at 34 Sclater Street. The meeting-place used here by the Mission was the famous "Room behind the Pigeon Shop," so named in a pamphlet with that title by Railton (1878). At the request of William Booth, George White and his family [1] transferred their service from the Holywell Mount Chapel to the "Pigeon Shop," and in the beginning White had charge of the work there. From the Bishopsgate Street end, Sclater Street had been widened ; the shop was the first on the left going east, on the still narrow portion of the street, but the whole section has been destroyed by bombing. Of this station George T. White has written :

It was a little hotbed of Salvation ; several families were brought in ; later their children went out into the Mission work. My father was in charge at the Pigeon Shop. No official ever came there, and Mr. Booth but seldom. We paid our own way. The outlay could not have been much. The room was not worth

[1] Appendix B, Early Witnesses

more than 2s. per week. A woman was paid to clean it. There was gas. When Mr. Booth came to our home at Hackney, which he frequently did, all business was done by word of mouth. Our principal worker was Mr. Longmore, a goldbeater. While at work he thought out his sermons ; you could hear him singing while he thumped out the gold into leaf. On Sundays he wore a preacher's coat buttoned up to the chin, with a neat little white tie. He did most of the preaching ; then Mr. Joseph Jermy and father took turns. There was little Miss Jones who used to pray —talk about " pulling the glory down " ; she did !

To get to the room we had to go through the house by a narrow dirty passage. It opened on to a filthy yard. Formerly it was a furniture-maker's workshop. The seats had no backs ; there was coconut matting on the floor, and the roof was so leaky that when it rained heavily we used to get wet as we sat there.

On Sunday mornings Sclater Street was almost impassable ; it was crowded with men and boys buying and selling their fancy dogs, birds, and other live-stock. Gambling went on everywhere ; I remember seeing coppers thrown on to a board, which the winner would greedily scoop up.

The room itself was infested with vermin ; often we had to strip when we got home and hunt through our underclothes. The woman who kept it, and from whom we rented the room, sold white or coloured mice, rats, and guinea-pigs, but not pigeons. [The last occupier of the premises indignantly denied that it had ever been a " pigeon shop." Pets were still sold there.]

It is surprising that anyone came into the rough, dirty places of those days.

About 5.30 one Sunday afternoon we were getting ready to start for the open-air meeting when a knock came at the door. I remember saying, " That is Mr. Booth's knock." He had walked from the West End where he had preached in the morning. He asked at once how we were getting on at Sclater Street. Father told him that several families had got saved, and that the Sunday before, while we were marching to the hall, an old mattress had been thrown out of a second-storey window, covering us with dust and bits of straw. Mr. Booth soon forgot he was tired. Mother wanted him to rest and go in time for the indoor meeting after the open-air. But he had a hurried tea (he liked a good cup of tea) ; had two boiled eggs and some thin bread and butter, and then off we went. He listened with evident delight to the testimonies of the new converts. On the way to the hall we were baptised with tea slops ; winkle shells were also thrown at us from the same upstair window.

The interest of The Evangelisation Society extended farther afield than the East End. The next entry in the minute book (3rd July) recorded that £20 was granted to assist William Booth in taking the Assembly Rooms at Margate for services on the Lord's Day for three weeks. This was one of the special campaigns conducted during this period by Mrs. Booth ; among other good results it brought into the Mission two young women whose careers can be traced in its magazines from month to month over a considerable period, in a continual round of devoted service.

The first of these was Miss M. C. Billups [1] of Cardiff, whose parents were close friends of Mr. and Mrs. Booth. Giving up ambitions for a musical and literary career, Miss Billups, who sealed her consecration at the penitent-form on the stage of the Effingham Theatre, became a powerful preacher and led hundreds of souls to Christ. She helped William Booth with the preparation of the Mission hymn-book. Some years later (1876) she married a revival minister and went with him to Canada.

The other was Miss Jane Short, whose minister (Congregational) had advised his congregation not to be led away by a woman preacher ! This, far from achieving its purpose, made her decide to attend Mrs. Booth's meetings at Margate. Miss Short became one of the Mission's district visitors and in addition had charge of the collection and distribution of old clothing and boots.

Miss Billups and Miss Short entered the Booth home as paying guests, their contribution to the housekeeping expenses making it possible for Mrs. Booth to move to the

---

[1] Appendix E, Early Supporters

quieter neighbourhood of Victoria Park, away from the distracting noises of Hackney.

A report on the past eighteen months' work of the Mission issued by " a small committee of gentlemen "—un-named, but no doubt the regular Mission committee—stated that a thousand persons had professed conversion, and that " these have been so far instructed in the duty of working for Christ, that Mr. Booth has now a band of nearly 300 helpers in his Mission."

At a noonday prayer meeting held in July at 165 Aldersgate Street (Y.M.C.A.), William Booth said :

There have been many prayers offered in this room and elsewhere for the East of London. For the encouragement of those present I want to say that those prayers are being answered in some measure . . . some who have been notorious sinners are being turned from darkness to light. On last Sabbath some twenty open-air meetings were held in connection with my Mission alone, at all of which vast crowds of people listened most attentively to the messages of mercy.

In the evening some 2,500 people, the great majority of whom were working-men, were gathered in the Pavilion Theatre. This, considering how strongly these beautiful evenings must have tempted them away to the park, was felt to be very gratifying. Many came on to the stage to seek Jesus, indeed the theatre could not be cleared at 10 o'clock until the gas was turned off.

He added that a beer-shop [the " Eastern Star "] had been obtained in Whitechapel, and a few days previously had been opened for the service of God and the preaching of the Gospel.

The continued anxiety of William Booth that the Mission should do what it could for the relief of distress was shown by his repeated appeals to the public for help, and in the addition to its staff of a Mrs. James Reid, the widow of a Presbyterian minister, who came to reside in East London that she might give all her time to this work.

In the meantime William Booth and The Evangelisation Society had an interesting passage regarding the financing

Early Supporters of The East London Christian Mission
1 Henry Reed, 2 Samuel Morley, 3 John Cory, 4 R. C. Morgan,
5 Mrs. Billups, 6 Mr. Billups.   (*See* Appendix E)

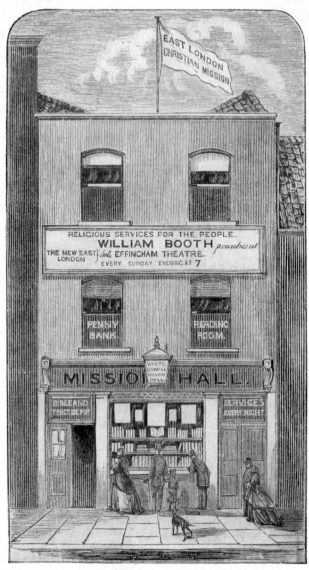

The Headquarters of The East London Christian Mission
(from the cover of the first Report of the Mission, 1867.
See page 88)

of the purchase of a site and the erection of a hall at Poplar. William Booth opened the discussion (31st July) by applying for a grant at the rate of a year's allowance, namely, £112. The secretary of the committee was instructed to say it " did not feel at liberty to entertain the matter at present." A month later William Booth returned to the charge. His application was then referred to a full committee. It would appear that the matter was then allowed to drop.

5

The names first applied to the Mission varied. There was The Christian Revival Association (describing the body William Booth proposed to establish in connection with the Tent Meetings) and there was also The East London Christian Revival Society of its first printed document. But a ticket of membership (September 1865) and a temperance pledge card (January 1866) both bear the designation, The East London Christian Revival Union.

At this time there were in various parts of London organizations known as Christian Missions, with prefixes denoting the districts in which they worked, or the churches with which they were connected ; for example, Cross Street Chapel, Islington, Christian Mission, the St. Giles Christian Mission, and Drury Lane Christian Mission—the last named at least having been " in operation for some years." This no doubt helped towards the choice of the name, " The East London Christian Mission." No statement was made regarding the Mission's adoption of this designation ; it first appeared, without comment, as a heading in press reports that on Sunday, 1st September 1867, the Mission had taken possession of the large lecture hall of the Edinburgh Castle Tavern, Stepney, as a preaching station, the first of a number of extensions of the work made in 1867.

The "Edinburgh Castle" was included in the list of stations given in the Mission's 1867 report, but not in that accompanying a survey of its work issued early in 1868. The reason for its abandonment, as given by Railton (1880), was that it was found " as difficult to attract people to the spot for living water as the publican had found it to attract customers for drink." To this he added :

A much more costly and protracted effort than the resources of The Christian Mission could then sustain was needed to fill it with the poor. The Mission had to be content in those days with little rooms in back streets.

But even so, in the short time meetings were held there a link was forged with great things of the future. In one of the first meetings held, a milkman named John Gore was converted. He emigrated to Australia, where his meeting in Adelaide with another Mission convert, Edward Saunders from Bradford, twelve years later, led to the unfurling of the flag of The Salvation Army in the Commonwealth.

6

The first of the Biblewomen employed by the Mission was Mrs. Eliza Collingridge, who came into touch with it at meetings held in the Dancing Academy in the autumn of 1865. She took no part in public service until some time later when at a holiness meeting held in the old wool-shed, Three Colts Lane, she " gave herself up to do and bear anything for Christ." After this she was " ready to speak in the open-air, the cottage, a mission hall or a theatre, in the midst of friends or foes." Her testimony, given at the opening of the " Edinburgh Castle," won " the first Australian Salvationist "—no doubt John Gore. Mr. Collingridge, a lamplighter, though not as gifted as his wife, was esteemed as a faithful Mission worker.

When Mrs. Collingridge died in 1872, William Booth wrote of her :

She was endued with useful gifts, and blessed with extraordinary grace. For a long time she devoted much time to the Mission, without fee or reward ; but to enable her to give a few extra hours in the middle of the day, to visiting the new converts and the sick and dying, we arranged to give her a trifle of money to obtain a little extra labour to supply her lack of service in her own home (1867). We remember how reluctantly she received it. Her heart was liberally disposed towards the cause of God, and had she possessed the ability to dispense with it, she would never have taken a farthing from the exchequer. Thus she became the first paid worker the Mission had . . . the whole of her time and energies for about five years afterwards were devoted to visiting the homes of the people, conducting private believers' meetings, dealing with anxious souls, and preaching.

Other points from William Booth's tribute were that she

understood and enjoyed real religion ; understood soul-winning work ; had skill in leading anxious souls by the nearest road to Christ ; was an acceptable and useful preacher ; in the open-air would hold a crowd of the roughest East End men breathless ; everywhere had souls for her hire, and had only to go anywhere once to be wanted again.

Another announcement of importance made at this time was that The East London Christian Mission had adopted as one of its " official preaching places " a room at the factory of Messrs. Owen, Merton and Co., Millwall.

Charles Owen, a partner in the firm, an earnest Christian, had established in the factory a Bible class for employees and their friends. One Sunday afternoon on his way to the London Hospital, Whitechapel Road, he saw a crowd gathered round a little woman who was standing on a chair, talking. It was Mrs. Collingridge, and she gave him a hand-bill bearing an invitation to " Come and hear William Booth in the New East London Theatre on Sunday at 7." He went, but at the moment he entered William Booth was warning his hearers of the danger of continuing in sin, and the first word Owen heard him use was " damnation." This so shocked him that he turned round and went out !

At a Christian Mission tea meeting at Poplar, a few weeks later, he again heard Mrs. Collingridge speak and then asked William Booth—whom he had come to understand better—to send her to hold a meeting in one of the rooms at the factory. At this meeting several men and women were converted. The next week Owen had a large packing-room cleared and seated, and such an awakening followed that still more accommodation became necessary and a coach-house was next set apart for the gatherings. Owen became secretary of the Christian Mission committee.

7

In September was issued a " Report of The Christian Mission under the superintendence of William Booth " which covered two years and two months. Its cover bore a picture of the former " Eastern Star," now the headquarters of the Mission. The flag shown flying over the building affords the earliest evidence extant that flags may have been used actually, as well as being mentioned figuratively when branches of the Mission were opened.

The report summarized all that has been set out as to the necessity for and purpose of the Mission, gave a list of the preaching stations—already mentioned in the order of their having been opened—and stated that seating was now available for 8,000 persons. Ten persons were wholly given up to the work in the various departments, nine of them being sustained by the Mission. Details of the accommodation provided by the Mission headquarters were also given. These last reveal the part William Booth designed the Mission should play in the life of East London ; some of these plans were never put into effect, others came to fruition only after the full development of The Salvation Army.

The long room, built for an American bowling saloon, and which will seat 300 people, is crowded to the doors every evening in the week [stated the report]. The shop is a depot for the sale of Bibles, Testaments, and soul-saving literature ; the parlour is a reading-room to which the people can come at any time, and in which we supply them with cheap refreshments ; in the concert-room we hold mothers' meetings, Bible classes, believers' meetings, etc., while in other parts of the house we have a residence for a Biblewoman and her husband and six brethren engaged in the Lord's work.

Mr. and Mrs. Collingridge occupied the " residence," but it does not appear that the " six brethren " ever did.

The weekly programme was very full. It was set out in detail.[1] The methods and agencies employed were described :

House to house visitation. Those willing to engage in this work go forth two and two, taking a small district, distributing tracts, conversing and praying with the people and inviting them to the meetings. . . . These visitors meet together weekly for mutual counsel and prayer and to report the cases of great temporal distress met with in order that relief may be given. To reach the masses of the people they must be visited personally.

We have also four Sabbath and two day schools, and it is one of our cherished purposes to enter largely upon ragged school work. Another important agency for spreading the truth is our Bible carriage, with which two brethren traverse the crowded thoroughfares selling Bibles, Testaments, and different kinds of religious literature, giving away tracts, publishing the different meetings, preaching Christ, and conversing with the passers-by.

[1] Appendix H, Programme of The East London Christian Mission

A postscript stated that the Bible carriage, a new one, had been destroyed by fire, and contained an appeal for help to buy another.

A special feature was the provision of a reading-room, it being urged that

a great barrier in the way of the poor man's rescue from the public-house, is the want of a place of pleasant resort and profitable and agreeable society. His own home but seldom offers him any attraction, consisting as it often does of but one small room of small dimensions, with six, seven, and sometimes as many as fourteen inmates !

After being accustomed to the exciting scenes and associations of a life of sin, he finds himself at the onset of a new career alone in the streets exposed to the full force of those temptations before which he has so often fallen. To meet and counteract these temptations, as we have opportunity, we wish to open comfortable rooms with books and papers to which converts can come through the day, or at its close, where they will meet brethren of kindred sympathy and purpose, who will cheer them on in the way of reformation.

The question naturally arises : what of the wives and the children ? There was no lack of sympathy for the man's family, but it was William Booth's view that what was essential to saving the man must be put first, for his salvation would change for the better everything in which he was concerned, whether in his home or elsewhere. Nor were the people at home neglected in the meantime. Under the heading " Relief of the Poor " the report stated :

Side by side with the sin and vice and crime which abound in the East of London, as a necessary consequence, the most painful poverty prevails. Since the last commercial panic this destitution has increased tenfold. Great numbers have been reduced from plenty to actual starvation, and at this hour in the richest city the world ever saw there are thousands who literally are pining away for want of bread.

Nine months ago our loving Father plainly indicated that we

were to do something for these suffering ones, and since then we
have been able to administer relief to the amount of about
£300. We are now distributing 240 tickets for bread and
meat weekly, in addition to which money is given where needed ;
sometimes money is lent, situations are sought out, and in various
ways a helping hand is extended to the afflicted and suffering
poor.
We have now in operation several maternal societies.
During last winter we had a soup kitchen at Poplar from which
we supplied about 140 quarts of soup with bread daily ; this
work we hope to resume there almost immediately, and also in
Whitechapel where such assistance will be equally needed.

Typical of the purpose underlying all these efforts for
the temporal benefit of the people, is the record of what one
of the Mission's visitors said :

How could I hope to impart any spiritual help if I could not do
something to alleviate the dreadful poverty ? Would they not
call it a mockery to talk about their souls whilst their bodies were
perishing with hunger ? But when I give them a loaf of bread or
a pound of meat their hearts are opened, and I can preach Christ
with some hope of success.

Considerable space is devoted to testimonies given by
converts, nearly all formerly drunkards. One woman had
been a notorious character ; when she was drunk, six policemen had been needed to take her to the station. In several
instances the conversion of a whole family had followed that
of one of its members.

It was proposed to provide a " new hall, ragged school,
soup-kitchen, Bible depot and reading-room " for Poplar.
The Mission had been established there for eleven months,
but for its

enlargement and perpetuation the present premises, which cost at
the rate of £125 per annum, are wholly unsuitable. . . .
I now propose to build a hall to seat 1,000 persons. . . . All the
seats will be free, and the place will be essentially a religious home

for the working people. A plain hall can be constructed for £500 . . . when completed we shall have premises of our own at a cost of not more than £30 per year.

The financial arrangements of the Mission were simple. It was essentially the day of small things, but in accounting for money received, and in providing for its proper use, nothing was lacking of the scrupulous care that characterized William Booth throughout his career. In the report he stated :

At the present time about £40 are required weekly and so far the funds necessary to meet this expenditure have been sent me. The Evangelisation Society has rendered very important assistance. . . . I propose shortly to publish . . . a full account of income and expenditure. The offerings sent have been appropriated in every case as desired by the donors and have therefore divided themselves into the following funds :

The General Spiritual Work. This money is applied to the salaries of Evangelists, Biblemen and Biblewomen, rent of theatres, halls, and general expenses of evangelistic labour.

The General Poor Fund. With this we help the poor, indiscriminately, that is, without regard to whether they belong to the Mission, the only condition being want. Inquiry as to need is always made before help is given.

The Destitute Saints Fund. For the relief of the members of the Household of Faith exclusively.

The Building Fund. After the erection of the hall and school at Poplar, we hope to erect a similar but much larger pile of buildings in Whitechapel.

The promised financial statement [1] was printed inside the back cover of the December 1868 number of the *East London Evangelist,* but may have been circulated earlier ; it disclosed that the Mission had paid its way. William Booth's heart had led to his over-spending on relief for the suffering poor, but on the whole turnover the Mission had finished the year with a little over £100 in hand.

[1] Appendix I, Balance Sheets

With regard to his own support, William Booth stated :

Having some years ago given up a stated income in the ordinary ministry for evangelistic work, I am wholly dependent on God for the support of myself and family. Hitherto I have not been necessitated to appropriate a penny of the general funds to my own support, the Lord having sent it specially for that purpose through a few devoted servants in different parts of the country.

The prime mover in thus providing for the support of William Booth had been Mr. Samuel Morley. The names of the gentlemen who had consented to be referees and of those who had become members of the Mission committee were given in the report.[1]

" In conclusion," summed up the report, " it will be seen from the foregoing " :

1. That this is a true Home Mission ; a mission to the heathen of London who are as ignorant, as besotted, as miserable, as wicked, nay more so, and in danger of a greater damnation than the heathen abroad.
2. That this work is in true sympathy with man as man, seeking to bless him in body and soul, for time and eternity.
3. That this is truly evangelistic work. As we stood at the corner of a densely populated thoroughfare in Shoreditch preaching not only to a crowd around but to an audience at every door and window in the street, a man cried out, " They cannot get the people into the chapels, and so they have come out here." That was just it. . . .
4. That this is an unsectarian mission. Our creed is the Bible, our work is to publish the Gospel, and we welcome as co-workers all who hold the word of God as the standard of faith and practice and whose hearts are in sympathy with revival work.

8

Towards the end of September, William Booth applied to the committee of The Evangelisation Society for assistance

[1] Appendix C, Membership of Committees ; Appendix E, Early Supporters

to enable him to carry on services in theatres. A grant of £100 for three months was passed, but when, early in October, the committee had before them another letter from him, asking for a cheque on account of this grant, the secretary was desired first to ascertain the financial condition of the Mission and report. At the next meeting of the committee, held on 16th October, the secretary reported :

that Mr. Booth's accounts differed from office books in consequence of his having continued the work at the Oriental Music Hall and Pavilion Theatre without requesting the committee to renew the previous grants, thus incurring liabilities amounting to £114 beyond what had been granted him, showing the Committee to owe him altogether £214.

There was no suggestion that proper accounts had not been kept ; the position had been ascertained from Mr. Booth's own books. A cheque for £50 was ordered to be sent on account of the grant.

The next paragraph of this minute would seem to show that the Mission's report and appeal had reached the committee—and had not altogether pleased them :

Secretary was requested to write Mr. Booth stating he had greatly alarmed the committee by sending forth circulars announcing that he required £40 per week for his work, and that they (the committee) feared he was involving himself so that their connection with him would bring them into discredit.

It is hardly a matter for wonder that the committee—few of whose members are likely to have had first-hand knowledge of the Mission, but who would all be fully aware of the poverty-stricken condition of the East End—felt some hesitation. Lacking William Booth's faith, vision, and conviction, they naturally sought assurance that money entrusted to their stewardship should not be squandered. The amount at their disposal was by no means unlimited ; indeed, by May of the next year the committee had to announce that the money contributed to the work by " one benevolent Christian merchant " had been expended and that £290 was the " full amount of free income." Between February 1867 and March 1868, six donations, each of £1,000, had been received by the Society from a Mr. Bewley, of Dublin. Mr. Pearse was again asked to investigate and report.

The services held in the Pavilion Theatre were markedly successful. At the final meeting, testimony was most effectively and impressively given by converted drunkards, blasphemers, gamblers, and infidels. At least 3,000 persons were present ; fifteen went on to the stage seeking salvation.

It was at the Pavilion that James Dowdle first attended a meeting of The East London Christian Mission. He had come to London from his Wiltshire village home to work on the Great Western Railway, but was now employed by Mr. Stevens, a builder, who was an enthusiastic evangelist with a hall of his own in Paddington. The two spent all their spare time in missioning among the roughest men they could find wherever their work took them.

Stevens had conducted services for the Mission, and William Booth asked him to put the " Eastern Star " into order for the Mission's use. Dowdle came with Stevens and was invited to attend the first meeting held in the Pavilion. He spoke at the great open-air gathering that preceded it and joined in the march to the theatre. That night some sixty seekers knelt at the penitent-form.

Later, when William Booth asked Mr. Stevens to recommend a worker for the Mission staff, he sent James Dowdle to him.

On 6th October, William Booth conducted the first of a series of Sunday evening meetings in the City of London Theatre, Shoreditch. The next Sunday, meetings were begun in the New East London (late Effingham) Theatre. Its site, adjacent to St. Mary's Whitechapel station, is now occupied by the Rivoli Cinema.

In the meantime Mr. Pearse had made his investigation of the Mission's affairs. That he had reported favourably is shown by this next extract from the minute book of the committee of The Evangelisation Society :

November 13. Resolved that Mr. Booth be informed that the committee recognize the importance of special help to the East London work, and also the efficiency of the efforts put forth, and agree to sanction the payment of the sum of £67, the sum asked for by Mr. Booth as an extra grant towards the expenses incurred in the late services held at the Pavilion and Oriental theatres.

To this, no doubt to meet the wishes of a still timorous minority, was added a cautionary suggestion that William Booth should revise his expenditure to avoid possible embarrassment.

An interesting possibility is pointed to by an entry (27th November) in the minute book of The Evangelisation Society :

Resolved that £10 be granted to Mr. Booth for evangelistic services at Store Street, Bedford Square, for a quarter.

Nothing has been found to suggest that this was a preaching station of the Mission, but a brief notice in the *Revival* (12th December) stated that " Mrs. Booth conducted meetings in the Concert Hall, Store Street, Bedford Square, on Sunday."

When, on that hot July day two years before, William Booth had walked to Whitechapel for his first meeting at the Tent, he had lunched " with a friend in the West End." He had also preached there " one morning on his way East." The Store Street Concert Hall may have been the place of his preaching, and his " friend " in charge of a mission there, in which he, as well as Mrs. Booth, may have assisted.

9

Mrs. Booth did not, at its beginning, take active part in the work in East London. Her first personal contact with the Mission is said to have been made on a Sunday at the end of October, or early in November, and the Oriental Music Hall, Poplar, was the station she then visited. Both the extent and the character of the work surprised her. On Sunday, 30th January 1870, Mrs. Booth gave the address at the New East London Theatre—this is her first visit to the Mission recorded in its magazine.

During the first years of the Mission, Mrs. Booth was very fully occupied with campaigns in various parts of London, as well as with others taking her as far afield as Ramsgate, Margate, and Brighton. The strain these campaigns imposed upon her was very heavy; the strongest could not have borne it without effect, and Mrs. Booth was far from strong.

Further, conditions in the East End were not such as could wisely be faced by a mother with young children—her youngest two were born in 1865 and 1867—herself in delicate health and in no way inured to infection.

Nevertheless, all accounts indicate that from the first Mrs. Booth took the keenest interest in all that pertained to the Mission. Her home was in a special sense its headquarters, even after this was officially provided elsewhere. For a lengthy period a prayer meeting was held there weekly for the Mission workers, and upon occasion the Mission committee sat there. Mrs. Booth, too, was the counsellor, upholder, and partner of her husband in all that was planned or done. And when, later, William Booth was absent from the Mission for months at a time, through illness, Mrs. Booth took his place at the head of its affairs.

When speaking at the yearly meeting of the Society of

Friends (1882) Mrs. Booth said of her experience in these days :

My husband took the lead. I stood back, having, perhaps, less of the power of adaptation in my composition. I said, " My dear, don't go too fast ; don't go ahead of the teaching of the Holy Ghost." But I went and saw the marvellous results. I saw 20—30—50 of the biggest blackguards in London broken all to pieces on a single Sunday night—just as much broken down as the Jews were under Peter's sermon. I spoke to them and applied the tests of the Gospel, and I was bound to say, " This is the finger of God ! "

CHAPTER TEN

PROGRESS AND ORGANIZATION : 1868

I

THE Evangelisation Society had finished 1867 by warning William Booth that it would not be able to help The Christian Mission to the same extent as previously. At the most, he was told, £4 per week could be expected, and for one quarter only. But hardly had 1868 dawned before the committee, at a meeting on 8th January, resolved to grant £8 per week for the two theatres for a month, instead of the £4 per week generally ; William Booth was to undertake to find money for his " other Missions." And when the month had expired the grant of £8 weekly was renewed.

William Booth was becoming recognized as an expert organizer of religious work among the poor. It was recorded in the *Christian Year Book*, 1868, that he was " carrying on evangelistic work on a large scale." Early in January he was one of the speakers at a meeting of the Evangelical Alliance. The subject under discussion was " The Evangelization of London."

In a review of the Mission's work, headed " The Heathen of Our Own Land," the *Revival* stated :

Twenty persons are wholly employed, assisted by a large band of devoted helpers. [In the *East London Evangelist* of February, William Booth stated " not a single official salary is paid," evidently meaning " office staff " as distinct from the Mission field force.] One hundred and twenty services outdoors and in are held weekly, at which the Gospel is preached on an average to 14,000 people.

The first number of the *East London Evangelist* had this heading : " The Heathen of Our Own Land " above the name of the Mission, but it did not so appear again up to the end of the year (1868). No covers are available after December 1868 until June 1876, when the heading had become "The Christian Mission *to* the Heathen of Our Land." A letter dated 6th February 1876 from Railton to William Booth was written on paper bearing a similar heading.

At this time sewing-classes were started at various East End centres in connection with public efforts for relief of the existing distress. One of these, "a sewing-class, District 12," had for superintendents "Mr. Skelton and Mr. Booth." The places of meeting were 43 and 188 Whitechapel Road. Later this class became the sole responsibility of The Christian Mission and was settled in rooms in Sidney Street, with Charles S. Mitchell in charge.

An endeavour was made to establish a home for women. An appeal for help for this purpose was issued by Mrs. Flora Reid. Mission leaders had been much distressed because sometimes women had presented themselves and prayed to be saved from a life of infamy, but after they had been sent in vain to refuges, they had again returned to the streets.

But the women's home did not materialize. By April only a little over £20 had been received, and this, with the consent of the subscribers, was paid over to the Rescue Society on condition of their accommodating girls sent to them by the Mission.

2

In February yet another Mission station was opened. Of this William Booth wrote :

In connection with these Lord's Day meetings [held in Cambridge Music Hall ; the City of London Theatre having been found too draughty and cold, a move had been made to this building], we have just taken and fitted out a Coffee-House on the corner of Worship Street, Bishopsgate, Shoreditch. Here we shall have a

Page from Minutes of the Shoreditch Elders' Meeting, 29th September 1868, showing emendations made by Charles Owen, Hon. Secretary of the Central Committee of The East London Christian Mission. (*See* page 109 and Appendix J)

Sunday Night Meeting in East London Theatre
(from an early drawing)

long room in the front that will hold 250 people, a shop for the sale of Bibles, etc., six rooms upstairs for private meetings, and, on a small scale, a temporary refuge for the poor, friendless, penniless girls who are so constantly crossing our paths.

To this was characteristically added :

In the hall downstairs the Gospel will be preached every night. I am of the opinion that in such situations congregations could be obtained in the day-time and propose by-and-by to try meetings through the day. The gin-palaces are always open. The emissaries of evil are always at work ; why should the ambassadors of Christ wait for the evening ?

This place had been nominally a coffee-shop and lodging-house, but in reality was of the vilest and most infamous character imaginable. When it was taken, the Mission's tenancy of the Holywell Mount Chapel was brought to an end. A fine place this had seemed to the missioners after the wretched holes and corners to which they had been accustomed ; at first meetings there had been well attended, but it never seemed to answer its purpose ; some thought this was just because it was a chapel. When a higher rent was asked it was given up. The chapel was then commercialized. It became a plywood factory and was burned down in the 1930's ; its silver communion service and offertory boxes were given to the Mission.

The combination of the coffee-house for week-nights and the Cambridge Music Hall for Sundays was a much better proposition than the chapel had proved to be.

In the meantime the work carried on in the room " behind the Pigeon Shop" had so prospered that it became desirable to obtain larger premises for Sunday evening meetings, and in February the Apollo Music Hall, Hare Street (a continuation of Sclater Street), which had seating accommodation for 600 persons, was occupied.

The services at the East London Theatre had more than

kept up their interest and power, and Sunday after Sunday, with scarcely any advertisement, even the top gallery had been crowded. Converts continued to be made ; the measures taken for their care were :

The name and address of every seeker was recorded, and a ticket given to admit them to a private meeting at the Mission hall on the following night, when they were met by experienced and sympathetic Christians who personally examined them as to the depth of their convictions and the ground of their hope, giving suitable counsel and placing them in touch with some duly qualified brother or sister whose work it was to watch over and counsel them. On the average about thirty persons attended this meeting.

What was being done by the Mission in the room "behind the Pigeon Shop" and at the Apollo was described in detail in a lengthy article in the *Christian World*. After noting the character of the neighbourhood and the pitiful trade carried on in small wild birds—even nightingales—the writer stated :

The E. L. Christian Mission have quietly established a preaching-room in a place where we should least have expected to find it, at the back of a bird-fancier's shop !

As we pass the doors, close to Club Row, the words of a hymn, perhaps that commencing,

A charge to keep I have,
A God to glorify,

may be heard ringing above the noise of chaffering . . . and higgling from the crowd assembled in the shop . . . we pass into a small backyard, some four or five feet square, where, opening a door, we find ourselves in a roomy outbuilding, which has been formed into a preaching-room capable of holding 150 or 200 persons . . . sometimes there is a sudden irruption of bird-fanciers who, placing their bird cages, tied up in coloured handkerchieves, under the rude forms, listen with strange attention to the proceedings.

The writer also visited the Apollo Music Hall. He noted that, whereas on week-days the hall is densely crowded by young people of both sexes who amuse themselves by mimicking and listening to the popular comic songs of the day, on Sunday evening all is changed. The mirrors and gas-lamps are as resplendent as ever ; the greasy benches are as densely occupied ; but the waiters, the orchestra of three performers, and the comic singers have disappeared. . . . Instead of roaring noisy choruses of popular songs, those present devoutly raise their voices in gladsome notes of praise to their Maker . . . even the unwashed, grimy-looking idlers who lounge at the public-house bar appear somewhat touched. They certainly seem very uncomfortable. They slowly put down their pipes, leave off drinking their beer, and either enter the hall from the bar or else betake themselves to the tap-room.

Because its week-day character was so bad, the proprietor of the Apollo lost his licence, and the building was bought by Messrs. Hanbury, Truman and Buxton. The Mission was shut out when the place was closed ; but William Booth, George White with him, went to the brewery office and in the end the new proprietors let the Mission have the hall free of charge, for week-days as well as Sundays, and erected a partition closing off from the bar a passageway to the hall.

We were allowed the use of the music hall by the brewers after they bought the house [commented Railton later] because they wished the latter to be decently conducted. The idea of decency as in any degree connected with any public-house in such a neighbourhood was horribly amusing.

Before concluding his report, William Booth stated that the room " behind the pigeon shop " was given up entirely when the Apollo became available for week-nights. The last reference to this station (Sclater Street) was its inclusion in the list of " Weekly Offerings " printed in the East London Evangelist for October 1869. The Mission was turned out of the Apollo without notice at the end of 1875.

A hall was opened in Shoreditch on 8th September 1867. This was said to be the tenth station of the Mission. Its exact location was not given. When the Worship Street coffee-shop, after nearly three years of occupation by the Mission, was taken over by the Board of Works to be demolished for street-widening (1870) a building in Hare Street—No. 18, formerly a furniture store—was used in its place. As Mission references loosely placed Hare Street in Shoreditch, though actually it is in Bethnal Green, this may have been the hall that was opened in 1867. It had three floors and sometimes meetings were held on all three simultaneously. At the end of 1871 it was given up and what belongings of the Mission were there were removed to the Apollo.

3

Hardly a month of this year passed without an innovation. March was opened with the announcement that Sunday morning services had been started at the East London Theatre. The experiment was to be tried for a month. A thousand persons had been present on the previous Sunday. Before long, three meetings were being held in the theatre on Sundays, that in the afternoon, at 2.45, being for converts. Later reports show this to have been a testimony meeting ; it may be regarded as the first " free-and-easy " on a large scale —a " free-and-easy " being the Mission's spiritual counter-attraction to the public-house " sing-song " to which the term was customarily applied.

A suggestion in keeping with the current practice of other religious bodies was contained in the next entry in the minutes of The Evangelisation Society's committee :

March 6. Mr. Booth's work to be continued until the end of this month on which date his case will be further considered, when it is hoped that the weather will allow of the services to be held in the open-air.

It may well be imagined, though no record has survived, that William Booth protested at once on the ground that it would be a fatal error to return to the old " seasonal " plan, which, with such good results, the Mission had abandoned. Entries for the summer months, covering April to August, record the continuation of the £8 per week grant.

Free breakfasts for the poor were frequently provided on Sunday mornings. A thousand residents of the neighbourhood were gathered into the Cambridge Music Hall for a breakfast and a

service presided over by Mr. T. B. Smithies, editor of the *British Workman*. Among the speakers were a lady member of the Society of Friends, James Dalton [no doubt James Dowdle], formerly a railway guard, and the Rev. William Booth.

The *Morning Advertiser* published a lengthy account of another of these breakfasts, in April of the following year (1869) at the East London Theatre, to which between 800 and 900 persons sat down :

The congregation . . . had come from the back slums, from foetid courts and alleys, from the casual wards, from the registered lodging houses, from sleep on doorsteps and in railway arches . . . a mixed multitude ; the negro, the mulatto, and other denizens of distant countries were there . . . every variety of feature . . . all were thinly clad, the bulk in rags and tatters.

The close co-operation between Friends and the Mission is further shown by the proceedings at a meeting held in the Friends' Meeting House, Bishopsgate, in May 1868. It was called by Mr. Smithies and Mr. Bastin—Friends who were united " in a feeling of deep concern for the teeming multitudes of the vast city with desires for their temporal and spiritual good." A report stated :

Mr. Hamilton, one of Mr. Booth's helpers in Whitechapel, who usually met inquirers on Monday evenings, related several remarkable cases [conversions] resulting from the breakfasts in the theatre.

Mr. Smithies introduced Mr. Booth by saying that he had been prejudiced against him, but since he had known him and seen his work all that had passed away. He had learned more the last six months of the people of London than in the previous sixteen years. Mr. Booth said he had noticed a difference between the poor of Millwall and of Whitechapel and Bethnal Green. The former had their recent recollections of better days, but the latter were the children, grandchildren, great-grandchildren of starving people, consequently they were physically and mentally depressed. They wanted heart. They wanted Christians to go and lay their hands upon them and let them feel the touch of warm sympathy.

William Booth concluded :

Christian men, come and lay hands on them, giving us one, two, or three days a week ; come and do the work altogether ; there is an open door ! Your friends go to China—is not a poor English brother or sister as worthy of your kindness as a poor Chinese ! Come, and God will richly repay you here and in the world to come !

Neglect of home heathen greatly disturbed William Booth; the constraint immediately upon him was to help and save them.

A further appeal for contributions towards replacing the burnt Bible carriage set out tersely the objects of this agency :

1. The word of God circulated.
2. Religious and healthy literature is spread abroad.
3. Good Bible pictures circulated.
4. Opportunity for continuous preaching of the Gospel by those in charge.
5. Profits made small but helpful towards the remuneration of the labourers who when not employed with the carriage are engaged in visiting the sick or conducting religious meetings.

The aggressive virility of the Mission found yet another outlet, described in an announcement by William Booth, that on 16th March special week-day services in the open-air at noon would be commenced on the Mile End Waste, a short distance east of the spot where the Mile End Gate formerly stood, in addition to services in the same place every night at seven, Fridays excepted.

On Good Friday a tea meeting at Poplar was attended by 300 persons ; another in the East London Theatre, by 1,000. As open-air services were held while these teas were in progress it would seem they were provided either for the needy poor, or to attract people to the indoor meetings held afterwards, or for both reasons.

It was different on Easter Monday evening in St. Mary's Schoolroom, Whitechapel, loaned by the Rector, the Rev. J. Cohen, when about 800 members of the Mission took tea and at the meeting which followed 1,500 were present, the majority of whom had been brought to Christ through the instrumentality of the Mission.

Before the end of April another enterprise had been set on foot, first referred to as being at Shalfont, but later named as at Stratford. A few weeks previously meetings had been started in a room. But a Unitarian church was for sale ; William Booth wanted it for the Mission in order to " publish a Divine Jesus, almighty to save." May had not closed before William Booth had secured it and had reported :

For the opening meetings the hall was crowded in every part —vestry, lobby, and yard—and souls found Jesus.

Also that in the East London Theatre on " last Sunday evening, thirty-four souls sought mercy."

The *Saturday Review* had criticized the East London Relief Committee's use of " religious instruments " (The East London Christian Mission was one of these) for the distribution of temporal relief. At a meeting of the committee William Booth stated that the writer of these criticisms had come to the Effingham Theatre to get material for another article, but had remained to pray.

The weekly outgo of the Mission had by now risen to

£50, and the balance with which the year had been started had gone. William Booth found it necessary to make an urgent appeal for help in order that he might not be compelled to close down some of the Mission's stations and agencies. This was backed by the *Revival* (20th June 1868) in wholehearted manner :

There is not in this kingdom [it said editorially] an agency which more demands the hearty and liberal support of the Church of Christ. . . . Mr. Booth's operations are unparalleled in extent, unsectarian in character, a standing rebuke to the apathy of Christians, and a witness to the willingness of God to show His work unto His servants and to establish the work of their hands upon them.

In striking contrast was a letter addressed to the editor of the *East London Observer* (20th June 1868) by " Anti-Humbug," the first of a long line of supercilious objectors to methods that offended their ideas of good taste :

I beg to call your attention to the disorderly mob which nightly parade the Mile End Road and its vicinity singing some rude doggerel verses which doubtless they please to style hymns. There must be, surely, someone in authority who has power to put a stop to such profanity and vulgarity, etc., etc.

Evidence of advance in organization is to be found in the minute book of the elders' meeting of the Shoreditch Circuit.[1] The first entry is dated 26th August 1868. There were intervals, some of considerable duration, when the elders did not meet. At one time Mrs. Collingridge was superintendent of the circuit and presided at the meetings, being thus the first woman to hold office in The Christian Mission. During her term of office a Drunkards' Rescue Society was put into operation. An interesting sidelight on the practices of those days is that J. C. Moore, one time chairman of the trustees of Holywell Mount Chapel, was treasurer of the Shoreditch Circuit, with but a short interval,

[1] Appendix J, Minutes of the Shoreditch Circuit Elders' Meeting

until September 1874, though he was at no time a member of the Mission : indeed, he regularly conducted open-air meetings which were entirely his own concern. The minutes show that he took a keen interest in the affairs of the circuit, and was by no means silent with regard to the direction of its work and workers. James Flawn was a member of the meeting and Peter Monk was one of its secretaries. William Booth took the chair on 30th July 1874 when " complaints were presented." At the next meeting (18th September) Brother Moore's resignation was accepted from " all his offices as regards Shoreditch station." It would seem reasonable to conclude that the " complaints " had included protests by members of the Mission against control by an " outsider." W. J. Pearson (later Colonel Pearson) was then chairman.

The minutes appear to have been submitted to the central authority of the Mission for approval or otherwise. Not only are they signed—or when he was not present, countersigned—by William Booth, or by Charles Owen, who was secretary to the central committee, but emendations were made. When, for instance, upon the motion of its secretary, the elders' meeting had proposed to modify the programme of open-air activity, the alteration was disallowed.[1]

In September the Mission first ventured outside the East of London. A gentleman of Upper Norwood, feeling anxious about the spiritual welfare of a colony of working people which had sprung up at Gipsy Hill and were without church or chapel, had built a mission hall for them, but had had small success. A few services held there by Mrs. Booth led to The East London Christian Mission being invited to take it over. This was done, but when under Mission guidance conditions improved, the originator wanted to resume control and the Mission withdrew.

[1] Minute of 29th September 1868 ; Appendix J

109

4

The most important event of September was the submission to the public by William Booth of a proposal for the " conversion of a penny gaff (known as The Eastern Alhambra) opposite. Limehouse Church into a mission hall." Disclosing that he had earlier made other attempts to bring this about, he wrote :

By the common consent of the whole district this place has been a moral pest-house . . . the place is offered to us on a lease of three years at £52 per year . . . it is near good stands for the open-air work, and with a resident population ignorant as heathens and black as night it will be one of the most important mission stations in London.

The Limehouse penny gaff was not singular in its bad character, the *Christian World* (2nd October 1868) declared :

Of all the numerous demoralizing things to which the children of the poor are exposed none have proved more thoroughly mischievous . . . entertainments consist of dancing and singing. County magistrates issue licences, and police cannot interfere unless theatrical representations are ventured upon. The frequenters learn to mix with the criminal population. The penny gaff has been largely instrumental in supplying recruits to the ranks of those who procure their livelihood by the practice of vice and crime, forming, as it does, an efficient school for the drunkard and the thief.

Regarding in particular the gaff at Limehouse, this journal added :

It bears a most disreputable look. The roof is merely three or four feet above the level of the pavement, the entrance door being gained by descending several steps. The interior . . . a low, badly lighted and badly ventilated hall about sixty feet long and twenty in width, fitted up with boxes, stage, and orchestra, all being as dirty as possible.

The floor is bare earth, and under the gallery opposite the stage is a small dark cellar in which the boys and girls waiting for the second performance are crowded together in the most indecent manner. The language and actions witnessed were horrible and filthy in the extreme . . . it was the black spot of the district.

The opening of the gaff as a Mission station took place on Friday 2nd October 1868. It continued to be used until December 1877, by which time it had fallen into a condition beyond repair. A new hall, to accommodate about 500 persons, was erected on the site and opened on Good Friday (19th April) 1878 ; it cost £710.

William Booth and Dr. Barnardo met at the gaff. Seeing The Christian Mission operating at the street corners, Mr. Barnardo—he was then a student at the London Hospital —threw himself heartily into the work and helped the missioners, assisting also at the indoor meetings.

One evening he told William Booth of his intention to do something for homeless boys, and that he had taken a house to begin in.

" Where is it ? " asked William Booth.

" Hope Place, Bull Lane, Stepney," was the reply.

" What is the rent ? "

" Eight shillings for the downstairs, and we shall get the upstairs, which is another four shillings."

They shook hands and parted with mutual expressions of thanks, and wishes for each other's success.

To bring the yearly closing of the Mission's accounts into line with general financial practice, the next statement of income and expenditure issued covered nine months, from 1st January to 30th September 1868. Including amounts received for special purposes, the income of the Mission had in this period reached nearly £2,500. A balance of £42, 2s. 3d. was left, in addition to monies held in trust. Offerings had reached a weekly total of between £30 and £40, and the subscribers' list was also assuming encouraging proportions.

5

In October the first number of the Mission's own magazine made its appearance. William Booth, as editor, dedicated the *East London Evangelist*

. . . to all those who, obedient to the Master's command, are simply, lovingly, and strenuously seeking to rescue souls from everlasting burnings, through His own precious blood, who, believing in the promise of the Father, are seeking with strong cries and tears for a mighty outpouring of the Holy Ghost to stem the rising tide of error and superstition, break up the slumbers of the professing church, arrest the attention of a dying world, and clothe the religion of Jesus with its primitive simplicity, fervour, and energy. . . .

The magazine was issued monthly, the price being one penny per copy. Messrs Morgan and Chase were the publishers. Fortunately its earlier numbers on file were bound with individual covers intact, preserving information not otherwise available.

For the first few months reports from other missions and revivalists were occasionally inserted, but they did not amount to much, and soon the only work recorded was that of The East London Christian Mission.

Intimation that much space was to be devoted to the topic of personal holiness was accompanied by a statement that the importance of this theme could not possibly be over-rated. In this connection, when reviewing the lessons of his fifty years of salvation service (1894), William Booth declared :

There came another truth which had much to do with the experience of these early days—the willingness and ability of the Holy Ghost to make men entirely holy in thought, feeling, and action in this life. This truth laid hold of the very vitals of my new religious experience. . . . I saw that Entire Holiness was insisted upon in my Bible ; while my hymn book, composed chiefly of precious hymns of Charles Wesley, was all aflame with the beauty and value of it. . . . I saw thousands seek it and testify to having found it. How could I doubt but that God was willing and able to sanctify any and every man, body, soul, and spirit, who trusted Him to do so ?

Mrs. Booth early became a contributor to the magazine. Her first article, " Prevailing Prayer," occupied the place of honour in the December issue.

From the time the Mission published its own magazine it was able to record its doings in greater detail than could be expected from other publications. It gained great advantage from this, as well as from the inspirational value of the exhortations and directions that its leader could now address to his followers without restriction of character, length, or frequency. On the other hand, the Mission lost the intimate touch it had enjoyed with readers of various religious journals, for after 1868 the religious press made comparatively little mention of the Mission's work. The *Revival* was an outstanding exception to the general rule ; it graciously and warmly welcomed what was in effect a rival journal, and continued to give much space to reports of the Mission's activities.

The great development of The Salvation Army's use of its own press in later years immeasurably compensated for any disadvantage that may have attended the first days of the Mission's own venture into this field.

Before lengthy reporting of the Mission's doings had been left, with the exception indicated, almost entirely to its own journal, another most informative survey of its work was printed in the *Nonconformist* (4th November 1868). The writer—signing himself " P "—had already in a series of articles in the same periodical presented its cause with ardour and understanding ; he now showed, especially, that he had grasped the significance of the principle upon which The Christian Mission acted in setting its converts to work :

The working men and women joining the movement [he wrote] instantly become its most efficient assistants, devoting all their spare time to the labour—unpaid and too often unpraised—of rescuing multitudes of their fellow-workers from the depths of social degradation into which they have too frequently become plunged.
Careless of rain or cold, of wind or storm, these faithful and devoted servants of religion are always to be found at their posts, never flinching from their self-imposed tasks, thereby affording not merely an example which might be beneficially imitated in higher quarters, but also a significant commentary on the common but not always correct assertion that the working classes are naturally irreligious.
Every success of the whole movement has been due to its working-class character. The great bulk of its advocates are working people, its leaders never forget that they have to deal principally with the working people ; in fact it is rendered so completely working-class in all its numerous ramifications that to all intents and purposes The East London Christian Mission can be regarded as an essentially working-class religious movement. . . . What work could be more useful or praiseworthy than this ? . . . are not these men and women true Christian patriots ?

It is strange that the Mission's Annual Reports did not refer to these articles, and that the *East London Evangelist* did not mention, let alone quote from, the one now noted.

The *Revival* printed at this time a long description of a Sunday afternoon testimony meeting (" free-and-easy ") in the East London Theatre, contributed by Gawin Kirkham, Secretary of the Open-air Mission. The testimonies were reported in detail :

The meeting commenced at three and lasted one hour and a half. During this period forty-three persons gave their experience, parts of eight hymns were sung, and prayer was offered by four persons.

Among those who testified was :

One of Mr. Booth's helpers, a genuine Yorkshireman named Dimaline, with a strong voice and a hearty manner.

Testimonies were given at this meeting by " all sorts and conditions " and many were stories in brief of remarkable conversions. The report concluded :

Mr. Booth led the singing by commencing the hymns without even giving them out. But the moment he began, the bulk of the people joined heartily in them. Only one or two verses of each hymn were sung as a rule. Most of them are found in his own admirably compiled hymn book.

The first record of a public utterance by William Booth's eldest son, William Bramwell—afterwards his Chief of Staff and his successor in the Generalship of The Salvation Army—was given in two lines :

A little boy, one of Mr. Booth's sons, gave a simple and good testimony.

Bramwell Booth has left on record that when he was twelve or thirteen years of age—8th March 1868 was his twelfth birthday—he was taken by his father late one Sunday night into a drinking saloon, a little known beer-shop in Cambridge Road. Of his impressions he wrote in later life :

The place was crowded with men, many of them bearing on their faces the marks of brutishness and vice, and with women also, dishevelled and drunken, in some cases with tiny children in their arms. There in that brilliantly lighted place, noxious with the fumes of drink and tobacco, and reeking with filth, my father, holding me by the hand, met my inquiring gaze and said, " Willie, these are our people ; these are the people I want you to live for and bring to Christ."

At the end of the year came the last grant from The Evangelisation Society. At the August meeting of the committee it had been decided that the grant for the next quarter could not be more than £20, but when September came £50 was provided ; in December another £50 was found. These amounts were for the respective quarters in advance, taking the record up to the final entry in the minutes :

April 7, 1869. The hon. secretary was requested to inform Mr. Booth that the committee find themselves compelled to relinquish the pecuniary grant hitherto made to him, and trust from the several previous intimations that he is quite prepared for this decision.

One of the factors that brought about this cessation of financial help was the good use that had been made of that already provided ; The East London Christian Mission had definitely become a permanent, organized institution, and as such was no longer within the scope of the constitution of The Evangelisation Society.

It would be difficult to write too warmly of the aid the Society gave the Mission in the days of its struggle for existence, and, consequently, to its preparation for becoming The Salvation Army.

CHAPTER ELEVEN

"ACTS OF THE APOSTLES": 1869

I

ENTIRELY unaware that they were doing anything beyond giving themselves to the work of the moment with full intent and devotion, the early Christian Missioners set up enduring standards of soul-saving effort. By 1869 the principles underlying the work of the Mission—and that of the succeeding Salvation Army—had found full expression. Wider variety of development was to come later, but the germ of all that has followed was by that time present. It is the purpose of this chapter to put on record not only the larger events of this year, but sufficient detail of the everyday work of the Mission to show the spirit and purpose of the missioners. It will not be possible at any future stage to give so detailed an account.

On the cover of the *East London Evangelist* was printed : " And the hand of the Lord was with them, and a great multitude believed and turned to the Lord."—Acts xi. 21.

It was, indeed, an appropriate motto ! Unceasingly proclaiming the apostolic message, that Jesus is mighty to save, the fervent missioners filled pages of the *East London Evangelist* with accounts of miracles of grace. This notwithstanding bitter opposition and great difficulties. R. C. Morgan was moved by his knowledge of the missioners and their work to use as a heading to his report in the *Christian* of the Mission's tenth anniversary meeting the words " Successors of the Apostles."

To begin with, conditions of life in the East End continued

to be appalling. To the weakening effects of near-starvation and the terrifying prevalence of epidemic disease were added discouragement and dismay born of lack of hope of betterment, a dark background against which the devotion of the missioners stands out in amazing contrast. At the end of 1868 William Booth had made an urgent appeal for help for the starving poor :

Already the workhouses are crowded and cases of death from actual starvation are occurring. The tales of distress we are called to hear are harrowing in the extreme.

In one paragraph there was a note akin to despair :

Only the Government can give effectual assistance ; but it is to be feared that, in the coming short session, too many things of national importance will crowd on the attention of Parliament for the East of London to get even a passing notice. It appears certain, therefore, that between hundreds, if not thousands, and slow starvation, there is only the scanty pittance of parish relief when it can be obtained, supplemented by the contributions of those whose hearts have learned, from the practice and precepts of Jesus, to pity and remember the poor.

Members of the Mission were among the sufferers :

One of our members and family go into the workhouse next week. A dear sister, awakened and saved in the Mission, after many weeks of lingering disease has just died in Jesus, and her mother, utterly destitute, knows not how to get her into the grave.

In the following number of the *East London Evangelist* (January 1869) an even more dark and dismal picture was presented :

Day by day the mass of pauperism is becoming intensified. Hunger and misery reign supreme in the homes of the poor . . . sickness and fever tread closely on the heels of want, and in the thin pinched features of many a little one, in their wasted arms and shrunken hands, we read the saddening story of parental privation and suffering.

Another danger is springing up. Large numbers of young women, usually employed in the manufacture of articles of clothing, find themselves deprived of work, and, having no friends or resources, are being helplessly driven into a life of shame and misery.

All the poverty of the metropolis, together with no small proportion of that from the provinces, seems steadily gravitating towards East London.

Unspeakably anxious as William Booth was to relieve the distress he saw all round him, nevertheless he did not allow his mind to be turned from what he believed to be the fundamental remedy :

Legislation [he added] may do much to counteract the mischief, but the spread of religious feeling will do more. The true Christian is a real self-helper. In bringing the truths of religion before the suffering masses we are also assisting in the great work of social reform . . . when we have taught people to be religious, half the battle has been won.

Again in July, William Booth wrote of the privations of some of the missioners :

Many of our poor people are pining away in dreadful poverty, and many of them are sick. The fund from which we help the poor of the household of faith is overpaid, and we have had to adopt the painful alternative of stopping the trifling weekly allowance we make to a few of these suffering ones.

One missioner—" her life a fair sample of the darkness, poverty, misery, and suffering so common in the back streets "—was known to have walked about for three days without breaking her fast rather than ask for help, and was one day found with a small crust of bread on her table, about to make tea with *old* tea leaves. Another missioner, to provide for her husband, five children, and herself, had 7d. per day and two quartern loaves weekly from the parish.

Notwithstanding all this, reports aglow with holy joy gave the year's records a good start :

Whitechapel (Dimaline) : A few of the baser sort would fain break up our meetings [in the open-air, of which work Dimaline had charge] ; but with hearts filled with the love of God we are more than a match for all the opposition men and devils can raise . . . oft-times the power of God manifestly rests upon the people, and tears are seen to flow on every side.

Almost every report was accompanied by information about converts. Among those mentioned in these were :

" one of the chief persecutors," and " a man who has been one of the most wicked of drunkards and blasphemers that ever trod Mile End Road." Also " a bricklayer's labourer, a rough, burly man," whose conversion had stood the test of persecution emphasized by " brick ends and pieces of mortar," and who had been re-united with his wife and children as a result of the change in his life.

Limehouse (Gaff) (Stephen Knott) : Seldom a service is held without seeing someone come out on the Lord's side . . . not only have they given themselves to God, but they are trying earnestly to get their friends and companions to join them . . . they work with ungodly men and women but they are enabled to stand fast.

Three Colts Lane (Joseph Jermy) : As we have made fresh inroads on Satan's territory we have had increased opposition . . . open-air meetings have of late been much disturbed by the police . . . people listened most attentively, and some followed us indoors who professed to find salvation. Among Sabbath school scholars we have some decided conversions.

" *Behind the Pigeon Shop*," *Sclater Street* (George White) : Great improvement in attendances both indoors and in the open-air . . . hall crowded, many having to go away. Three found mercy.

A series of stories of " Trophies of Grace " included :

. . . a professed infidel, a coloured man, converted at a meeting in the East London Theatre . . . after giving good testimony for several weeks, disappeared . . . later letter from him stated he had obtained berth on a ship to earn money to pay debts and was still serving God. Rather than beg from the Mission he had tramped to Sunderland, spending fifteen days on the road, often with nothing to eat, sleeping in fields, yet was happy, for " God was with me ! "

Others were a drunken butcher, and a backslider who had been a persecutor.

An adventurous "band of brethren" for the last three Sundays in February had

gone out to labour in Ratcliffe Highway . . . beyond comparison the foulest sink of moral corruption in the metropolis. At first persecutors contented themselves with ridiculing and mutilating the tracts that were given . . . next Sunday they threw one brother down three times. . . . On Sunday 21st, a crowd of men, women, and children fell to howling and yelling in the most frightful manner. While Brother Rose was speaking about a hundred fell upon him . . . one young man seized him by the throat, another tried to trip him up, another struck him a heavy blow on the cheek, and the whole party were being much knocked about when four policemen came and compelled the preachers to desist, dragging them away and threatening to lock them up. . . . In obedience to the police the brethren departed, greatly rejoicing that they were counted worthy to suffer for the sake of Jesus.

This year was, indeed, marked by outbreaks of open and violent opposition. A year or two before his death (1939), the Rt. Hon. George Lansbury told a Salvation Army officer that, when a boy in Whitechapel, he had often seen William Booth and his followers mishandled by the mobs, and he used to wonder whether they would come out alive. Typical of this phase was a report from Poplar :

We have to listen to the vilest oaths and at times calmly bear a few blows. On Saturday evenings the arch-fiend rages most ferociously . . . a week ago we were beset by a gang of six or eight mechanics emptied from a public-house, but God restrained their violence. Several of them accompanied us to the temperance meeting, signed the pledge, and are now sober men. Amid all this opposition God keeps us strangers to fear . . . though often prevented by the cries and yells of wicked men from making ourselves heard by the people, a calm endurance for truth's sake creates conviction.

Publicans, on the Mission's final Sunday at the Three Colts Lane wool shed, stirred up the police to interfere with an open-air meeting on the ground of " obstruction." Two of the missioners were taken to the police station. Followed by a great crowd they sang, as they went :

> I will sing for Jesus,
> With His blood He bought me ;

and then,

> Jesus, the Name high over all,
> In hell or earth or sky !

At the station they gave tracts to each of the policemen who were just going on their beats. They then commenced reading the Bible, but being told to sit down they knelt down and prayed aloud. They were afterwards dismissed with an intimation that they would be summoned.

At the hearing a publican, the chief witness for the prosecution, averred that the preaching was a nuisance, that the singing, prayers, etc., disturbed the quiet of his customers, would not let his children sleep, nor him and his wife read. The policemen declared there had been an obstruction of the thoroughfare, whereas there were but some two dozen people present when the preachers were interrupted.

The magistrate . . . said he was sorry for the police to come into collision with the open-air preachers, but thought, on the inspector's statement, there had been an obstruction, that the young men had shown too much zeal, and they must be bound over in their own recognizances not to repeat the same offence in that particular locality for six months.

To the report in the *East London Evangelist* William Booth added :

We very much regret this collision ourselves. We think our brethren on this occasion should immediately have yielded to the request of the inspector to desist and gone elsewhere. It is better to suffer than to contend. If we have not had much protection from the police—and with a few exceptional cases they have rendered us no assistance whatever—still, they have not, as a rule, hindered us, as no doubt they have often been strongly tempted to do, and as our report of Ratcliffe Highway shows they did last Sabbath morning. We are on the side of law and order and wish to work harmoniously with those who are the paid guardians of the same ; and we hope our brethren will obey them so far as they can with a good conscience.

A month later it was reported from Ratcliffe Highway that, while bitter persecution continued, the police, instead of opposing, had protected the missioners. It would seem that William Booth's " olive branch " was bearing fruit. But the time came when to keep " a good conscience " men and women by the hundred submitted to the despoiling of their goods and to imprisonment rather than cease preaching the Gospel on the streets. The fighting—and winning—of this battle is one of the major issues of the history of The Salvation Army.

The missioners of Three Colts Lane set to work to find another hall and

after some little search found premises which, after considerable alteration, have been admirably adapted for Mission work. We have a large room that will seat 300 people, a smaller one that will hold 200, a soup-kitchen and other rooms. These premises we opened on Lord's Day, 14th February, when Mrs. Coates preached morning and evening.

Characteristic of their spirit was the manner in which the missioners set to work to break down indifference :

As the hour approached for the morning service, there were only a few people present, but the friends went out into the street and sang and invited the people into the hall, while a brother and sister went from door to door. . . . The place was three parts filled in the morning, while at night it was crowded right out into the street . . . so powerfully did the Lord work on the hearts of the people that the place was filled with weeping, and some were constrained to cry for mercy while the dear sister was preaching. We are already visiting from house to house, and shall at once open schools for the children, classes for ignorant adults, Bible and believers' classes, and set to work all the evangelistic agencies the Lord has blessed so much elsewhere.

This hall—an old tin-plate factory—was at the corner of George Street and Old Bethnal Green Road ; a year later it was taken over by the railway company and demolished. After two or three weeks' occupation of a small hall in Thomas Passage—since built over—a chapel in Hart's Lane was used until a move was made to the Railway Arch, which became famous in Salvation Army history as the home, for a considerable period, of the Bethnal Green Corps. The Three Colts Lane wool-shed, though first occupied as a week-night meeting-place for the parent (Whitechapel) station, was situated in Bethnal Green and had been later designated the Bethnal Green station.

2

A report from Poplar (July) reflected the exigencies of the times :

Poverty has sent several of our friends to the workhouse ; sickness has laid others up in hospital ; and emigration has taken away others who were noted for their piety, and praiseworthy for the service they gave at our meetings.

But notwithstanding all the difficulties,

converting power is felt in our meetings almost without exception, and strangely diverse are the characters brought under its influence. Formal professors, depraved young men, loose young women, and aged profligates are alike smitten, broken, and blessedly saved.

Among recent converts were

a robust young navvy who when cursing in High Street turned in at the hall attracted by singing . . . and went out himself singing praises of Jesus.

"Wooden-leg Sweety" who, obliged to close his stall by rain, came into the hall. He, too, went home rejoicing . . . has never opened his toffy stall or sold a farthing's worth on Sunday since. An old man (74) who, to get a moment's relief from "devilism," as he called it, had crept out of one of the narrowest, darkest dens of drink, prostitution, and blasphemy . . . in his life there had been tragedy unspeakable. Drink had swallowed up his wages, broken up his home seven or eight times . . . his wife had several times become a harlot on the street. For the safety of his own life he had to pay for her keep in the workhouse, and then for neglecting to pay had been sent to prison. At last his wife lost her life in a drunken row. Since then he has been living with a daughter in whom the wife's bad qualities seem more fully developed. She takes up his money at the Union, spends it in gin, goes home drunk, swears most awfully at the old man, then leaves him for days without fire or food. Yet notwithstanding all the horrors of such a miniature damnation as this place is, when I called unawares (writes the Mission leader) the old man had his Bible by his side. Since then the daughter has been to the hall and has signed the pledge. Oh, may God have mercy on her soul !

Two ship's captains had been among the converts at the Gaff, Limehouse.

While missioners were singing down a Bethnal Green street,

some half-drunken men jeered and mocked and threw water over them. When they knelt to pray the men fell upon James Dowdle, but he remained on his knees and answered all their jeers and oaths with prayers for them. Some of the persecutors followed to the hall, and at the close of the meeting one of the ringleaders asked if he might speak. With tears in his eyes he said he felt the missioners were right and he was wrong, and if they would forgive him he hoped the Lord would have mercy upon him.

A glimpse of Mrs. Collingridge at her work of visitation is given :

I was requested [she wrote] to visit an aged man, seventy-nine years of age, by his niece who, with her husband, had been very much blessed at our meetings at the theatre. I found the old man's mind very dark. He was an entire stranger to God, and I spoke to him as the Spirit enabled me.

When I called again he said to me, " Until I saw you I had never given religion a single thought, but thank God since then I have thought of nothing else. . . . He has pardoned my sins and now I am not afraid to die." . . . The following morning at three o'clock the summons came and he went to be for ever with the Lord. Oh, what a miracle of Grace !

Abundant evidence of the aggressive spirit of the Mission was provided by continual " new departures "—Mrs. Booth's epithet for fresh ventures. In her first of many reports, Mary C. Billups told of the formation of a band of " Female Pioneers " :

In connection with this Society (Whitechapel) fourteen of our sisters have banded themselves together to strengthen each other's hands in the Lord's work.

And :

A children's service is held every Sunday evening at Whitechapel Mission Hall, and two weekly juvenile classes for those who are seeking Jesus. . . . Many children come in from curiosity, frequently shoeless, bonnetless, ragged, and dirty in the extreme.

Another agency being fully worked was tract distribution :

About fifty of our brethren and sisters are engaged in distributing 2,000 tracts weekly from house to house. In face of much discouragement and at times persecution, they pursue their way regularly and bravely ; and although most of the streets which they visit bear a very bad character, for we aim at taking up the courts and alleys left by surrounding places of worship, they meet with a measure of success.

Some of these tracts were written by William Booth.

Stratford and Poplar missioners went together, under the leadership of Evangelist W. J. Sheehan, to Epping Forest for a camp meeting during which some of " the roughest and

rudest men and women in the East of London were constrained to listen for hours in unbroken attention." For the
second day's meetings a tent was pitched in the field. In the
evening, at a service conducted by William Booth,

speakers put the plainest truths in the most homely way. But
gradually a crowd gathered who were evidently bent on mischief.
Outside half-drunken fellows beat the tent with sticks, threw
stones, and flung children through the canvas. Inside a number
of youths intoned amens at the end of every prayer, laughing at
the sport, and others made most awful mockery. One batch of
men who had come to cut the ropes, caught in the act, came by
invitation inside and these unexpectedly took up cudgels for us,
and spreading themselves throughout the tent did good service in
ejecting four or five roughs and holding in awe most of those who
remained to annoy.

By this time many hundreds had come together in the field, and
it became necessary to close the meeting. This was the signal for
a general tumult in which the ropes were cut, the lamps seized
and emptied on the ground which set fire to the grass ; and but
for the diligent care of many hands would have burnt up the tent.
Several of our friends received heavy blows. Several things were
stolen, the tent sorely rent, and much crockery smashed. About
ten-thirty the police came to our assistance, and very near midnight we returned to our homes with hearts full of gratitude to
Him who had restrained not only our enemies but the hearts of
many of His own children who, with far less provocation, a few
weeks ago would have fought like demons.

The significance of the last remark lies in the fact that a band
of " converted navvies and coal porters were present."
Their leader was John Allen.

Of all the " trophies " of The Christian Mission, Allen was
regarded, with good reason, as the outstanding instance of
the " rescuing and transforming power of God." " For him,"
wrote William Booth after his death, " to stand and say
' Look at me ! ' was an argument neither sceptics nor devils
could answer."

John's foreman, who had been converted a fortnight

before him, had started on him directly. But he yielded only inch by inch. When, at length, he was got to a service at the Oriental Theatre, it was by his having been *dared* to go ! His conversion, some twelve days later, was graphically described by Railton :

When Jack came in [to the Temperance Hall, the week-night meeting place] with trousers-knee patched, coat elbows torn, the top buttons of his trousers undone, and a belt round his waist, his face and hands all black with coal dust, he looked indeed an outcast.

At the close of the meeting, knowing how deeply he was convinced of sin, but finding him still unwilling to come out to the penitent-form, they " mobbed him," as one who was present eloquently described the process. That is to say, twenty or thirty men and women of God knelt all round him where he sat near the door, and began to plead with God for his salvation. How thoroughly natural for a gang of converted roughs to mob anybody they wanted to see converted !

After a long time spent in prayer, he began to groan and bellow like a bullock for mercy himself, and this continued for about twenty minutes.

He then sprang to his feet, and stretching out his long arms he cried, with glaring eyes, " I do believe ! I do believe ! " The tears had made two clear alleys down his face.

And then he jumped, and shouted, again and again, " The blood of Jesus cleanses me from all sin ! "

" There's a Mission man for you," roared the ex-railway guard Evangelist [Dowdle] to his delighted followers.

It was not long before Allen was made leader of the " Navvy Squad " and with his men went from station to station of The Christian Mission, everywhere winning converts, among them numbers of men like themselves, convinced by their testimonies and the change in their lives.

In 1870 Allen became an evangelist. After a short time at Stratford he was sent to take command at Stoke Newington, and till his death in 1878 he was prominent in the service of the Mission.

3

Throughout the year meetings were continued in the theatres. Typical reports of these were :

After Mr. Booth had preached at the East London Theatre one Sunday evening in April, among others, three men, all confirmed drunkards, came on to the stage seeking salvation.

On 16th May we reopened the City of London Theatre (Shoreditch). St. Leonard's Music Hall was too small and badly ventilated. Mr. Booth preached a powerful sermon on profit and loss. There was a large congregation . . . eighteen came to the stage and with tears and prayers sought Jesus.

East London Theatre. The congregations here keep up wonderfully in the hot, sultry evenings, averaging on four Sabbath evenings in the past month (July) nearly 2,000 people, and there have been at least sixty anxious inquirers in that time.

On 23rd June, Mr. and Mrs. Reed entertained at Dunorlan seventy of the principal workers of the Mission. Then Reed conducted, on the afternoon of Sunday 18th July, an experience meeting of the whole Mission, held in the Wesley Chapel, Approach Road, Bethnal Green. About 1,500 persons filled the place. Mrs. Reed also preached at Limehouse on this Sunday evening. These were the first public tokens of their renewed interest after the rejection by William Booth, in January, of an offer by Reed to build a hall for the Mission.[1]

The missioners were to have gone to Upton Park for their annual excursion, but Reed next invited them all to come to Dunorlan, undertaking to pay the difference in the railway fares. Accordingly, on Monday, 19th July, 1,420 members went in two special trains to Tunbridge Wells. The day proved to be no unworthy forerunner of the great

[1] See Chapter 12, Market becomes Mission Centre

annual gatherings of later years. During the morning, meetings were held in various parts of the spacious grounds. In the afternoon :

. . . the great meeting of the day, the large experience meeting was held on a slope. Not less than 2,000 people gathered. . . . There for two hours testimonies were borne by converted infidels, drunkards, blasphemers, formalists, and Pharisees. . . . Many wept and every now and then some fell out from the crowd and went aside to pray and believed unto the salvation of their souls.

There was a procession back to the station. On the way home,

in most of the carriages prayer meetings were held and seven or eight sought salvation, one the wife of a most earnest worker whose conversion has been long sought and prayed for. In Cannon Street and Broad Street stations hymns were sung and the different bands sang as they walked home through the crowded, gaslit thoroughfares. Our Poplar friends began with prayer at the station at 7.30 in the morning, and ended with prayer outside the station at eleven at night.

Next year missioners had another similarly large and successful gathering at Dunorlan.

At this time the *East London Evangelist* first mentioned " newspaper abuse."

During the last month several slanderous letters and articles have appeared against us in the newspapers.[1] Reference to the services at Dunorlan, the camp meetings on London Fields, and other meetings have been specially distasteful, and misrepresentations of the most scurrilous kind have been written and freely circulated. We have not replied, neither have our hearts fainted ; we have fallen back upon Matthew v. 10, 11, 12.

Indication of the nature of at least some of these attacks is given by a passage in Mrs. Reed's life of her husband :

[1] Appendix T, Relief of Distress in East London

The behaviour of this crowd of people from the east end of London was most praiseworthy; they had the free run of the gardens, yet not a leaf was touched, though the newspapers gave a very different account of their conduct.

The Mission operated all the year round, *indoors and out*, but under William Booth's masterly leadership advantage was also taken of special opportunities for reaching the people. He called for a special month of prayer—September—preliminary to " the Winter Campaign " which, he went on to say,

fairly commences with October. Although soul-winning should be, and thank God is, always in season with The Christian Mission, yet there are the long evenings of autumn and winter peculiarly favourable to religious meetings. The unconverted attend more freely, not having the same outdoor attractions. Consequently we regard it as our harvest time. Oh, to enter upon it endued from on high !

4

It was at this time finally established that, notwithstanding the previous abortive experience at Norwood, The East London Christian Mission was destined for wider service than its limiting name implied. Mrs. Booth had preached in the Croydon Public Hall in 1866. In 1869 she conducted another campaign there, this time of three months' duration, concluding at the end of June. Many remarkable conversions had taken place. Ivo Cobet and Henry Holmes, acting on behalf of other Christian friends who had been prominent in these efforts, requested that a branch of The Christian Mission should be established in Croydon. William Booth consented, and the Workmen's Hall (seating 700 persons) and two small mission halls in different parts of the town were occupied. Cobet and Holmes became secretary and treasurer, respectively.

James Dowdle conducted the first week's meetings. When laying the foundation stone of a new hall (1872) Cobet stated that the opening date was Saturday, 3rd July. Mrs. M. Coates was the preacher on Sunday, 11th July, and Mrs. Collingridge for Sundays, 25th July and 1st August.

Preachers were supplied from week to week until January 1870 when Alexander Ritchie was appointed resident superintendent. The Workmen's Hall was used until 1873 when the Mission moved to its own building ; in 1887 this was replaced by the Croydon Corps' present Citadel in Elis David Road. Among the most notable of early superintendents were John Allen (1871–1873) and William Corbridge (1876–1877).

In November 1868 a Mr. P. Stuart, of Edinburgh, visited East London. William Booth being laid aside, he took his place, and conducted meetings almost every night. Stuart had originated the Edinburgh Christian Mission (it had been so named from its beginning), reports from which were printed in the *East London Evangelist*. The Booths visited Edinburgh the following July (1869) and conducted meetings there. Union of the Edinburgh with The East London Christian Mission followed at once. This continued until July 1870 when it was announced that financial considerations had compelled the withdrawal of the representatives of The Christian Mission. One of the provisions agreed upon at the time of the union was that the Edinburgh Mission must be self-supporting, William Booth stipulating that money contributed by friends for The East London Mission could not, rightly, be diverted to Edinburgh. The local missioners continued their work under unpaid leadership and, from time to time, reports from them appeared in the *Evangelist*.

In the meantime, and before Edinburgh had withdrawn, with his flair for recognition of the fitness of things, in the September number of the *Evangelist* William Booth announced under the heading, " Our New Name " :

As we have now branch missions at Croydon and at Edinburgh, the name first adopted by us is no longer strictly applicable. We have overstepped our boundary and gone out of our parish. We think we should now be more correctly termed—*The Christian Mission.*

With the first number of 1870 the title of the Mission's journal became the *Christian Mission Magazine.*

The probability of still further extension, to which these movements outside London pointed, evidently stirred William Booth to consider future financial policy. In an appeal to friends for help, after stating his conviction that spheres of work were opening for the Mission " as rapidly as we have the right kind of worker to fill them," he set forth, as a guiding principle, that " any philanthropic or religious work, to be widely useful, must be largely self-sustaining," adding, as a ground of appeal for help, that the Mission was already achieving a good measure of self-support, though

our extensive operations, and their *purely missionary character*, render the work very costly, and only help *from without*—from those whose hearts yearn for the salvation of the heathen of their own land—can enable us to go forward.

This policy, set out here for the first time, and pursued ever since, to the degree which in any branch of the work has been possible, has been the basis, financially, of the progress of The Christian Mission and The Salvation Army.

Before 1869 had ended, three more new openings had taken place. First, *Bow Common* (River Street) :

Here, amidst manure manufactures, gas works, chemical works, match factories, and other similar establishments, live thousands of persons in utter indifference and ignorance of spiritual things. Having at last the opportunity of taking a good hall capable of seating nearly 300 we at once secured it ; and on Sunday, 17th October, we opened it.

Then, *Old Ford* (Three Colt Street—not to be confounded with Three Colts Lane, Bethnal Green) :

Two of our people [wrote William Booth] moved away from Whitechapel here . . . they had two rooms they could knock into one, and these they invited us to occupy. We consented, and on Sunday, 14th November, the flag of The Christian Mission was unfurled.

And *Canning Town*, of which it was stated :

Three or four brethren residing here have attended meetings at Poplar . . . they implored us to open a branch. They were willing to take the financial responsibility. Public rooms have been taken for Sabbath services and four nights a week, and were opened on Sunday, 21st November.

But all was not plain sailing. The human element had to be reckoned with. Even in the midst of such religious fervour as characterized the Mission as a whole, trouble could, and did, arise. From Stratford came this report :

Some time ago a misunderstanding arose at this place and the brother who had the oversight of this station left, with the greater part of the people. Since then we have had uphill work, but the few left behind have kept struggling on. Now, converts are being made at nearly every meeting.

William Booth sent out an appeal for Christmas help for the poor, suggesting it should be handed round at the breakfast table on Christmas Day. A postscript stated that he had planned to distribute 4 pounds of beef, a plum pudding, and 1 ounce of tea to each of three hundred families on Christmas Day.

About £100 was sent in. Three hundred dinners were provided and a number of destitute families were helped over the worst part of the winter.

This effort was the outcome of William Booth's experience of the previous Christmas, which Jane Short thus movingly described :

The General had determined that the children should have a thoroughly happy old-fashioned Christmas, and for a week beforehand every preparation was made for a great family festival. . . . I really thought it would be a day of the purest happiness. But when the General returned from his preaching in Whitechapel on Christmas morning he was pale, haggard, and morose. He did his best to enter into the children's fun and frolic, but it was no use ; he kept relapsing into silence and gloom. . . . And then suddenly he burst out, " I'll never have a Christmas Day like this again ! " and, getting on his feet and walking up and down the room like a caged lion, he told us of the sights he had seen that morning in Whitechapel, indignantly saying, " The poor have nothing but the public-house ! "

Chapter Twelve

MARKET BECOMES MISSION CENTRE

I

BY the end of 1869 The Christian Mission had become well established—but it still had no central hall.

Two years earlier, on Whitechapel Road, a building had been erected " with a front not unlike a chapel, and an interior bearing a strong resemblance to a music hall minus ornament." Public speculation had included its being " the future field of labour of a well-known evangelist " or " an off-shoot of the Newington Butts Tabernacle."

Eventually it had been announced that the building was to be " a People's Market where provisions of all kinds, not to mention boots and shoes, would be sold, of the best quality." The market was the property of a limited liability company originated by John McCall, manufacturer of preserved provisions, of Houndsditch. McCall was a member of the central committee of The Christian Mission and co-treasurer with Powell. Stalls were provided, but the main idea was that costermongers should wheel in their barrows and take station round the ground floor. Advertisements contained this strange statement : " Real butter 1s. 2d. (warranted not English-made Dutch with its beastly adulterations of pulverised flints and horse fat)." But the costermongers did not wheel in their barrows. Before a year had passed, the People's Market had been closed. The *East London Observer* (3rd October 1868), announcing this, stated :

Since the attempt to provide cheap food for the body has failed, an attempt is to be made to provide cheap food for the soul. It is currently reported that the Rev. William Booth . . . has made an offer for the building.

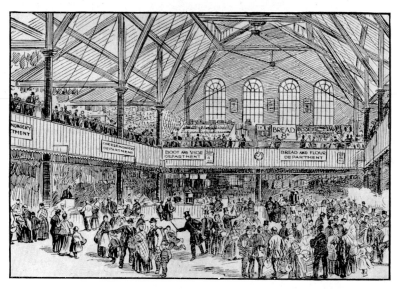

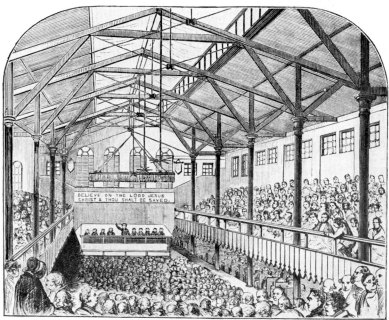

(*Above*) The People's Market   (*Below*) The People's Mission Hall
(from *How to Reach the Masses with the Gospel*, 1870)

The People's Mission Hall, Whitechapel Road : midday porch meeting
in progress
(from *How to Reach the Masses with the Gospel*, 1870)

The report was true. The minute book of the Mission's central committee recorded, under date 28th August 1868, that an offer was made to Mr. McCall, who forthwith resigned from the Mission committee, to rent the premises from him at £300 per annum, and that, this having been declined, it was decided to offer to buy them from him for £2,500.

The first public presentation of the scheme was made in the *East London Evangelist* for November 1868, when William Booth addressed an appeal to the friends of The Christian Mission for financial aid towards the purchase of the building and its " conversion into a People's Mission Hall." He wrote :

Ever since the commencement . . . the work has suffered greatly and been prosecuted with difficulty from the want of suitable premises. While our Sabbath evening congregations range from 2,000 to 3,000 [that is, individual congregations ; the aggregate accommodation of the buildings in use was 8,000], our largest room for week-night work will not contain more than 350 people. This room is packed from end to end on week-nights, and could we accommodate them we could readily obtain three times the number. Moreover we have not nearly the rooms required for the private meetings such as Bible classes, believers' meetings, evening educational classes, mothers' meetings, and others of kindred character without which any and every mission work will be a rope of sand.

And yet, insufficient as is this accommodation, it is fearfully expensive, the theatre and mission rooms costing over £500 per annum.

The People's Market will seat on the ground floor and in the galleries around it 1,500 people with comfort, while 2,000 may be crowded into it.

In addition to the hall there are ten small rooms. . . . There is also a large shop to the front and a soup-kitchen admirably fitted up with steam-engine, coppers, etc., capable of supplying 1,000 gallons of soup daily.

The entire premises are offered for £3,000.[1] They are held on

---

[1] Neither this figure, nor the stipulation (*E. L. Evangelist*, February 1869) that the offer was open only until Christmas 1868, was recorded in the minutes

an unexpired lease for thirty-nine years at a ground rent of £135 per year.

Giving up the theatre for morning and afternoon and other premises altogether would at once effect a reduction in annual expenditure of £250.

The poor people of the Mission have been contributing for some time towards a place, and have stored up something like £300 which it is felt certain they will make up to £500.

This first attempt to secure the People's Market ended in February 1869 without the parties reaching agreement. Other sites were viewed; all without result. In the meantime McCall had become financially embarrassed, and some eight months later he approached the Mission with a reduced price. The amount he offered to accept was not recorded, but the Mission committee approved purchase of the market if it could be obtained for £2,000. At a second special meeting it was resolved " that the lease of the market should be forthwith purchased for £1,750." The dates on which these meetings were held were not recorded, but would be between 27th August and 29th October 1869, when meetings held before and afterwards took place. Mr. Hamilton, the member of committee to whom the negotiations had been committed, had evidently bargained with McCall to good effect.

In his public announcement of the revival of the scheme William Booth stated :

Seeing that we are not only hindered from effectively carrying on evangelistic operations, but are suffering daily the most serious loss for want of better accommodation, and as this place appears to have been kept open for us, *and no other can be had*, we have been led to think, after much prayer and deliberation, that Providence points this way.

Meanwhile it had been ascertained that the acoustic properties of the building gave no reason for fear.

The market was stone-paved. At a meeting of the committee, one of the members suggested that the floor should be asphalted. To this William Booth replied quickly, " No, poor people feel the cold quite as much, if not more, than do rich people. We shall have a wooden floor and the place shall be heated by hot water apparatus. No one gets a blessing if they have cold feet, and nobody ever got saved while they had the toothache ! "

First it was proposed that the names of all members of the committee should be attached to the assignment of the lease, but eventually the number was reduced to seven, namely, " Messrs. Booth, Baxter, Hamilton, Morley, Powell, Reed and C. Owen."

Immediately the market had been taken over, the soup-kitchen that had been operated on the premises was transferred to the old Mission hall, 188 Whitechapel Road, and for the meetings being held there on Sunday mornings and afternoons the " Skittle Alley " was again used, also " a shop on week-nights fronting on Whitechapel Road, although a miserable place for Mission work."

When the architects (Messrs. Haberton and Pite) sent in the bill for the repairs and alterations to the market, it disclosed that the Mission had been committed by them to an outlay that " far exceeded the limits to which Mr. Booth had stated . . . his means would allow him to go." The total was over £1,500. Protest was at once made, and an itemized account demanded, but the matter dragged on for more than two years. It does not appear that the Mission was able to obtain redress, and its statement of income and expenditure showed payments, in 1872 and 1873, that brought the total outlay to £3,577, 10s. 10d.

William Booth made a special appeal for help towards meeting this additional cost, and the Mission's subscription list for 1870 showed that among the donations received were two of £500—one from Mr. Morley, the other from " An Old Disciple."

Henry Reed had at first refused to have anything to do with the People's Market scheme, considering the building unsuitable and the lease too short. He then made a counter-proposal. On a site in the heart of the population the Mission desired to reach he was ready to erect a building that would include a hall to seat two thousand persons and facilities for carrying on all the Mission's departments of work. The cost would be about £10,000. He offered this to William Booth on two conditions : that if the Mission should at any time be conducted in a manner of which he did not approve, he should have power to resume possession ; and that William Booth should settle down in East London. Seeing at once that the first condition meant that the control of the Mission would not be in his hands, William Booth declined the offer.

For a time after this rebuff Reed kept aloof from the Mission, but after a few months he renewed his interest in it. This he continued until, probably as a result of receiving an appeal for help towards the overspending on alterations to the market, he wrote to William Booth a remarkable letter (15th April 1870) on the sin of going into debt.[1] No record exists of William Booth's having replied to this letter, but explanations that satisfied Reed must have been made, for in many ways he later showed that his confidence in The Christian Mission, and in William Booth, had become firmly re-established. Further, when an address was presented to Reed in 1873, on his leaving Dunorlan for Harrogate, generous help in securing the People's Mission Hall was acknowledged. His name nowhere appears in the subscription lists, so that it would seem more than likely that he was the " Old Disciple."

[1] See Appendix E, Early Supporters

2

Sunday, 10th April 1870 (William Booth's 41st birthday), was the day of the opening of the People's Mission Hall. "At last," began the *Christian Mission Magazine* report of the proceedings, "the result was gained for which so many efforts had been made, and so many prayers offered, and a large and commodious hall was ours—actually ours."

A seven o'clock prayer meeting—"knee-drill" it would now be called—was the first engagement ; 250 persons were present. At the morning service Mrs. Booth preached. William Booth was ill ; he presided at the afternoon experience meeting, but could do no more. About two hundred missioners took tea together, and after singing and prayer some of them went out to hold an open-air meeting on the Mile End Road. Others remained in the building, praying and preparing for the evening meeting, for which the hall was crowded. William Booth was to have been the preacher, but Mrs. Booth again took his place. The "communion rail" (penitent-form) was crowded, first by persons who responded to Mrs. Booth's appeal that the occasion of the dedication of the building should be made one of personal re-consecration, and later by unconverted persons seeking salvation. The number of these was estimated to be 150, in addition to many seekers who knelt in other parts of the hall.

One of the advantages of having a place of their own was specially noted by the missioners :

It was late before the meeting closed, it being a matter for exultation that the service could not be abruptly ended, as at the theatre, by the punctual turning out of the lights.

Representatives of a wide range of religious endeavour took part in the meetings held at the Mission hall during the

141

opening and Eastertide, which fell in the following week. Among these were Rev. W. Tyler, R. C. Morgan, Lord Radstock, John Hilton and members of the Temperance League, Rev. G. Scott, Rev. W. Pennefather, Gawin Kirkham and William Carter. The Rev. William Cook, the revivalists Isaac Marsden, John Hambleton, Mr. and Mrs. Neal (from the U.S.A.), and the singer Philip Philips had helped the Mission earlier.

Summing up the advantages provided by the new premises the *Christian Mission Magazine* said :

They form, in the estimation of all who have seen them, the best adapted pile of buildings for evangelistic work to be found in the three Kingdoms. Oh, may we have grace to use them for good to the very uttermost !

And in conclusion :

We feel that these services and the character of the premises augur a future of brighter usefulness than we have ever dared to hope for. We are greatly encouraged, and knowing that a wholehearted people in the cause of the Saviour are in possession, who have confidence in His word and in His Spirit, we doubt not but that it will be found in the last great day that thousands of immortal souls have been born for Glory there.

It does not appear who wrote the report of the opening of the hall, but that final declaration bears the stamp of the faith of William Booth himself !

The People's Mission Hall scheme had been warmly welcomed by the *Revival* (29th October 1868). In a leading article it had quoted the Rev. Baptist W. Noel's " prophetic words," " I believe we are on the eve of a greater work than England ever saw," and had continued :

But of all the evangelistic organizations in the East of London one of those most recently commenced has also become by far the most acceptable and, we have every reason to believe, useful in proportion to its extent—we refer to the Mission committed by the Lord to William Booth. We well remember how long and anxiously he hesitated before he resigned his ministerial position with the income attached thereto and threw himself into the work of the Lord in sole dependence upon Him ; but little could anyone have supposed that so many places could have been efficiently worked under the superintendence of one individual, or that funds could have been found to meet so large an expenditure. . . .

It is a noble movement in furtherance of the grand purpose inaugurated by Baptist Noel and Reginald Radcliffe.

Although so much had been achieved in fulfilment of that historic prophecy, at the time these words were written The Christian Mission had not reached the fifth anniversary of its birth in that humble and dilapidated tent !

CHAPTER THIRTEEN

THE SECOND FIVE YEARS : 1870-1875

I

THE illness that had prevented William Booth from taking active part in the opening of the People's Mission Hall kept him away from East London until the end of July 1870. The minutes of the central committee of the Mission record his attendance at two meetings in April (probably before he went away) and at an urgent meeting on 11th May. Two other meetings were held, the dates of which are not given ; nor is it stated whether William Booth was present or not— they may have been held after his return to London in July. The next meeting minuted was held on 16th September, and William Booth took the chair.

An event of 1870, of even greater importance to The Christian Mission than the acquisition of the People's Mission Hall, received no notice whatever in its public records. This was the constitution and first meeting of the Christian Mission Conference.[1]

Again, in 1872, William Booth was forced into temporary retirement ; this time for more than six months. His doctors pronounced his trouble to be a nervous breakdown, resulting from overwork, and expressed fear that it would be impossible for him to return to duty.

The Mission had attained to new and large responsibilities. Its members were becoming practised in their vocation and its stations were beginning to give evidence of realizing their relationship to one another and to a central administration.

[1] Chapters 15 and 16

The Bethnal Green Railway Arch, used as a meeting-place by
The Christian Mission and The Salvation Army

An Evangelist of The Christian Mission
Commissioner John Lawley, A.D.C. to General William Booth

But so far as this had been achieved it had been under constant strong leadership. Had this now come to an end and with it the progress which had been made ?

Misgivings were quickly proved to be unfounded. Mrs. Booth had still to be reckoned with.

A Swedish writer, Dr. Laura Petri, after close study of Mrs. Booth's share in the making of The Salvation Army, declares :

To decide whether William or Catherine Booth was the Founder of The Salvation Army is to venture on the speculation whether a child derives its being from father or from mother. The Army was started, not on one motor, but on two.

Earlier, W. T. Stead had written :

Mrs. Booth when she died was universally known as the Mother of The Salvation Army ; and no mother ever magnified her office more constantly and consistently.

And to the same point William Booth addressed himself in the *War Cry* at the time of her promotion to Glory :

She was the *Army Mother*. This relationship, almost universally recognized, had grown up like so much of the Army, without any set arrangement or design. Other religious organizations cannot be said to have a Mother ; their guides and authorities are all *Fathers*. The Salvation Army has, of God's great mercy and wisdom, and we think through His own leading and inspiration, felt its need of the more tender, feminine side of human character, as well as the more robust and masculine element. . . . The Army will mourn her loss and has reason for doing so ; but she will live on, and on, and on in the hearts and lives of thousands and thousands of her daughters.

During William Booth's first absence Mrs. Booth had assumed control of the Mission ; now once more, vigorously and skilfully, she undertook its oversight, abating nothing of full devotion to its affairs on account of either her own weakness or her gnawing anxiety for her husband. This latter, notwithstanding, she declared at a united Mission meeting that even were he to die the work should, with God's blessing, be carried forward. The only notable omission from the Mission's normal programme was that Conference did not meet in 1872.

In a printed letter " To the Readers of the Magazine and Friends of The Christian Mission," Mrs. Booth expressed her thanks for " the many kind assurances of sympathy and intercession in this time of trial." She went on to say :

I have found my position trying and arduous in the extreme since my dear husband was compelled to leave us ; but the Lord has wonderfully strengthened me . . . it would be too much to say that the work has not suffered ; but . . . all our workers have been kept in unity and love and the usual services have been sustained *without diminution*. It is our one absorbing desire the *work should grow*, whatever instruments should be laid aside.
We want more of the Holy Ghost. Our difficulties in this East London you cannot possibly estimate unless you were in the fight. It seems sometimes so hopeless a task to make any great inroads on this mass of wickedness that we are tempted to despond. . .

2

William Booth returned in October. There were still to be periods when he, and Mrs. Booth also, were compelled by ill-health to be absent from the Mission—notably for three months after the 1876 Conference, and again after that of 1877—but before these further breakdowns took place a strong and capable helper had arrived to share the oversight.

While recuperating at Matlock in 1870 William Booth first heard of the dynamic personality and aggressive spirit who was destined to be his second in command during these crucial years. The Rev. Launcelot Railton, a Wesleyan minister, told William Booth that he had a younger brother, George, who would just suit him. He described some of the adventures George had already met with in preaching the Gospel, including an attempt to make his way to " some un-known part of Africa to which no missionary had penetrated," which had ended with his becoming stranded in Morocco.

Two years later William Booth received a letter from George Scott Railton. He had obtained a copy of the Mission's second report, *How to Reach the Masses with the Gospel*, and it had so stirred him that he offered himself to William Booth. As soon as he could honourably leave his employment, in March 1873, Railton, being 24 years of age, entered the service of The Christian Mission as its Secretary. To his brother, the Rev. Launcelot Railton, he wrote (1872):
When you pointed out to me Mr. Booth's work I at once said that was *the Way* and that I couldn't see how to refuse if asked to assist in it, understanding by that if I were asked to be one of his missionaries. But instead of this I am asked to take a place by his side and to be his lieutenant-general.

On his first visit to the Mission, October 1872, Railton had been impressed by the vigorous faith and earnestness of its converts, and was satisfied that the work was of the Holy Spirit. He had expected to find " a mere community en-joying a common vitality," but instead had seen evidence of " a real individual life which would propagate itself." He had also been convinced that The Christian Mission had solved the problem of combining liberty with order :
I expected [he further wrote at the time] to see a company of powerful but irrepressible volunteers, whereas I found myself in the presence of a battalion of trained male and female soldiers, quite as remarkable for their steadiness as for their readiness.

Railton grasped at once William Booth's great idea :
The charity of . . . England may pour ceaselessly into " the East End," and yet be lost in its ocean of drink and vice ; but when the working classes, on the spot, become the workers together with God, we have reached the goal of a " native agency," and hope finds a solid resting-place.

It does not come as a surprise, after this, to find that when Railton wrote to William Booth (January 1873) about the final arrangements for his coming to London, he began " My dear General " and concluded " Your ever-to-be-faithful Lieutenant."

William Booth was commonly designated " the General " in the early days of the Mission, alike in his home and by the missioners, though it is said that this was nothing more, at the time, than a handy abbreviation of " General Superintendent." No doubt Railton heard him so called on his visit to the Mission, but that he associated " lieutenant " with " general " would seem to imply that the military idea was present in his mind. This finds support in the phraseology used by him at various times, and in his songs.

As its Secretary, Railton served the Mission ably, seconding William Booth in every effort to maintain and increase its usefulness. At times, indeed, he was the pioneer who blazed the trail ahead of his leader. His fertile brain (it was stated in a sketch of his life which was printed in the *War Cry* in 1880) was always at work in developing new schemes that were presented to the General in such a convincing manner and with such a show of practicability and sound judgment that he almost invariably came out with orders to go ahead. His utter selflessness was seen not only in his devotion to duty while Secretary of the Mission, but in his acceptance of the new conditions created for him when William Booth's eldest son, Bramwell, after the Mission had become The Salvation Army, became the Chief of the Staff of the organization.

Beginning before he was officially connected with the Mission, Railton wrote for its magazine articles that were ablaze with the fires of holy energy and aggression that consumed him.

His first contribution was entitled " God's Fools." (Incidentally, the title was provided by comment in the *Pall Mall Gazette* on a fraud practised upon members of The Christian Mission, in which they were stigmatized as being fools who might expect to be taken in easily.) In a letter written in 1872 to his brother Launcelot (copy of which has been preserved), Railton told him that William Booth had stated that his duties in The Christian Mission were to include the editing of its magazine ; but as the title page of every volume (1868-1878) bears the legend, " Edited by William Booth," and there are many internal indications that its leading articles were usually written by him, it would seem that Railton's position was rather that of sub-editor, though perhaps his responsibilities were greater than those of most sub-editors.

Railton also gave to the movement some of its most stirring war-songs. One of the earliest and best known of these was either written or adopted by him—which it was is not clear. It was printed, with music, in the February 1874 issue of the *Christian Mission Magazine*, headed " A Christian War-Song," without any indication as to authorship. It was given prominence in all editions of *Heathen England* as " Our War-Song " ! Written to be sung to " Men of Harlech," it began :

> Soldier, rouse thee ! War is raging,
> God and fiends are battle waging ;

and for chorus it had :

> Through the world resounding,
> Let the Gospel sounding
>   Summon all, at Jesus' call,
> His glorious cross surrounding,
> Sons of God, earth's trifles leaving,
> Be not faithless, but believing ;
> To your conquering Captain cleaving,
>   Forward to the fight !

Whether written by Railton or not, the spirit of the composition was entirely in keeping with his own ; to him the battle for souls was *real* warfare.

Railton wrote several books, two of which especially helped to bring about an understanding of the aims and spirit of the organization—*Heathen England* (1877) and *Twenty-one Years Salvation Army* (1886). The first of these was dictated by Railton when he was in bed with smallpox. " I knew what was the matter with me, and fully expected to die," he said later, " and therefore the book was to constitute a sort of testimony to my generation."

With a characteristic touch of sardonic humour, Railton, when his nurse tried to bring animation into his chilled extremities with hot-water bottles, feebly protested : " It's no use trying to warm up Jordan ! " He was terribly ill and all were amazed that he recovered.

3

Till the opening of the People's Mission Hall, meetings were continued in the East London Theatre. On Sunday 30th January Mrs. Booth had preached there to " an unusually large congregation." There is, however, no further mention of the Mission's using East End theatres, though the original proposal provided that the Mission Hall should be used for week-day and for Sunday morning and afternoon meetings, and the theatres on Sunday evenings.

Several reasons for this change of plan are apparent. The People's Mission Hall—provided people could be attracted to it ; as at first, at least, it seems they were—had considerable seating capacity. As already noted, meetings could be prolonged to any time desired ; and rent that would have had to be paid for theatres was available for other Mission use.

Moreover, William Booth was too ill at the time to conduct theatre meetings himself, and there had not yet come to the front other leaders able to sustain such campaigns. Perhaps another reason was the strong objection held by Reed to helping theatres, by paying rent for them on Sundays, to provide on week-days entertainments which were considered objectionable. His influence in this direction would no doubt be associated with his renewed interest in the Mission generally and his having provided substantial help for the People's Mission Hall scheme. In any case, from this time forward the Mission's efforts in East London were concentrated upon securing buildings that would be entirely at its disposal, whether rented, purchased, or erected by it, and on the formation of its forces into self-contained units of an organization more and more acquiring definite and permanent form.

Later, when branches of the Mission were established in the provinces, much use was again made of public buildings to which the people were accustomed to resort for entertainment—and this with excellent results.

How Secretary Railton would have used his influence had he been with the Mission in 1870 was made very evident when he wrote on the subject in 1877 :

Here is a theatre full of people, the vast majority of whom are sinners in danger of burning in hell, for ever. We cannot possibly provide another building of such capacity for them in the town, even supposing that we should be sure of securing their attendance there . . . then, is it not our bounden duty to gather them where alone we can get so large a number of them ?

And again :

What more suitable building could we possibly have for close, thorough dealing with the heart ? Every eye can see the preacher's face . . . every ear can catch his slightest whisper. The people seem all close around him, piled together like an open-air crowd. . . . Everyone seems to be facing you, as if there were only the two of you present. Now, for life or for death, deal with that poor soul !

It was characteristic of William Booth's readiness to adopt methods that were proved successful, even when it meant acknowledging mistakes had been made, that six years after the holding of meetings in East London theatres had been abandoned he wrote :

The anniversary services at Middlesbro' have brought into prominence the enormous advantage of having a place of amusement for our Sunday services, and we trust will for ever banish from the heart of everyone connected with the Mission any spirit of contentment with small congregations, such as we needs preach to where we have only halls of our own wherein to gather the people. The very same labour which is necessary to gather a few hundred working people into a building set apart for religious service, and to set Christ before them there, would fill a large theatre or music hall, and send home conviction to the hearts of thousands. The Lord has called us to a great work. We must not be content with a small one. . . .

The People's Mission Hall possessed a unique feature ; the one-time market drive-in had been altered in such a way that it could be used as a semi-open-air preaching place, or be added to the hall itself when extra accommodation was required. When it was used for open-air preaching there was room in the porch for 150 persons as well as a sufficient number of missioners to give effective backing to the preacher. The footpath was wide enough for a considerable crowd to stand around without causing obstruction. For many years meetings were held in the porch at one o'clock every week-day except Saturday. At first Mrs. Collingridge was usually the speaker ; when her health broke down, Mrs. Reynolds took her place. Within three months of the opening of the hall it was recorded that :

Men and women who live at a long distance, but whose business has brought them this way . . . have been led to the Saviour and have gone home happy. These services have been attended by some who have come in their carriages, as well as the poor of the neighbourhood.

Meanwhile the members of the Mission as a whole continued to go about their ordinary work with vigour, showing enterprise in devising, and perseverance in putting into effect, measures for the advancement of the Cause. At several places " pioneer bands " were formed ; these were parties of men and women missioners who went from station to station. Tract distribution societies and sick visitation societies were in full operation. Gipsy encampments were visited with exceptional success ; at one, out of a total of 60 souls, 16 converts became Mission members.

An original salvation song set to a secular tune, the first to be printed, appeared in the *Christian Mission Magazine* (March 1870) under the title, " Victory or Death ! " The tune was " Young Recruit " ; the writer J. A. Jermy.

Millwall Station so outgrew the candle factory coach-house that in June 1870 Charles Owen sought financial help from William Booth in securing a larger hall. " We shall without difficulty be able to furnish any needed labour," he wrote. Foremost among the members who worked on the alterations when a building was secured was Frederick Coxhead, a builder who had been converted in a meeting at the factory two years before and who later had charge of the station. The building was a cow-shed in Cheval Street. This was in use until a larger place, a box factory, was leased in 1879. Working at night by lamplight because the building was urgently required, Coxhead was a mark that the roughs could not miss, though happily the stones and brickbats thrown did not seriously injure him. In his later years he erected many buildings for The Salvation Army. Coxhead was on the plan in 1870 for the Poplar Circuit as preacher, exhorter and prayer-leader ; Millwall was a station of this circuit.

It is not peculiar to modern times that there should be "ups and downs" in the prosperity of stations (or corps). One instance has already been recorded ; there were more as time passed. Not only in private records, such as minutes of elders' and committee meetings, but in frank public statements was this made clear.

In a survey of "The Present Position and Prospects of the Mission"—in connection with its sixth anniversary in 1871—William Booth, in the *Christian Mission Magazine*, wrote with "deepest thankfulness" of many aspects of the Mission work ; but he also stated :

In looking over our numerous Stations we see with grief two or three at which the work appears at a standstill. Circumstances over which we have no control bar our way, or brethren have been removed, or Satan has successfully withstood us ; but even here we do not despair. We continue our ordinary measures and wait our opportunity for extraordinary operations.

Summing up the reasons for declension in one instance (Croydon), William Booth went on to state in the same issue of the magazine :

Here, for some time now, there has existed a division of feeling and opinion, which has greatly retarded the work. . . . The Station has been unfortunate in the brethren appointed to manage it. Zealous, pious, and affectionate though they have been, and blessed with success in winning souls, they have lacked the power to guide and control the society. Discipline has been wanting. Under new leadership we trust everything will be changed for the better. Already there is a great and perceptible difference.

Later, dealing in general terms with the causes of occasional declension, William Booth declared :

It is one thing to attract hundreds of people to witness some strange and unusual religious service ; it is another and a very different thing to drag men and women out from among all their associates and associations to commence a new life, and to maintain that life steadfastly. . . . Who can wonder if hearts grow weary and hands hang down—if even desertions take place in the midst of such a conflict ?

No stations were opened in the years 1871 and 1872. Suitable leaders could not be found and—perhaps partly, at least, accounting for this—William Booth was absent from the Mission for lengthy periods. Even when not absent, he could not have been fit for strenuous work. Moreover, as a result of his ill-health, Mrs. Booth was kept busy at home with the direction of Mission affairs ; with one exception she was unable to conduct campaigns such as, earlier and later, resulted in the establishment of new branches of the Mission. The shortage of suitable evangelists is emphasized by the fate that befell this one exception—Tunbridge Wells. Following Mrs. Booth's one month's campaign there, in July 1872, a station was established—but in October 1873 the *Christian Mission Magazine* announced :

Our hearts have been saddened during the month by the necessity forced upon us of parting from our dear poor people at Tunbridge Wells, owing to the departure of Brother Cameron, the missionary there, who is going with Mr. Reed to Australia . . . but in this we are thankful to be able again to turn over to a Christian Church a large contingent of souls rescued by the instrumentality of the Mission from the very jaws of hell.

Following a campaign conducted by Mrs. Booth at Brighton, and at the urgent request of many local people, a station had been established there in December 1869. Long and glowing accounts of its progress appeared in the *Christian Mission Magazine* until the autumn of the following year, when it was announced that

this branch of the Mission, which God enabled Mrs. Booth at great personal sacrifice and labour to establish, has, without any *justifiable* cause being assigned, and as we are satisfied time will show, been *very unwisely* and, we may add, *very ungraciously,* separated from us.

The evangelist placed in charge—a comparative stranger to The Christian Mission—had been engaged under stress of lack of helpers. Carried away by the prospect of becoming independent, he had persuaded the treasurer, a wealthy man, and the majority of the members to join him in a secession. Mrs. Booth went to Brighton and remonstrated with the treasurer, but without effect. Eventually the evangelist left the country in most discreditable circumstances and the mission was broken up.

This pause in extension and accompanying setbacks were succeeded by advances. In his preface to the 1873 bound volume of the *Christian Mission Magazine* (written at the end of that year) William Booth summed up the position thus :

Here we have no mere spasms of devotion, but a great work steadily advancing—a progress of victory almost unbroken, and continuing now with increasing power.

More and more space was needed to record the manifold activities of the Mission's stations ; its magazine was doubled in size. Organization also was proceeding apace. A " Plan of the religious services to be held in the Whitechapel Circuit—1872 " was most comprehensive. First it set out in tabulated form for three months—May, June, and July ; the Plan would seem to have been issued quarterly—the places of meeting (indoors and out), the leaders and the bands that were to support them. Preachers (22), Exhorters and Prayer Leaders (45), belonging to the home stations, were listed with their postal addresses, as well as nine " from other places." Thomas W. Cameron was the superintendent of the circuit. Quarterly sermons, watch-night services, fast days and " private believers' meetings " were provided for. Open-air meetings were held as far away as Peckham Rye on Sunday afternoons and evenings. Breakfast meetings—tickets 3d. each—followed by " Essay and conversation on some profitable topic" were held on Sunday mornings at Whitechapel, also tea meetings for workers and friends.

At the Conference of 1873 a proposal was adopted for the establishment of what was termed " A Christian Mission League." A form of covenant and " classification of labour " were provided, but it was only in two particulars that these went beyond the obligations already attendant upon membership in the Mission ; the exceptions were pledges " not to drink any intoxicating liquor except under medical advice or for sacramental purposes "—office-holders were already so pledged—and " not to use tobacco." There is no indication that the League was put into operation. It was probably realized that to do so would have implied that the Mission itself was decadent, or would have tended to create and foster an idea that full consecration to the objects of the Mission was not obligatory on all its members.

4

During the latter part of this second five years' period, buildings were erected or purchased for Mission use in numbers remarkable in proportion to existing stations. The first hall to be erected by The Christian Mission was opened at Ninfield, Sussex, on 10th August 1871. A revival had taken place among the Wesleyans, but the converts were not given the freedom they desired in the Church—they were too lively for the older members—and they held meetings for themselves. When William Corbridge was in charge at Hastings they invited The Christian Mission to assume control, in fact they had from the first called themselves The Christian Mission.

Some time after the erection of the hall there was a division in the Mission, and after it became The Salvation

Army the corps dwindled and eventually was closed. The building is now a United Methodist chapel.

A second hall, erected at Canning Town, was opened on 23rd December 1872. The following year—1873—saw the consummation of five schemes, some of which had been under consideration for lengthy periods. They included new buildings at Croydon (opened 12th January), Poplar (20th January), North Woolwich (8th April), and the acquirement of a church at Plaistow (6th July) and of a chapel at Buckland (7th December).

Occupation of the famous Bethnal Green Railway Arch was the outstanding event of 1874. Of the genesis of this it was said :

During the summer we secured a piece of ground together with a railway arch at the east end of the Bethnal Green Road, opposite one flaming gin-palace, and next door to another. On this piece of ground we erected the tent formerly used on the London Fields. So prominently situated . . . it could not fail to attract attention, and be thronged with people night after night. . . . We are arranging for the erection of permanent premises on the spot.

The arch had been lengthened to provide a hall with seating for 400 people, with vestry and other accommodation, and Mrs. Booth conducted the opening services on 17th March. The noise made by the trains passing overhead, it was noted, does not seriously interfere with the comfort of speakers or hearers, and the singing can be heard from within, above even the noise of the great thoroughfare close at hand, so that the building is eminently a success, and with the large space facing the road for open-air services there can be no question of our having gained one of the best positions in London for our work.

Until the widening of the railway brought to an end the use of the railway arch as a Salvation Army hall, every anticipation of its usefulness was fulfilled. Many of the converts made there went out to usefulness in wide spheres of influence as Christian Mission evangelists or Salvation Army officers. The most notable was James Barker, who pioneered The Salvation Army in Victoria, Australia. Passing on a bus, he had been attracted by the fervency of a speaker at an open-air meeting conducted from a rostrum in front of the railway arch. Mrs. Barker—Alice Sutton—was converted at a meeting held in Hart's Lane Chapel, which the Mission occupied before moving to the railway arch.

The first of the other halls to be occupied in 1874 was an old place at Chatham which was purchased and renovated. William Booth conducted the opening meetings.

At Stoke Newington a brewery had been leased and transformed into a house of prayer . . . the result is as complete a hall for salvation work as could well be desired.

Finally, a hall erected at Wellingborough was opened on 6th December.

Only one hall was completed in 1875—at Hackney; the most substantial that had then been built for the Mission, it was in use till bombed. Mrs. Booth opened it on 29th April. The main hall seated 600 persons; school and class-rooms beneath it made provision for young people's work, the earliest instance of this being done. Part of the cost of this hall was met from a loan of £300 from a friend, which was to become a gift at his death, interest at the rate of five per cent. per annum to be paid as an annuity.

The Rev. Charles Spurgeon was much interested in The Christian Mission and during this period twice went to East London to give his noted lecture, " Candles," to help its funds. When the Bethnal Green station, then using the Hart's Lane Chapel, was endeavouring to raise money to fit up the railway arch, a number of young people (George T. White was one of them) were formed into a committee to approach Spurgeon. He invited them to come and see

him at Stockwell, sending his coach and liveried coachman
to fetch them. They sang and gave their testimonies in his
study, and Spurgeon prayed for God's blessing on the undertaking. Spurgeon complied with their request and later
(19th May 1874) repeated the lecture at Whitechapel in aid
of a fund for repairing the roof of the People's Mission Hall.
So bad had its condition become that during a heavy shower
rain poured through in every direction. The glass alone
cost £200. Mrs. Booth, Mr. R. Pearsall Smith, the Rev.
Brewin Grant, and Henry Varley took part in the reopening
meetings.

In 1874 the Rev. J. E. Irvine, "a revival minister," conducted meetings at the Whitechapel and Chatham stations
of the Mission. Early in 1875 he and Miss Billups were
married ; in July they went to America, continuing in
revival work there.

5

In October 1874 William Booth was impelled to write
that one of the chief features of the previous month had been
the violent opposition encountered in the open-air, the police,
the publicans, and lewd fellows of the baser sort having in turns,
and in some instances all seemed to combine, to defeat and drive
us from the ground.

Commenting on the cause of these attacks generally, William
Booth continued :

The public-houses are the difficulty . . . drunken men are
bribed with liquor to annoy and if possible break up the meetings.

There were, however, gleams of commonsense. At Strood
(Kent), when rowdyism threatened to stop the work, an
appeal to the mayor brought immediate police protection.
At Hastings the persecutors, after trying "everything their
hearts and Satan could suggest," petitioned the magistrates

"to remove the noise." But the magistrates, instead of taking arbitrary action,

appointed police officers to inquire into the disturbance and, finding it was yells, and howls, and shouts, and shrieks, and old tins, whistles, trumpets, and squeaks in opposition to the Gospel of Peace, they decided to let us keep our stand—and police protection was given.

The Hastings bench was much influenced by the conversion, through the Mission's efforts, of a notorious character who had been often before the justices.

Not all these incidents were as picturesque, or as harmless in effect, as one reported from Harrogate, where Henry Reed, having left Dunorlan, had built himself a house attached to which were rooms "expressly devoted to the Lord's service." Two Christian Mission evangelists had been sent down to help him with the work he was carrying on. Sanger's Circus was in the town. When these brethren were conducting an open-air meeting on the Stray, the circus employees (the meeting seems to have been held in the vicinity of the circus tent) pelted the missioners with clods; this not driving them away, the next move was to try what effect a brass band, doing its worst with discord, would have. "But they found we were brass-band proof," reported the evangelists. Next bass and side drums were beaten in front of the speaker, while cymbals were clashed behind him—still to no avail. An elephant and two dromedaries were paraded up and down while roughs shouted and women and children shrieked. This was too much for the police, who interfered and ordered the beasts to be taken away; but the drummers, reinforced by "hundreds of roughs" with tin kettles, renewed their annoyance till they found that a bystander ostensibly helping to beat the bass drum had slit the head with a penknife, whereupon the drummers hastily retreated. After an hour and a half the missioners formed a procession and went singing to their hall, sweeping a crowd of people with them.

An attempt to stop Sunday open-air meetings was neatly circumvented at Limehouse. John Allen, the evangelist in charge, reported :

Salmon's Lane is the Sunday market of the poor . . . who regularly buy their food while we are preaching the Gospel. Of course the Sunday traders were dreadfully annoyed, and most bitterly opposed to our carrying the message of Mercy into their very midst. On the Sabbath . . . we had no sooner commenced the service than up walked three policemen. . . . The inspector said, " You must move off here." " All right," said our brother in charge, and immediately the door was thrown open of a fish shop kept by one of our friends, and down came the shutters . . . and from it sounded forth the same blessed words of Salvation, while policemen, and publicans, and shopkeepers and customers looked on in wondering amazement.

Bramwell Booth knew the owner of this shop. He was, he has stated, formerly " a wild, dissolute man, reckless, worldly, self-indulgent, pleasure-loving," who " on Sunday mornings did a roaring trade." Roughs had so ill-treated a notorious character—who had been converted—that the then unconverted fishmonger had taken him under his protection. This man's influence brought about the conversion of his protector, who closed his shop on Sundays and joined the missioners. Alterations made the long fish-slab removable when the shop was used for preaching.

The next week the missioners had the shop licensed so that they could not be legally interfered with in using it as a preaching station.

A later report stated :

While the butchers and greengrocers, and others, are crying loudly " Buy ! Buy ! Buy ! " we cry to numbers of working people who stop to listen, " Buy, buy our wine and milk, and that without money and without price ! "

This perfectly innocent, indeed apt allusion to Isaiah lv. 1, may have been the basis of later charges that Salvationists made blasphemous references to " the Lamb of God," being obtainable cheaply. Again, when Evangelist Annie Davis was at Shoreditch (1876), the Mission was ejected from the Apollo hall, and " an old pudding shop " in Brick Lane was occupied, which had a front giving opportunity for preaching in " no way inferior to Whitechapel porch." Efforts were made to stop the missioners using this, but the evangelist asked : " If they allow the butchers to stand in their shops and on the pavement all the Sabbath morning, crying, ' Buy ! Buy ! Meat fourpence-halfpenny a pound ! ' why may we not stand and offer Salvation cheaper still ? "

At Cardiff, in October 1875, John Allen, who had been appointed there from Limehouse, was proceeded against by the police for obstruction. A protest meeting called by the ministers of the local churches, coupled with newspaper agitation, caused such a stir that the watch committee demanded an explanation from the police who, finally, were ordered to protect the open-air services.

The earliest instance of a turning of the tables had occurred during Eastertide 1868. A Brother Totman, of Stratford, was locked up all night on a charge of obstruction, but when he was brought before the magistrate in the morning he was discharged—with a contribution of a guinea for the Mission funds from the magistrate !

Chapter Fourteen

FIELD STATE : 1875

I

AT first the control of Christian Mission stations was entirely centralized. Preachers and local preachers were appointed on a " plan " to conduct meetings, but had no further responsibility. In a few instances only, a local member of outstanding ability was recognized as the leader at his own station, and on one occasion William Booth asked a member to transfer to another station (George White, from Holywell Mount to Sclater Street) for purposes of leadership.

By November 1868 an evangelist (Richard Dimaline) had been placed in charge of open-air work in connection with the Whitechapel station. Biblewomen had been engaged earlier still. But not until January 1870 was there any mention of an evangelist having charge of the station as a whole. The first " stationing " of a leader in a circuit as a superintendent was of James Dowdle to Poplar, but although " stationed " was the word used in the report, Dowdle's work in this appointment was voluntary and "spare time"; not until November 1873 did he become a full-time evangelist.

Transition from itinerancy to fixed appointments, when it did come, was quickened by the taking over of stations from other missions, and the beginning of work at certain places during the latter part of 1869 and throughout 1870, where the appointment of a full-time evangelist was required by the circumstances.

From 1871 onward the minutes of the proceedings of the Annual Conferences, as well as reports in the *Christian Mission Magazine*, indicate progressive decentralization. The minutes of 1873 record that four districts (Whitechapel, Shoreditch, Poplar and Limehouse, and Hastings) were represented at the Conference by superintendent preachers. By this time the term " itinerant preacher " had been dropped. The number of superintendents had, by 1874, been brought up to eight by the addition to the list of districts of Croydon, Wellingborough, Tunbridge Wells, and Portsmouth.

By 1875 the "Field" had been thoroughly organized and a full complement of whole-time leaders appointed, each responsible to the Mission headquarters for the conduct of the affairs of his (or her) station. Conference for this year issued a statement showing " Appointment of the Evangelists and Workers of The Christian Mission " which conveniently provides occasion for surveying the stations and personnel of the Mission at the end of the second five-year period of its existence. The statement had three sub-headings :

I HEADQUARTERS

The Rev. W. and Mrs. Booth

Treasurer
Nathaniel J. Powell, Esq.

Hon. Secretary
Robert Paton

Secretaries
George Scott Railton and Thomas E. Hedley

At a meeting of the Christian Mission committee on 12th June 1874 it was agreed that, "subject to Mr. Powell's approbation, Mr. Paton should be appointed honorary secretary to the Mission."

Charles Owen, having failed in business and suffered a breakdown in health, had withdrawn from this office ; a farewell meeting and presentation to him took place on 10th February 1873. To give him the benefit of a sea voyage, it was arranged that he should travel as a welfare officer—by authority of the government—with 300 emigrants to Australia. While proceeding to Sydney after landing the emigrants at Rockhampton (Queensland) the ship was wrecked, fortunately without loss of life. After his return to England, Owen served as a secretary in connection with Dr. Barnardo's work for boys and went to Canada. Robert Paton, of 43 Highbury Quadrant, London N., was prominent in many evangelistic enterprises. He was honorary secretary of the committee that arranged Moody's and Sankey's London mission during their visit in 1875.

George Scott Railton was *the* secretary of The Christian Mission ; thus designated he signed the deed poll of 1878. Indeed, in the *Salvationist* (November 1879), William Booth wrote of " shaking hands with Mr. Secretary Railton " when leaving London for Wales. Thomas E. Hedley was a clerk and accountant. In reply to a " friendly criticism " of the books of the Mission by Mr. S. Beddow, of the firm that audited the Mission's accounts, William Booth explained (5th January 1876) that the fault complained of had been due to the incompetence of Hedley, but that he was no longer in the employ of the Mission and " a perfected portion of the accounts " would shortly be supplied.

II FOR EVANGELISTIC WORK

Mr. W. Bramwell Booth
Miss Pollett
Miss Booth

This was the first appearance of Bramwell Booth's name in a published list of Mission workers, but that he had not even yet decided to devote his whole life to work in the Mission is made evident by a letter (27th August 1876) in which William Booth wrote to him :

Your future, *i.e.* your life-work. How can I divine this ? You ought to have convictions yourself. . . . My own and a growing conviction is that God wants you to assist me in directing and governing this Mission, and at my death, if it should anticipate yours, to take my place.

As late as October 1877 Bramwell Booth wrote to " the General " :

In my present condition the *burden* of fatigue of preaching positively unfits me to do anything else much, at any rate compared with what I might do without it. . . .
The present state of things coupled with the fact that I do not achieve anything—if it was anybody else they would have to resign—is unbearable. . . . I do not feel I am called to preach . . . so this is why I again come to propose going with Katie [his sister]. However, if you refuse I must submit. The Lord knows I am willing to be a doorkeeper, or a door mat, if I can have Him and peace . . . even if with them I cannot have many very desirable things and cannot be all I would wish to be. . . . And perhaps I could be of more real use to the Mission than if I *was* a regular preacher, or even a great preacher—anyhow we shall see.

Foreshadowing of the part he was to play in the advocacy of holiness—in particular the series of holiness meetings conducted by him in the Eighties at Whitechapel—was found in another passage in this letter :

I am nearly come to this, that I will not preach to sinners any more. Sunday morning, or night, or any other time, I will confine myself to preaching Holiness and Holiness alone.

But neither his doubts of his capacity to serve, nor the handicap of deafness which was now growing upon him, was allowed to make his service in the Mission anything less than the best of which he was at any time capable.

Bramwell Booth's first introduction to East London conditions had taken place three or four years after The Christian Mission had been established. When thirteen (1869) he had assisted in Children's Mission meetings in Bethnal Green, but shortly afterwards became so ill that for the best part of two years he was unable to do anything at all.

In September 1870 a Christian Mission station was established in Hackney, the district in which the Booth family lived, and by this time Bramwell had sufficiently recovered to begin active work there. Of this period he afterwards wrote :

For some time I was what we now call a ward sergeant, and from this work I entered into a more responsible position as an employed official of the Mission. It was in 1874, when I was eighteen years of age, that I came thus definitely into the Mission service. I did not consider that my entrance into that service pledged me to a life of public ministry. . . . I was in the midst of a great controversy with myself, which continued for at any rate three years.

In a letter he wrote to Railton (6th October 1874) he described an attempt he had made, at a quarterly meeting of the Shoreditch Circuit, to prevent open-air meetings being limited to half-an-hour apiece, in which time, he had argued, all that could be done was to have a " walk round and a holler ! " He had been outvoted.

Bramwell's name does not appear in the records of the Shoreditch Circuit elders' meeting ; he no doubt attended the quarterly meeting (a more widely representative committee) in virtue of his connection with the Hackney station.

In 1871 Bramwell Booth was appointed treasurer of the Preachers' Beneficent Fund, James F. Rapson being secretary, and two years later he became *ex officio* a member of Conference. He forthwith took active part in the proceedings and served (1874) on a committee that had in hand the preparation of a concise set of Rules of the Mission. In 1875 he was appointed a member of the Conference committee, the body dealing with the business of the Mission between Conferences.

Miss Pollett had been appointed in April 1874 to supervise the starting of a Mission-wide Drunkards' Rescue Society. After service in this appointment and as an evangelist, Miss Pollett was married, in 1876, to Railton's uncle, Mr. R. Ward, of Stockton.

Miss Booth was Catherine (Katie), the oldest daughter of William and Catherine Booth, nearly seventeen years of age, in later life to become known, when she pioneered Salvation Army work in France, as *la Maréchale*. After having led with success a number of isolated public meetings, she was beginning to conduct evangelistic campaigns lasting for three weeks or a month. Her first address, apart from speaking at meetings of the Children's Mission, was given, at the suggestion of Bramwell Booth, at an open-air meeting held outside an East London public-house. Though then only fourteen, Catherine had spoken " with such sweetness and power " that the request that she should speak was often repeated.

When Mrs. Booth was holding services at Ryde (August 1874), Catherine spoke at a large open-air meeting conducted by the united churches. This led Mrs. Booth to raise objection to such early publicity. But Bramwell protested. " Katie," he said, " is as surely called and inspired by God for this particular work as yourself." Mrs. Booth accepted Bramwell's remonstrance in good part and withdrew her objection.

III DISTRICT SUPERINTENDENTS AND HELPERS

WHITECHAPEL : William Bamford, A. Peters, and Ellen Hall
SHOREDITCH : Henry G. Waters
BETHNAL GREEN : Supply
POPLAR AND CUBITT TOWN : James P. Grey
LIMEHOUSE AND MILLWALL : John Tetley
CANNING TOWN : J. Watts
STRATFORD : Supply
CROYDON : William Jones

Of these, Cubitt Town is the only station not previously mentioned. An unsuccessful attempt was made to establish a branch of the Mission here in July 1871 ; some two years later, however, work was again started. The revival of trade, it was noted, had brought people back to the place, and crowds—which before could not be obtained—attended the meetings.

Other stations added to the list since the opening of the People's Mission Hall were :

STOKE NEWINGTON AND TOTTENHAM : Trenhail
Mrs. Booth concluded a campaign at Stoke Newington on Sunday, 2nd May 1870. The opening of a branch of the Mission was announced in the July *Christian Mission Magazine*. Tottenham was opened on Sunday, 16th October 1870.

HACKNEY : Richard M. Lane
A shop on Hackney Road near Cambridge Heath station was occupied as a preaching station as early as January 1867, but the opening of Hackney station proper dates from Sunday, 11th September 1870, when John Eason (formerly a member and a superintendent of The Christian Community), who had established a mission with a hall on Loddiges Road, Hackney,

and an auxiliary tent on London Fields, joined forces with The Christian Mission.

When Eason died (1887) it was said of him that he had been " friend, supporter, sympathizer, and comrade to every Salvationist with whom he had come in contact." Like William Booth he had begun life in a pawnbroker's shop, but had afterwards prospered, though not without reverses, latterly as a photographer. He was an enthusiastic student of the Revelation of St. John, and published a book thereon, but events did not bear out his interpretation of the Apostle's prophecies.

HASTINGS : William J. Pearson
Following a campaign conducted by Mrs. Booth the first meetings of this station were held on Sunday, 18th December 1870.

WELLINGBOROUGH : William Corbridge
A member of the Croydon Mission, Ireson, having moved to Wellingborough, stirred up local Christians to seek the establishment of a branch of The Christian Mission. Twenty of them met on 7th April 1873, and so earnestly pressed for this that an evangelist was sent at once.

PORTSMOUTH : Job Clare
Mrs. Booth began a campaign here on 2nd March 1873. This was continued for four months; at the conclusion a Mission station was at once opened, seemingly on Sunday, 6th July.

The 1875 Conference brought to a head incipient trouble at this station. The stationing committee decided that the evangelist (J. M. Salt) should be included in the changes for the ensuing year ; but immediately following the adoption of the stationing committee's recommendations Salt handed his resignation to the General Superintendent.

Twice the Mission had allowed branches (Norwood and

Brighton) to secede without asserting its rights ; but in this instance, for the welfare of the whole Mission and the discipline necessary to good government, William Booth—supported by Conference, and subsequently by the Conference committee—took a firm stand. The stationing committee presented an amended list providing for the manning of all stations without Salt, and this was at once accepted. Secretary Railton was despatched to Portsmouth with another evangelist (Job Clare) and was able to rally the majority of the Mission members to loyalty to the organization.

Mrs. Booth also helped to save the station to the Mission. The Conference committee (17th March 1876) recorded its thankfulness at " the blessing that has attended Mrs. Booth's labours at Portsmouth and trusts . . . that the Society will now be able, leaving behind all the unpleasant circumstances of the past, to give themselves entirely to a grand and glorious extension of the work of God."

The disaffected missioners attempted to seize the Lake Road hall, but legal proceedings resulted in favour of The Christian Mission. The point that carried the day was that in the leasing of this building the name of William Booth had been associated with those of members of the local committee, the corporate entity of The Christian Mission being thereby established.

PLAISTOW : Alfred Russell

The trustees of a Union Church at Plaistow having offered the building to the Mission, it was accepted and a branch was opened on Sunday, 6th July 1873.

KETTERING : William Ridsdel

A committee on which various denominations were represented was in control of work carried on at Kettering in a hall built by a local gentleman for the purpose. Seeing the success attending The Christian Mission elsewhere the committee invited it to take this over. That the Mission had done so was announced in the *Christian Mission Magazine* of November 1873.

STOCKTON : Abraham Lamb

Mr. Secretary Railton went on a "Mission Tour" in September and October 1874. He began at Enfield and finished at Stockton, holding meetings at almost every place of size on the Great North Road as he proceeded.

Alone, a perfect stranger in almost every town visited, without any introduction of friends, often unannounced, save by the banner which he carries in his hand, he has [reported the *Christian Mission Magazine* for November 1874] borne our message of mercy to thousands of people in the open-air, and pressed home upon the hearts of numerous churches and congregations of almost every denomination the importance of actively caring for the souls of the working classes.

At Stockton (where Railton's uncle, R. Ward, lived) he found that some Christian workers were holding meetings in an old theatre—" a dilapidated building which had become a penny gaff of the worst description." This was secured and opened as " The People's Hall " on Sunday, 22nd November.

MIDDLESBRO' : James Dowdle

In his review of the doings of January 1875 William Booth wrote :

The success so suddenly crowning our labours in Stockton, as reported last month, demanded we should follow up the advantage gained with vigour. We scarcely knew where to turn for a suitable man for Middlesbro', as there seemed to be no possibility of our getting one without taking a missionary from one of the stations. It was no small request to make, but it afforded to Brother Dowdle and our friends at Chatham an opportunity of manifesting a missionary zeal worthy of apostolic days. Thus set free, Brother Dowdle left for Middlesbro' on the 23rd [January 1875] and reports over 2,000 people present at his services on Sunday.

Other instances are recorded of stations and leaders having been consulted before changes were made.

BARKING : Annie Davis

Preachers of the Canning Town branch of the Mission had been invited by Barking acquaintances to preach in the open-air there ; this led to demands being pressed for the establishment of a local branch, the first meetings of which were held on Sunday, 30th November 1873.

CHATHAM : Charles Hobday

A campaign by Mrs. Booth was the prelude to this branch of the Mission being opened. James Dowdle, the first appointed evangelist, announced that he had " raised the Christian Mission flag " there on Sunday, 30th November 1873.

NORTH WOOLWICH : Charles Panter

Reported in the *Christian Mission Magazine* for March 1874 as opened, but not mentioned again until a year later, when some outstanding instances of conversion were described.

HAMMERSMITH : William Garner

Miss E. A. Bazett and Mrs. Saunders (the latter a Christian Mission convert employed as a Biblewoman by Miss Bazett) had established a mission, but it was being threatened with extinction by priestly interference. The Christian Mission was pressed to go to their assistance. Union took place, and the first meetings of the new régime were conducted by a band of converted gipsies from Whitechapel on Sunday, 28th February 1874.

SOHO : George Mace

Grafton Hall—originally a Baptist chapel, but designated as " for two or three years occupied by the party devoted to Home Rule (*sic*) and infidelity "—was to let. Friends entreated that the Mission would begin work there. William Ridsdel conducted the first meetings on Sunday, 2nd August 1874.

CARDIFF : John Allen

The trustees of a Gospel hall " fully and freely " gave it to The Christian Mission. It had been built by a Christian lady and her brother (unnamed), but failing health had rendered them incapable of carrying on and the work had slackened. John Allen took over on Sunday, 15th November 1874.

In addition to the places named in the list of main stations, others were worked either in full association with them or as outposts. Among these were :

HASTINGS : Ninfield, Boreham, Rye, New Romney, and St. Leonards

PORTSMOUTH : Buckland and Southsea

CARDIFF : Canton

CHATHAM : New Brompton, Strood, Rochester, and Beacon Hill (Luton)

HAMMERSMITH : Fulham

CROYDON : Penge, Bromley, and Carshalton

Some names had disappeared ; Bow Common, Globe Road, and Old Ford were among these. The Christian Mission had withdrawn from association with the Edinburgh Mission ; Norwood and Brighton had seceded.

2

Some of the appointed evangelists have already been referred to incidentally. Others were associated with the Mission only for comparatively short periods. Those not previously mentioned who subsequently became noteworthy as leaders were :

John Trenhail. Had just entered the work. As at some other stations of the Mission, the members at Stoke Newington had settled down into a quiet routine ; they were averse to being disturbed by the efforts made by young Trenhail, a Cornishman imbued with the true missioning aggressiveness, to apply the newer methods so strikingly successful elsewhere. Much that he tried to do was condemned as not being " our way." This so discouraged the young evangelist that when after six months a good situation was offered him he resigned. Within two years, however, he was again in the work. His first appointment then was to Portsmouth, not very long after the " split " had occurred, and where he had as helpers Henry Edmonds and John Roberts, both of whom eventually attained the rank of colonel in The Salvation Army. William Booth's letter to Trenhail announcing his re-acceptance and appointment to Portsmouth throws light upon financial arrangements of the period :

I think it well to say in writing that we have received you on trial as an evangelist of this Mission. That your salary will be 25s. per week. But seeing the house at Portsmouth where you have been appointed is too heavy rent, you are at liberty to receive 30s. per week while it remains empty, but we wish you to let two or three rooms at once. . . . I will write you again as to your furniture to-morrow.

Trenhail—until his voice failed, comparatively early—was conspicuous in opening new stations when the Mission became The Salvation Army. He was over 90 years of age when promoted to Glory from Truro, where he was living in retirement, though still an ardent and active Salvationist.

William Corbridge. Was born in a Leicestershire village —Somerby—in 1843, and at the age of 15 was converted when kneeling under a hedge. Three months later he began to preach. After working with the Hallelujah band at Leicester he entered the service of The Christian Mission in November 1869. Had charge, among others, of Hastings and Leicester stations. At the latter he put into effect the methods of the Hallelujah bands, with outstanding success.

William Ridsdel. William Booth had heard that a young local preacher, working as a grocer's assistant, would be likely to make a good evangelist. He wrote to him, enclosed a copy of *How to Reach the Masses with the Gospel*, and asked him to come to see him. Before the end of that year (1873) Ridsdel had been appointed assistant evangelist at Portsmouth. He was the first missioner to become a Territorial Commander—the officer in command of Salvation Army operations in a country or countries included in a " Territory."

Annie Davis was the first woman evangelist to be placed in command of a station, having been appointed by the 1875 Conference to Barking. Railton afterwards wrote of this " daring experiment " :

Annie Davis, in the streets and in the little upstairs Bethel of Barking, effectually settled the question whether a woman was capable of managing a station successfully.

According to the same authority, she was the pioneer of the cloud of women officers who three years later were suddenly sent flying all over the country with full power to attack and take possession of towns, just as the men had done.

In September 1878 Annie Davis and William Ridsdel were married at Stockton ; William Corbridge conducted the ceremony.

CHAPTER FIFTEEN

CONSTITUTION MAKING: 1870–1875

I

THE first constitution of The Christian Mission (1870) [1] was a self-denying ordinance on the part of William Booth. By it Conference was made the final authority in the affairs of The Christian Mission. There is nowhere any suggestion that William Booth at any time regarded The Christian Mission, or The Salvation Army, as being his in any other sense than that he was the instrument used by God to bring the organization into being, and that as a trustee he was responsible for taking what measures seemed necessary to secure its success and permanency. When his followers urged him to do so, because in their judgment it appeared to be advantageous to the cause, he resumed sole leadership as their commander, the change being made in accordance with the provisions of the revised Constitution adopted in 1875. With characteristically direct and plain speech he disposed of any idea that The Salvation Army was ever " a family affair " when he wrote to his son Herbert (16th September 1902) :

If you suppose that our children were the earliest if not the chief helpers your mother and I had in laying its foundations, I think you are mistaken. We had able and faithful workers (some of whom are with me to-day) before you were out of the school-room—I might say the nursery.

If you assert that as my children you possess some inborn right to superior position and power over your comrades and over the organization, I . . . say that I entertain no such opinions. . . .
In this matter I have not been willing to recognize any " right

[1] Appendices L, Rules of The Christian Mission, 1870 ; M, Conditions of Membership, 1870

inherited by birth." The only right I have been disposed to regard is that which comes of devotion to God, loyalty to our principles, and faithfulness to me, that is I have striven to treat you, in your relation to me as Officers, after the same fashion and by the same rules as I have treated others.

Speaking at the marriage of his eldest son, Bramwell, in 1882, William Booth emphasized that while it was both possible and probable that his son would step into his place, the generalship of The Salvation Army was in no sense hereditary, nor was it contemplated to make it such.

In November, William Booth assembled the first Conference of The Christian Mission to consider the elaborate constitution that he had devised [1] ; this was based mainly upon liberal Methodism, but with one radical difference— women were admitted to full participation not only in the work of the Mission, but in its government. Comparison of the rules of The Christian Mission (1870) with those of the Methodist New Connexion shows a strong family likeness, though William Booth did not slavishly follow his model. For instance, that the Mission did not change leaders annually necessitated important differences in provision for procedure at conferences. In addition, total abstinence from the use of alcoholic beverages was made a condition of holding office.

Conference was composed of the General Superintendent of the Mission, the secretary, the treasurers of the Conference Fund, the life members or "guardian representatives" (appointed in 1874, Mrs. Booth being the first), evangelists in charge of districts and two lay delegates, elected by the society meetings, from each district.

Records of Conference proceedings have been preserved in a MS. minute book, *The Conference Journal*. The only other contemporary references to the first Conference extant

[1] Appendices L, Rules of The Christian Mission, 1870 ; M, Conditions of Membership, 1870

are in the minutes of (a) the Shoreditch Circuit elders'
meeting [1] of 4th November 1870, recording the election of
Brothers Longmore and Moore as representatives to attend
the "Whitechapel Conference on 15th November"; and
(b) the central committee of The Christian Mission of
November (date of day not recorded), when William Booth
informed the members that during the previous week he had
held meetings with representative members of the Mission
and had presented to them "the general rules of the Society
in a consolidated and collective form, that some rules had
been amended and others added, and he, Mr. Booth, hoped
that since the rules had been accepted by the members they
would tend to the better regulation of the Mission."

The minutes of the first Conference are, in the *Conference
Journal*, dated 15th, 16th and 18th *June*, but this is obviously
a mistake. Among indications, other than the above, that
November is the right date are (1) that William Booth was
absent from London for the whole of June, and (2) that the
evangelist (Mackson) who was appointed secretary to the
Conference (but who did not act and who withdrew from
the Mission, at the instance of William Booth, in January
1871) did not join the Mission until September. The
Conference Journal names thirty-four members, six of them,
with Mrs. Booth at their head, being women. [2]

The Rules (1870) set out that "the Mission shall be
under the superintendence of the Rev. William Booth, who
is spoken of hereafter as the General Superintendent." He
was to

possess the power of confirming or setting aside the decisions and
resolutions of any of the official, society, or other meetings held
throughout the Mission, which in his judgment may be in any
way prejudicial to the object for which the Mission was first
established.

[1] Appendix J
[2] Appendix K, Membership of the First Conference

But this power did not include that of over-riding Conference. This was not conferred until 1875.

With regard to a successor to William Booth in the office of General Superintendent, the rules (1870) provided :

1. If the General Superintendent shall resign or die, or, in the unanimous opinion of the Conference, become incapacitated to continue the general superintendence of the Mission, then the duties, powers, and responsibilities of the office shall pass into the hands of Conference.

2. That the General Superintendent " may if he think proper appoint a successor to his office, but in such case the appointment shall be approved by at least three-fourths of the Conference."

This first constitution was comprehensive ; the table of contents of the 34-page closely printed octavo book in which its provisions were set out contained no fewer than thirty-eight headings.

The conditions of membership in the Mission were exceedingly complicated and detailed in their requirements, but while it was insisted that members should not in any way traffic in intoxicating drink, personal abstinence therefrom was not more than strongly urged.

Provision was made for setting up a trust to hold the property of the Mission.[1]

2

The climax of the first attempt to provide a satisfactory form of self-government for The Christian Mission was reached with the enrolment in Chancery of a deed-poll dated 5th June 1875, signed by William Booth as " President or Chairman of Conference," and by George Scott Railton as " Secretary."

The deed was prepared by Thomas Whittington, solicitor to The Christian Mission, with the advice (gratuitous) of

[1] Appendix O, Mission Property

eminent counsel, Mr. Cozens Hardy, afterwards Master of the Rolls. The preamble sets out that William Booth had " commenced preaching the Gospel in a tent erected in the Friends' Burial Ground." Read one way this dates William Booth's beginning to preach as from the tent, in another, that there was no preaching at the tent until William Booth went there ; the fact differs from either interpretation and was better stated in the introduction to the " Rules and Doctrines of The Christian Mission," also printed by order of the 1875 Conference. This read :

The Christian Mission was founded by William Booth, who preached the Gospel in a tent erected in the Friends' Burial Ground, in the summer of 1865.

To this deed-poll was attached a certification that it had been " duly presented to Conference and approved as the Foundation Deed of The Christian Mission." In it appears for the first time the provision :

THAT THE SAID CHRISTIAN MISSION IS AND SHALL BE HEREAFTER FOR EVER UNDER THE OVERSIGHT DIRECTION AND CONTROL OF SOME ONE PERSON

The position of William Booth was considerably re-inforced. His power of veto was extended to cover " all or any of the decisions and resolutions of any Conference " in addition to those of " official society or other meetings." Power was also given to him to appoint his successor by deed.

In the event of William Booth's not exercising his power to appoint his successor, a candidate for the office could be nominated by any twelve members of the last preceding Conference (or by a General Superintendent who had succeeded William Booth). Election was then to be by ballot, the highest number of votes to be decisive.

A General Superintendent appointed by deed by William Booth was to hold office for the term of his natural life subject to the provision, as with William Booth himself, that if he became incapacitated he could be removed by a unanimous vote of Conference. In all other respects in regard to holding office he was to be subject to the provisions applicable to a General Superintendent elected by Conference.

A General Superintendent elected by Conference was to hold office for five years, but could be re-elected.

Official, society, and other meetings were given right of appeal to Conference against the veto of any succeeding General Superintendent not appointed by William Booth, a vote of two-thirds of Conference being required to nullify such veto. Any veto of resolutions or decisions of Conference could be likewise set aside.

A General Superintendent not appointed by William Booth might be removed before the expiration of his term of office by a vote of three-fourths of Conference.

But to William Booth was given power, at any time during his continuance in office, with the concurrence of three-fourths of the members of Conference, to annul or alter anything contained in the deed.

Power was given to Conference to consider at the end of five years, " the propriety of any alterations in or modifications of the constitution or government of the said Christian Mission and so periodically at the end of every succeeding ten years . . . and if two-thirds in number of the two annual meetings of Conference next ensuing shall decide upon the adoption of such alterations then the same shall be made."
Excepted from this power of alteration were :
The doctrines of The Christian Mission
The position, office, or powers of William Booth
Continuance of the elective character of Conference
Prohibition of the letting of sittings in any halls of the Mission [Within three months of the starting of the Mission

some of the members had proposed the letting of sittings in their little halls.]

The right of females to act as evangelists or class leaders ; to hold any office ; to speak and vote at all official meetings of which they might be members.

If Conference did not meet for three years successively, or the membership of the whole Conference became less than twenty for five successive meetings, Conference would be extinguished and all property would vest in " trust or trustee for the time being."

3

Quite as remarkable as this constitution making was the manner in which Conference conducted business. A few of the members had had previous experience of the mechanics of debate—resolution moving, seconding and voting—but the majority had not ; many had had but the rudiments of education—some were admittedly illiterate. Nevertheless, from the first, the minutes show a wholly admirable orderliness of procedure. There are no traces of acrimony; the nearest approach to crisis was seen when, after the appointments committee had announced its decision to remove an evangelist from a certain station, he had tendered his resignation. This was accepted in due form, and the necessary rearrangements were made. On another occasion an evangelist was charged with having been lax in regard to the financing of his station and with not making proper reports to the central authority. William Booth, it would appear, cleared away personalities, quietly questioned the supposed delinquent " from the chair," and elicited from him information which exonerated him.

The records of Conference were excellently kept. The minutes of the 1870 and 1871 proceedings are in the handwriting of Rapson, who would seem also to have been Secretary to the Mission. The Conference committee, on 2nd October 1871, recorded :

In appreciation of the business-like manner in which the books of the Mission have been kept by the Secretary, Mr. Rapson, and an expression of their esteem for the satisfactory manner he has discharged his duties generally, agree to ask Mr. Booth to advance his salary to 42s. per week from and after the first day of January 1872. To this arrangement Mr. Booth concurred.

Conference did not meet in 1872, and by the time the 1873 Conference met, George S. Railton had become Secretary of The Christian Mission. Rapson continued to be a member of Conference, and was appointed minutes secretary as well as secretary of the Preachers' Beneficent Fund, of which Bramwell Booth was treasurer, but by 1874 another secretary had been appointed and Rapson's name had disappeared. He had left the Mission. Later he went to the United States of America and entered the ministry of the Baptist Church.

Chapter Sixteen

DISAPPOINTMENTS

I

GREAT things had been hoped for from the institution of self-government for The Christian Mission. It was confidently considered that with the enrolment of the first deed-poll (1875) a climax of effective and stable government had been reached.

Commenting on the Conference at which this instrument had been completed, William Booth wrote :

Our blessed unity found a happy and, we trust, enduring legal expression in the deeds for the settlement of our property, which were unanimously accepted and executed. . . . We have at length completed and enrolled in Chancery a deed [1] which will, we think, render the use of our halls for other than a purely evangelistic purpose utterly impossible. . . . The strong and hearty manner in which the deeds were adopted by the Conference leads us to entertain the most sanguine expectations of the perpetuation of the Mission spirit.

But it was not very long before disappointment began to overshadow satisfaction. Not only was the hoped-for progress not made, but slowly, though surely, it became evident that retrogression had set in.

The dreary record of attempted government by resolution filled pages of the *Conference Journal.* Even members of Conference who had not had earlier experience of like procedure quickly developed an avid appetite for it. All seem to have felt that the safety and progress of the Mission depended upon the readiness with which each could detect

[1] Appendix O, Mission Property

some seeming defect in its rules, or departure from them, or threatened danger for want of legislation to provide against it, and the plans for remedying defects which each could present !

This plethora of discussion prevailed throughout the Mission. The minutes of the Shoreditch elders' meeting [1] were no doubt characteristic. Railton has also left on record a vivid description of the position :

For years past the Founder and General Superintendent . . . had been inventing scheme after scheme for the consolidation and perpetuation of the work, and the result was an amount of organization at which we can afford to laugh nowadays, but which implied a total of patient toil it would be impossible now to estimate.

. . . In connection with halls that would not hold a hundred people, you might find as many as half a dozen different official bodies meeting every week. The poor convert who had been brought to the penitent-form two months since must appear trembling before an elders' meeting. If he ventured to aspire to public speaking he must pass another examination before the exhorters' meeting. Did he wish to distribute tracts, then he must see the tract committee. . . . If the tract distributor came across cases of extreme need, then he must apply to another committee for the help to the extent of a shilling or two which he might be allowed to give. By-and-by would come round the solemn day for the local preachers' and the quarterly meetings. . . .

The amount of time spent in official meetings of this description after their day's work was done by these hard toilers in the factory, the street, and the workshop seems almost incredible. . . . Oh, those elders' meetings ! . . . prolonged till midnight many a time !

In Conference, rules of debate were closely observed. Alterations, small or great, were made the subjects of formal resolutions. There are to be found, in the *Conference Journal*, instances where the adoption of a resolution and its rescission took place in the same session !

[1] Appendix J, Minutes of the Shoreditch Circuit Elders' Meeting

Examples abound of the wasting of time in needlessly formal procedure :

In the 1874 minutes four separate resolutions were recorded regarding the Conference committee : (1) that it should consist of four persons resident in London ; (2) that they should be elected by open vote ; (3) that the committee should be elected as a whole ; and (4) the names !

Again, at the 1875 Conference No. 1 of the " New Rules " —a shortened and simplified version of the 1870 code—as first adopted read :

Anyone may become a member of the Mission who is converted, and who lives consistently.

Before the session had closed this had been amended by the addition of the provision :

That no person be returned as a member until they have been in membership six weeks, being of the age of fifteen years.

And again :

By the substitution of the words " turned from darkness to light, and from the power of Satan unto God " for the word, " converted " !

This taking of the wrong turning inevitably affected the general work of The Christian Mission. On the one hand the energies of the older missioners were absorbed by the committees—they had become committee-men rather than active workers. On the other hand, new-comers were deterred from becoming workers by fear of the examinations which they were required to undergo before acceptance as such.

In the twelve months completed by the meeting of the 1876 Conference (5th June) one station only had been opened —at Leicester, following a campaign there by Mrs. Booth. A return submitted to Conference showed that the nominal membership of the Mission was 2,455 ; at the next Conference (1877) William Booth had to take to task those responsible for this return because, for one thing, when evangelists had gone into their new stations many members recorded could not be found.

Many of the matters dealt with by Conference were, of course, of importance, and at times discussion could not be otherwise than helpful ; but a vital link was missing. Railton pointed out the greatest weakness of all when he wrote :

As each Conference came round, it became more and more evident to everyone that what was done or not done during the year had little or no connection with any resolution of the Conference.

Conference was not only the cradle but the grave of its multitudinous resolutions !

But, comparatively barren as they were of practical issue, the meetings of Conference were by no means devoid of spiritual value. It was the practice to pause at the end of every hour for singing and prayer. One year (1874) it was said :

We all felt this to be not merely a great refreshment to our hearts and minds, but again and again difficulties and doubts seemed to fly in a moment under the influence of our devotions, and so much time was saved, as well as spiritual blessing received.

Even in 1876, the year in which the futility of Conference as a governing body made itself fully apparent, official comment claimed " the harmonising and invigorating influence of these gatherings will be blessedly felt all the year."

One of the foremost in spiritual influence on these occasions was " praying John Smith," a lay representative from Hastings. Smith was a navvy, " a hard worker with pick and shovel," who had been converted when a young man—" a simple, humble follower of Jesus, who longed to do his utmost for Him " ; and the Church, for 44 years, had left him without any special commission—would not let him even be a pew-opener, and refused the request of 30 members that he should be made their class leader. He found a sphere of usefulness when the Hastings station of The Christian Mission was opened five years before his death, and though pelted with rotten fish, rolled in the mud, haled before the magistrates, was always ready, radiant with joy, to take part in any effort to save sinners. Of him Railton wrote :

If he was little qualified to represent the refined tastes of that remarkable watering-place, and little inclined to enter into any of the niceties of debate, John was . . . a thoroughly sensible, shrewd old countryman. He was perfectly able to deal in a commonsense manner with almost any subject that came before us ; and many a time gave hints that were of great practical value. He could not always influence every mind ; but he never failed to move every heart and, as he went on, glowing all over with heavenly ecstasy, the old man would jump from gladness and spread the contagion of his joyous tears on every hand.

It was men like " Praying John " William Booth no doubt had in mind when he said (1877) after bemoaning that talking at conferences was largely monopolized by " dried-up theoretical legislators " :

I want the holiest and most devoted men and women to come to the front. They have a right to speak. They have something to say. I want them round me, and then we will cry together to the living God, and He will give us a gloriously successful Conference.

Regarding the general position in 1876 and the earlier part of 1877 William Booth stated :

In many of the old stations we appear, from the returns, to have had something like *stagnation* during the year. We have only got a net increase of 200 members . . . I should conclude I was out of my place if I spent twelve months at a place and did not leave it tangibly, unmistakably, visibly better than I found it.

Another factor contributing to the general slowing down was that, where buildings had been erected for Mission use by aid of money obtained on mortgage, members lost sight of the advantages of the change from their old rough accommodation —which indeed, from many indications, did not prove to be as great from the point of view of effective pursuit of their objects as had been anticipated—when they found they had to raise money to pay interest and repay borrowed capital. The burden became irksome, they grew discontented, lost heart and looked back, longingly, to those " good old days " which have, in every age, been so attractive in retrospect !

William Booth remarked at the 1877 Conference :

how often have I heard people say, " If we could only get a new chapel we should get on." But they have got the new chapel and have become deader than ever, besides having a debt to grapple with.

Some stations, too, had gone deeply into debt for current expenses.

2

In view of the extent and efficiency of the young people's work of The Salvation Army it makes strange reading that, at the 1877 Conference of The Christian Mission, William Booth ordered the abandonment of Sunday schools. " We have not yet," he declared, " any real plan to propose for dealing with the children. So far as our experience of Sunday schools has gone, they have been an injury to the Mission wherever they have existed." This order was also printed in the *Christian Mission Magazine*.

A report on " The Coming Army " (1888) stated that " in the earlier days of the movement it had become apparent that this great work could not be carried on efficiently without a separate organization under leaders willing to devote themselves to the children . . . only the slow process of years could produce the necessary staff."

At first the Children's Mission had done well under

James F. Rapson, of whose work in this connection William Booth in 1872 wrote in high praise. The Booth children had taken part in the Children's Mission under Rapson's direction. Bramwell had sometimes led meetings in the small hall situated in Thomas Passage, Bethnal Green, which was used between May and August 1870, and in the Fieldgate Street building to which the Children's Mission moved in August.

In one report (November 1869) initials and ages are given which clearly indicate that the simple testimonies quoted were given by the Booth children. They were B. B. (12)—which would be Ballington ; C. B. (10), stated to be a little girl—Catherine ; E. B. (9)—Emma ; and W. B. (13)—Bramwell. To his testimony Bramwell was reported as having added :

I have never been to any of these meetings before ; but I am glad I came to-night and I think I shall come again.

Brother Rapson was in charge ; Miss Billups was present and spoke. The meeting was held in " our lower hall " (188 Whitechapel Road).

A special hymn-book for the use of " The Children's Mission " was published in 1870 or 1871.

After Rapson left, efforts were made to reorganize the work, it being announced (June 1873) that " Mr. Booth's sons " and other young people had undertaken this work in association with Miss Billups.

There is nothing to indicate how the new arrangement worked until two years later, when in a report Ballington Booth wrote :

The dear friends who have been patiently labouring here for a long time had become almost disheartened. We have succeeded not only in restoring order but in largely increasing the numbers in attendance. At my first Sunday evening service over 250 were present and 13 came out for salvation. We are training a force of children to carry on the work.

Quotations from the few reports of meetings of " The Children's Mission " which appeared (1868–1877) indicate that the methods then employed were far removed from those of the present day. Children's meetings were " conducted on the same principle as our ordinary revival services " (1869) ; a children's " experience meeting " was opened by singing :

> We are waiting by the River,
>   We are watching by the shore,
>   Only waiting for the angel ;
>   Soon he'll come to bear us o'er !

The testimonies that followed all bore relation to the idea of this verse. Speakers at children's meetings took such subjects as " What wilt thou say when He shall punish thee ? " (1871) and " Death on the Pale Horse " (1874) !

The only other reference to young people's work during this period was that made when the Hackney hall was opened (June 1875), when it was stated :

The extra expense and trouble in erecting schoolrooms and class-rooms . . . will be amply repaid. Such quantities of bareheaded, unwashed children we never saw as preceded and accompanied our procession . . . there seems to be no prospect of difficulty in getting either congregation or attention.

After this there was silence until William Booth's order for discontinuance of all Sunday schools.

3

Among the auxiliary enterprises of the Seventies which had promised well but which were abandoned were the soup-kitchens and food shops. The People's Market had been fitted up with the appliances necessary for carrying on a soup-kitchen on a large scale. When it was purchased by the Mission at the end of 1869, it was decided to transfer the fittings to the " 188 " premises, as the space occupied was required for extension of the People's Mission Hall auditorium. This and all the relief work of the Mission were at that time directed by Charles S. Mitchell, who had previously been associated with other philanthropic work in East London, principally in connection with the Rev. W. Tyler's church. Flawn worked with him as manager of the soup-kitchen, which by this time (April 1870) it was shown by a comprehensive report had become a considerable undertaking. This read :

During the short time this has been open we have supplied 5,000 families with soup and bread *free*. The sick have been visited and parcels of tea, sugar, arrowroot, mutton, tripe, rice, sago, cornflour, and bread given gratuitously. We sell soup to 600 or 1,000 persons *daily* at one penny per pint and a large slice of bread for one halfpenny, much of which is taken home to families ; also mutton (cooked) free from bone is sold in small quantities at the rate of sixpence per pound, and beef marrow at the rate of sevenpence, which the poor use instead of butter. We sell a pint of tea for three-halfpence, half a pint for one penny. Coffee for one penny per pint, half a pint for one halfpenny. We also sell large quantities of boiled and baked pudding at a penny a large slice.

Our soup hall will accommodate 150 ; the tea, coffee, and reading room 100. We can bake for 250 people and boil for as many more.

The whole affair when in operation will be *self-supporting*. For every guinea we receive we send 100 tickets to the various clergymen and dissenting ministers, scripture readers, missionaries, and Biblewomen, to be distributed among the starving poor (of which there are thousands), which entitle the bearer to one quart of meat soup and a slice of bread.

When the funds from which the sewing classes had been supported failed, friends, prominent among them the Hon. Mrs. Hobart, had turned their attention to emigration and at the Mission's Sydney Street rooms Mitchell, on their behalf, attended to the fitting out of the emigrants. But the soup-kitchen plant had hardly been set up at " 188 " when Mitchell died from overwork, William Booth wrote.

Subsequently the Mission committee unanimously determined that the soup-kitchen should no longer be carried on by the Mission, but that both the plant and the lease of the " 188 " premises, for which the Mission had no further use, should be offered to William Booth. He accepted the proposition ; at the next meeting of the full committee (16th September 1870) a valuation, amounting to £140, presented by a sub-committee, was agreed to. A receipt for payment of this amount by William Booth, dated 10th September, signed by N. J. Powell, treasurer, has been preserved.

William Booth's reasons for accepting the offer were set out by him in a circular to friends of The Christian Mission in 1877. In it he explained that some of the gentlemen who, when he first went to East London, had undertaken to provide for his support, through adverse and other circumstances some two or three years later had failed him, and that, for a time, he had been very much tried.

At this juncture [he continued] it appeared to me that the Lord opened my way to a business which I entered into in the hope that I might no longer be chargeable to my friends and yet continue to devote myself as fully as ever to the work of the Mission. . . .

At the outset everything seemed to betoken success, but soon afterwards unforeseen difficulties arose, principally from the very limited amount of capital employed, the difficulty of obtaining conscientious and competent managers, and my own inability to give a personal oversight to the undertaking. The result has been a positive and continued loss for more than twelve months.

He had come to the determination, reluctantly, he said, to relinquish this enterprise, and was expecting, almost every day, that the last of the shops would pass out of his hands.

The soup-kitchen had been expanded into the setting up

at one time of five shops for the provision of cheap meals, with " Food for the Million " as a slogan.

Contemporary directories show " 188 " Whitechapel Road to have remained a soup-kitchen, with Flawn as manager, till late in 1871. In the 1872, 1873, and 1874 editions the description given was " Dining Rooms, William Booth." In 1875 " Cooper " was substituted for " William Booth " ; he was brother-in-law to Mr. Billups, who had purchased the business from William Booth.

A letter from Bramwell Booth to Mr. (or Mrs., it is not quite clear which) Billups (22nd August 1873) throws light, first on the date when William Booth began to dispose of the shops, and second on the relationships of Bramwell and his father to them. The Billups had asked William Booth for some advice for Cooper. In reply Bramwell stated this letter had been given to him for attention because his father knew very little about the matter :

He has never [wrote Bramwell] come into it, not so much as to give advice or sign me a cheque. The fact was he said to me at the first that unless I could do and manage the business without him, I was no good and he must give it up. . . . Papa has never had time to attend to the matter in any way.

With regard to the unreliability of employees he recalled that when Cooper took over the place he had told him he must handle the money himself, since they found they were robbed every day that they did not do so.

General relief work seems later to have been abandoned by The Christian Mission,[1] for writing to the Rev. Arthur Wedgwood (hon. secretary of the Whitechapel Union Division of the Charity Organisation Society) in June 1877 William Booth stated that the Mission had ceased almost entirely to administer relief to strangers, but instead referred them to the Charity Organisation Society.

[1] Appendix S, Relief of Distress in East London

4

Still another temporary disappointment concerned total abstinence. At the time the Mission was founded tea and coffee had been very dear to buy. Beer was cheap—and no trouble to prepare. The poorly paid workers of East London, consequently, made beer their common drink—and Mission members among them. William Booth was greatly shocked when at an outing (Epping Forest) in the early days of the Mission some members ate their lunch on tables outside a public house and had beer with the meal. Mrs. Booth and other members took loose tea and obtained boiling water—at a charge of 2d. per head.

At the 1876 Conference, Bramwell Booth had proposed that total abstinence should be made a condition of membership in the Mission and not incumbent only, as it already was, upon office-holders. An amending resolution was carried which went no further than to require that members should be " strongly urged " to abstain.

Later, William Booth wrote in the *Christian Mission Magazine* :

Our opinions upon the question, as it affects our societies, differ. Let us wait until we can arrive at something with unanimity ; until we have made up our minds to some definite plan it will be useless to talk. But in the meantime let us *make all our people abstainers*.

He was also determined that the energies of the missioners should not be dissipated in temperance advocacy divorced from religion. He insisted that there should be no " temperance meetings without God in them." There were to be none that were mere entertainments. " We will have," he continued, " no mere teetotalism. We will have godly meetings, and we will teach all our people never to drink or touch the stuff, *for Christ's sake*."

Chapter Seventeen

NEW LIFE : 1877–1878

I

RAILTON, Bramwell Booth, Dowdle, Ridsdel, Corbridge and other ardent spirits grew tired of the futility of attempted government by Conference and the slowing down of progress consequent on the lack of effective leadership inherent in that system. Headed by Railton and Bramwell Booth, they waited upon William Booth and protested : " We gave up our lives to work under you and those you should appoint, rather than under one another."

" You tell us what to do," said Ridsdel, " and we'll do it. I can't see the good of a lot of talk, with one wanting one thing and another another."

This would seem to have been late in 1876. William Booth called a meeting of the Conference committee, augmented by all the superintendents and evangelists of the Mission, for 23rd and 24th January 1877. It would have been held earlier, but for the need for the disinfection of the Booth house where Railton and others had lain ill with smallpox.

William Booth addressed this gathering on " The Constitution and the future of the Mission " and " several conversations followed." The conclusions reached, without a dissenting voice, were that government by committees was too slow and roundabout ; that decisions were continually required upon important matters ; that theirs was a war, anyway ; that the annual Conference should be continued, but as a council of war and not a legislative assembly.

By the time Conference met in June the change thus

originated had been formulated and was presented for confirmation. But the leaders of the Mission had not waited upon formalities—they had had enough of these and had broken with them for all time ! They submitted at once to everything implicit in the new system, and new life surged through the Mission.

The first notable indication that a new spirit was operating came from Leicester. Late in 1876, without any warning, the evangelist in charge of the local branch of The Christian Mission had declared it to be dissolved. Backed—as had been the case at Brighton—by a wealthy treasurer, he endeavoured to set up an independent mission. The special meeting of the Conference committee dealt also with this attempted secession—it may well be that the need for a strong central authority it revealed at least strengthened the desire for the change of system to which this meeting gave effect. This view is supported by what Railton later wrote : " The taking of the Exchange at Stockton contrary to the expressed wish of Headquarters, with one or two similar acts elsewhere," helped to bring matters to this crisis.

Stationed with Abraham Lamb, the defaulting superintendent, was a second evangelist, Arthur Russell.[1] He, said William Booth—when, at the 1877 Conference, he referred to the episode—together with " a band of brave, faithful people . . . had vowed with or without a place to cover their heads they would have a Christian Mission in Leicester."

Railton, with the precedent established at Portsmouth to strengthen his hands, dealt promptly and effectively with the business side of the affair. William Corbridge was sent to take charge. William Booth followed up with counsel and instruction, and in February went to Leicester to open the " Salvation Warehouse," a building larger than that

[1] Appendix B, Early Witnesses

previously used, which had been secured as a meeting-place for the Mission. He was delighted with the " sudden and extraordinary upward bound " of the Mission which had taken place. The proceedings on the Sunday began with a triumphant procession at six o'clock in the morning !

Evangelists Corbridge and Arthur Russell had put into operation, in full, the methods of the Hallelujah bands.[1] This had made a great sensation locally. The *Midland Free Press*, in the course of a long, racy, but on the whole sympathetic report of what was taking place, described a meeting at which

the " speaking talent " included a one-armed rag and bone man, a framework knitter, a burly Yorkshireman, a coal porter—who had been a thimble-rigging cardsharper—a cab driver (as he was likely to trench too largely on the time, he was quietly informed they had had enough of him), and a shoehand. Continued volleys of loud " Amens " and " Hallelujahs " burst forth with a vehemence actually startling !

There were plenty of hymns sung—to tunes that go with a swing and a bang—with a chorus that will force one to sing—and they did seem to strike a tender chord in many a breast that might never have vibrated to any other touch. To see them, to hear them singing the chorus :

> Let us never mind the scoffs and the frowns
>   of the world,
> For we all have our cross to bear,
> It will only make the crown the brighter,
> When we get the crown to wear

was exceedingly pleasing. There was not one, perhaps, in the room but had known more of crosses than anything else in the world.

A cordial shake of the hand by Mr. Corbridge and the blunt though well-meant question as to whether we had " found Jesus " brought us up all of a heap and dissipated all idea of further observation !

William Booth, in reviewing the doings of the Mission as a

[1] Appendix D, William Booth's Call to the East End and his Plan of Work

whole during March, found that considerable progress had been made towards the realization of his ideals of aggressive warfare.

We have been trying [he wrote] and, we thank God, with no little success, to break loose from all the trammels of custom and propriety which may in any degree have hindered or hampered us in the past. The dreadful tendency to settle down is apparent in connection with all religious work. . . . We mean to gain the ear of the people for our Master, and we are more than ever determined that no conformity to any Church forms or ideas shall hinder us.

Bramwell Booth leading Hallelujah bands of colliers in the East Hartlepool Theatre, and Brother Dowdle fiddling through the streets of Bradford and gathering thousands of hearers, have perhaps represented as perfectly as possible the progress of our Mission away from the commonplace lines of custom to the ears and hearts of those who will not listen to common ministrations. We shall gain more and more the contempt and hatred of men ; even a religious contemporary has thought proper to describe our operations at one station as " Pantomimic Missioning," but we shall by the power of the Lord, who so generously helps us, win more and more of those who prefer the pantomime to the ordinary preaching service ; and for that we live.

2

Of individual contributions to the rising tide of new life in the Mission at this time, none held greater significance than the entry into its service of a one-time sweep's climbing boy and drunken pugilist. Elijah Cadman had been converted and had, with characteristic thoroughness, started a mission at Rugby when he met William Booth and was convinced that under his leadership in The Christian Mission he would have wider opportunity for such work. He was now at his first station, Hackney, and from him came a report of stirring doings there :

At our open-air services, publicans, policemen, butchers, and quite a number of " lewd fellows of the baser sort " have combined to drive us from the field. . . .

. . . We were set upon by a band of ruffians shouting, howling, and pulling us about. Some of the sisters were very roughly handled indeed. One man was knocked down and left with a black eye, but we stood our ground. They pelted us with all sorts of things, and flour in abundance. I was as white as a miller. We had a good meeting, and one man professed to be saved.

During this adventurous nine months Cadman had rescued various intending suicides from their purpose, seen an organ grinder and potato man converted—in previous opposition the one had sought to drown the speakers at an open-air meeting with music while the other bombarded them with hot potatoes ! Also a very large number of infidels, drunken or vicious cabmen, carmen, bricklayers, factory workers, a detective, and others transformed . . . into sober, pure-living, hard-working citizens.

In one of his reports Cadman (October 1876) showed that in his mind the " army " idea was already at work—at least so far as phraseology was concerned. He wrote :

We are making a powerful attack upon the devil's kingdom . . . King Jesus is our great Commander. . . . We have an army here that will face the world, the flesh, and the devil. All are volunteers.

Of a " Great Salvation Fair " in progress at the People's Mission Hall, Whitechapel, the *East London Observer* (17th March 1877) said :

The promoters of the fair have not scrupled to enter the camp of the enemy and appropriate all that might be regarded as attractive, and in their announcements have so closely copied the music hall as to even deceive habitués of such establishments.

But while the *Observer* thus paid tribute to the effectiveness of the fair, its other references were anything but approving. Sacred things, it protested, were bandied about as if they were wares for sale. " The whole thing," it concluded, " would be rank blasphemy if the perpetrators knew the meaning of or had any reverence for what they utter."

This was not a bazaar or sale of work, but a method of presenting Salvation. Among other announcements was one proclaiming the virtues of " The Wines of the Kingdom," while at the open-air service and in the processions " we," said the Mission's Magazine report, " utilised as banners the boards carried by men throughout the East End on Saturdays, and which bore in type which every passer-by on the pavement could read :

SAVE

YOUR

SOUL

The crowd which followed was tremendous." Among the attractions were preaching by the Christian Mission giant (Dr. Morrison who weighed 33 stones) and " orations by all the best available talent."

Some of the older and more staid members of the Mission objected to the " fair " and left, among them George Hamilton who had been a prominent member of the Mission committee. On the other hand, among those attracted by it was young Hugh Whatmore, who in later years became a commissioner of The Salvation Army.

Commenting on these tactics, General Bramwell Booth stated :

We in the Army have learned to thank God for eccentricity and extravagance, and to consecrate them to His service. We have men in our ranks who can rollick for the Lord. Often they have blundered, and occasionally they land us in awkward places. Some of them have been very rough and uncouth, and all that. . . . Thank God for the dare-devils ! They led us on the forward march. Their freedom of attack has brought, and still brings, within our reach the very people we want most. They have helped to keep us free from shackles of respectability. They keep us passionate. So that even such a writer as H. G. Wells, after saying that our " shouts, clangour, trumpeting, gesticulations, and rhythmic pacings stun and dismay my nerves," can add, " I see God indubitably present in these excitements."

Evangelists vied with one another in the production of arresting announcements. William Corbridge was specially gifted in this respect, and word cartoons from his pen, designed to catch the eye of the indifferent with topical allusions that on closer inspection conveyed Salvation truths, were featured in the *Christian Mission Magazine*, as well as being reproduced as handbills and tracts.

Harold Begbie wrote :

We find the Mission adopting the traditional methods of Petticoat Lane to attract the spiritual attention of Whitechapel. Rewards are offered for " Lost Jewels," appeals made to help the Master to recover His " Lost Property," and invitations extended to " A Grand Banquet " in the Palace of God. But while these methods are employed—methods of an essentially English character and old as our English hills—the spirit of the missioners is deeply and grimly serious.

John Reid Morrison, L.R.C.P., L.F.P. and S., L.S.A. (Eng.), " The Mission Giant " of the fair, had obtained an appointment as doctor to the hundreds of navvies who were building the East London railway. He was fast becoming a slave to strong drink when one of his navvy patients persuaded him to attend a meeting of The Christian Mission in the Limehouse " Penny Gaff." He went to the penitent-form, joined the Mission, and became an out-and-out worker. After his conversion he never attended a patient without telling him of the plan of Salvation and reading from the Bible. To a doctor friend who repeatedly reasoned with him on the impropriety of his being advertised as the " Salvation Giant " or " The Hallelujah Doctor " his answer always was, " I am willing to become a fool for Christ's sake." To another, who urged that if he would " attend only to his practice and leave preaching to the clergy " he would be able to keep his carriage and pair, he replied that with a carriage and pair he might drive headlong into Hell ; he would rather walk steadily into Heaven. In 1880 he married a fellow Salvationist (Rachel Rich).

One day when he was being driven along Commercial Road, Whitechapel, in a four-wheeler, his great weight was too much for the rickety vehicle—the floor collapsed and until he could let the driver know what had happened he had to run along the roadway inside the cab framework as best he could !

Failing health led to his moving away from East London, and in 1890 he died suddenly, aged 55, and was buried in Honor Oak Cemetery. Elijah Cadman and others of his old comrades took part in the funeral service.

In April, the first evangelist of the Mission who " passed away to the everlasting reward while actually engaged in the work," Sister Anderson, of Barking, was given a " Mission funeral." She had been in the service only a few weeks. In deference to the wishes of her friends the procession to the grave was silent, and at the graveside, " in the absence of a thorough-going Burial Act we had to be grateful for the kind permission granted us to sing a favourite hymn." For the rest, all that was allowed was " a few words of exhortation."

James Dowdle was by this time the evangelist in charge at Bradford. In Pullan's Theatre of Varieties converts were being made by the hundred. Among them John Lawley, later a commissioner in the Salvation Army, and A.D.C. to William Booth. He became an evangelist in 1878. In a report of the opening of the theatre the check-taker is said to have averred that on the Saturday evening over 4,300 people had been in the theatre ; later William

Booth at Conference (1877) remarked that the theatre " seats over 2,000 people. They say it seats 4,000 . . . these theatre people I must say do sometimes make tremendous *mistakes* about numbers ! "

3

The plans adopted at the Conference committee meeting in January had at once been acted on, but Conference itself remained to be reckoned with. When this assembly met for its next session—12th to 14th June 1877—William Booth made explicit and unequivocal acknowledgment of the failure of his cherished plans :

We have [he declared] to a great extent abandoned the plans of previous gatherings. Much dissatisfaction had been felt, and in many instances expressed, at the controversial aspect it [Conference] assumed, so large a portion of time being consumed in discussion on comparatively trifling matters, while the mightier and practical questions, which intimately concern the work of God and the souls of our people, were left partially neglected. It became evident to me we were drifting in a wrong direction. I confess I have been much to blame in this matter. Under the idea that teaching my brethren management and law-making would increase their sense of responsibility and unite us more fully together, I launched the Conference on a sea of legislation which all came to nothing. . . . And yet here we were, with new men coming in thick and fast, leaving the most essential principles and practices to be mangled about and decided by mere majorities.

Seeing all this we asked, What shall we do ? There seemed only one course—to return to our practice at our earliest gatherings. Most of you were present at the Conference held in January, when I frankly and fully expressed the feeling of my heart and intentions as to the future, and my explanations appeared to be as frankly and cordially received.

. . . What then is the advantage of a Conference ? Much, I answer, every way. What is the good of a council of war ?

The Commander-in-chief calls the principal officers around him to receive information and counsel from all. Each brings his facts and expresses his judgment as to what is necessary and important to do, and then in view of all this he resolves upon a programme of operation. This is our council of war. We are here to consider practical questions and how we can best deal with them. To receive reinforcements and station our army, and above all we are here to help each other's souls, to cry together to the Living God for the rebaptism of the Holy Ghost.

The Conference committee would be given up ; for one thing it had been found impossible to keep in being a truly representative committee because so many of the leaders of the Mission were stationed at places distant from London. Evangelists would be accepted and appointments decided by William Booth.

" This is a question of confidence," concluded William Booth, " as between you and me, and if you can't trust me it is of no use for us to attempt to work together. *Confidence in God and in me are absolutely indispensable both now and ever afterwards.*"

William Booth's proposals were formally accepted by the Conference on Tuesday, 12th June 1877, by resolution :

That this Conference heartily endorsing the principle laid down by the President's address at the opening desires that the rules and resolutions of previous Conference respecting the mode of Conference procedure should not be allowed to interfere with the adoption of the programme he has set forth for the conduct of the present and future Conferences.

William Booth at the same time made it clear that he had seen and accepted that the new plans implied the adoption of a military form of government for the Mission :

We have been called [he said] by the arrangement of Divine providence to be officers and leaders in His army, and we are met to consider how we can best advance the interests of that army.

The contrast between conditions existing before and after the turning point of January 1877 was emphasized when William Booth announced at this Conference that already new stations had been established at Bradford, North Ormesby, Leeds and Hartlepool, at the same time reporting regretfully that as a result of the unsatisfactory procedure —which had made the opening of a station dependent upon a vote of Conference—no fewer than nine stations, with nominally over six hundred members, had had to be closed. Some of these, William Booth declared, ought never to have been opened.

This abandonment, he stated, had been taken exception to by some of their friends ; in fact, there were some who had energetically protested against the giving up of any ground once occupied . . . but, William Booth continued :

if we find that we have made a mistake and taken a stand which is not likely to prove spiritually remunerative—in which the results do not promise to answer to the toil and sacrifice called for—let us have courage to confess our mistake, and withdraw for more congenial and productive fields of labour.

It was no mere rhetoric when, four years later, he publicly declared :

Beginning as I did, so to speak, with a sheet of clean paper, wedded to no plan, and willing to take a leaf out of anybody's book that seemed to be worth adopting, and, above all, to obey the direction of God the Holy Spirit, I have gone on from step to step. . . . We tried various methods, and those that did not answer we unhesitatingly threw overboard and adopted something else. . . .

At this Conference William Booth dealt at length with three special subjects, leading evangelists following, in each case, with statements based on their own experiences in regard thereto.

His first subject was " Hallelujah Bands." He recalled what he had done at Walsall to originate the movement.

As a whole it had come to an untimely end because it had lacked organization and discipline, though lively and useful offshoots were still in existence. He analysed in detail the methods that he felt could with advantage be adopted in The Christian Mission.

William Booth's second subject was " Holiness."

Holiness to the Lord [he declared] is to us a fundamental truth ; it stands to the forefront of our doctrines. We write it on our banners. It is in no shape or form an open debatable question as to whether God can sanctify wholly, whether Jesus does save His people *from* their sins. In the estimation of The Christian Mission that is settled for ever, and any evangelist who did not hold and proclaim the ability of Jesus Christ to save His people to the uttermost from sin and sinning I should consider out of place amongst us.

The importance attached in The Christian Mission to the teaching of holiness was emphasized by the holding of a conference in the Fieldgate Hall (Whitechapel) in December 1876, at which the Rev. Asa Mahan, D.D.—holiness teacher and author of *Out of Darkness into Light*—had been the principal speaker.

William Booth's third subject, dealt with in an intensely practical way, was " Good Singing." Singing, to please him, must be congregational, hearty, and useful. He poured scorn on " buying a musical machine and getting some half-taught schoolgirl or ungodly musician to play it," and on " selecting a few people, converted or unconverted . . . to lead the congregation just because they happen accidentally to have melodious voices " :

I have [he added characteristically] ever found choirs to be possessed of three devils . . . the quarrelling devil, the dressing devil, and the courting devil.

At the 1874 Conference of The Christian Mission it had been resolved that " many of our female converts could be most profitably formed into bands of singers to visit the homes of the people as well as more publicly to sing of Salvation."

William Booth made no direct reference to the use of secular tunes. The nearest approach to a suggestion that they should be made captive to sacred words was a lament that the devil claims music as his own peculiar property ; from which he proceeded :

He only allows us the crumbs that fall from his table, such as the old hundred[th], and a few more funereal ditties. Of the soul and citadel of music he has taken possession . . . and with it he charms and chains and sways the world.

But if sensual worldly satanic music wields such a power, what might music not do when songs and hearts and voices were inspired and directed by the Holy Ghost. . . . That is a problem that has yet to be solved. . . . Let us swell louder and louder our triumphant songs, and to the sound of that victorious music let us go up to the conquest of the world for Jesus.

That " the devil has no right to all the good tunes," a saying sometimes attributed to William Booth and at others to Charles Spurgeon, is found in a collection of sermons by Rowland Hill. Railton had concluded an article " About Singing " (1874) with an impassioned plea, " Oh, let us rescue this precious instrument from the clutches of the devil, and make it, as it may be made, a bright and lively power for good ! " He also wrote (1886) : " The prophecy of the Brooklyn divine [unnamed, but generally supposed to have been Henry Ward Beecher] who declared, ' These people will sing their way round the world in spite of us,' is already being fulfilled, for on sea and on land our songs have been heard all round the globe already."

Evangelists spoke of their experiences of the use of singing to attract sinners and bring them to Christ. James Dowdle added a somewhat surprising aside, saying that the first time he had seen Mr. Booth (1867, Whitechapel) he

had heard him sing, " Oh, how I love Jesus ! " to the tune
" So early in the morning ! "

Bramwell Booth was now designated " Travelling Secretary," and Railton " General Secretary " ; they were listed
in that order.

In a review of the events of July (1877) William Booth
wrote :

We do not hesitate for a moment to say that we have commenced
the grandest year of the Mission's history. My eldest daughter
[Catherine] . . . proposes to give herself up to labour in the
Mission, and I trust by next Conference we shall have another son
[Ballington] ready for the work. I think you must all see that
the entering of our children into this enterprise is no small token
of our confidence in the future. . . . We have no greater joy
than to see our children devote themselves to the redemption of
the masses.

In August, William Booth, taking Catherine with him,
paid " a flying visit " to the northern stations. " I have," he
wrote, " never witnessed more precious conversions, nor seen
services that more blessedly indicated the possibility of a great
work than at Bradford." He was specially pleased all the
way through his visit by the fervour and energy of a band of
youths who gave good promise, he stated, if rightly trained
and kept at work, of providing some daring and successful
evangelists.

At Stockton he noted there was a larger proportion of
men at the meetings, both indoor and out, than he had ever
seen before. Week-day noon open-air meetings had never
failed a congregation and sometimes fifty men had followed
to the indoor meetings.

Then came the first contemporary record of the use of
a brass instrument in Mission proceedings :

The last Sabbath we had a little novelty, which apparently worked
well. Among the converts are two members of a brass band—
one plays a cornet, and to utilize him at once Brother Russell put

him with his cornet in the front rank of the procession from South Stockton. He certainly improved the singing and brought crowds all along the line of march, wondering curiously what we should do next.

Another direction in which the new spirit had found expression was in the extension of the holding of dinner-hour meetings.

During the winter months [wrote William Booth in approval] it is so much easier to get a crowd to stand in the middle of the day, than in the cold, dark, damp evenings. In the neighbour-hood of docks, factories, warehouses, workshops, multitudes of operatives can be brought together in the middle of the day with comparatively little labour, and our only wonder is that the idea of using such opportunities did not strike many of our evangelists long ago.

Such meetings were being held by the Mission on the old Blackwall Stairs, at the East India Dock gates, at Hackney outside a large factory and on the Triangle, and outside the gates of H.M. Dockyard at Portsmouth.

In December a second evangelist died, W. George Thomas. He was in charge of the Whitechapel station. " Promoted to Glory " had not yet become the accepted form of announcement for the death of Salvationists ; " Our Crowned Heads," used in connection with the passing of Evangelist Thomas, was not far from it. He was buried in Bow Cemetery, where the missioners were permitted to hold " something like an hour's service."

Thomas was an outstanding example of a preacher ob-tained from the public houses, he having been, before his conversion, " a drunken comic singer." At his death it was declared that " the Mission has lost a leader and a commander . . . who shared not merely the qualities of a Christian and a faithful soldier, but those of a general capable of accomplishing worthy achievements in the great warfare in which we are engaged."

Members of Conference of The Christian Mission, 1877, that ratified the change in form of government

Centre: William Booth. *Front*: 1 William Ridsel, 2 William J. Pearson, 3 Elijah Cadnan, 4 William Corbridge, 5 James Dowdle, 6 George Scott Railton, 7 Bramwell Booth, 8 Job Clare, 9 John Allen, 10 William Garner, 11 John Price Gray, 12 Charles Hobday, 13 Thomas Blandy. *Seated*: 1 Charles H. Panter, 2 Alfred Russell, 3 James Flawn, 4 Mrs. Dowdle, 5 Mrs. Ebdon, 6 Ernest Blandy, 7 Rodney "Gipsy" Smith, 9 Evangeline C. Booth (aged 11). *First row standing*: 1 Mrs. Reynolds, 2 Sarah A. Dexter, 3 Bro. Solway, 4 Bro. Collingridge, 5 Isaac Skidmore, 6 George Thomas, 7 William H. Ebdon, 9 James Pargeter, 10 Albing Toft, 11 John Eason, 12 Catherine Booth, 13 George (Jockey) Roe, 14 Emma M. E. Stride, 15 Mrs. Mary M. Goddard, 17 Annie Davis (Mrs. Ridsel), 18 Sarah Smith, 19 Mrs. Arthur Watts, 20 Mrs. Caroline Porter, 21 Agnes Pollet. *Standing at back*: 1 Bro. Jackson, 2 Jonathan Brock, 3 William C. Bennett (The Black Prince), 5 John Roberts, 6 Harry B. Tucker, 7 Frank H. Tucker, 10 Joe Hurrell, 13 Robert Ward, 14 Emma Booth, 16 Sister Pollard, 18 James Broadbent, 20 Arthur Watts, 22 John Borrill

Elijah Cadman, the Converted Sweep, and Dr. John Reid
Morrison, the Christian Mission Giant. Two of the
Attractions of The Salvation Fair, Whitechapel, 1877

From the first the Mission had taken advantage of the opportunities offered by the recurrence of special seasons and festivals—such as Christmas, New Year, Easter, and bank holidays—for the holding of meetings. By 1877 the "practice of singing in the streets on Christmas Eve" had "taken such a hold upon our societies" that it was felt to be necessary to issue special instructions for the guidance of those taking part in it. Such singing, it was laid down, must be exclusively for the glory of God and the salvation of souls and not for the gratification of any man or men.

In the same number of the *Christian Mission Magazine* (February 1878), under the general heading "Christmas Festivities," were printed reports of special meetings at many stations, but only in one instance was there mention of Christmas dinners for the poor—these were provided at Portsmouth for a "great many old and very poor folk."

A council of war, attended by some fifty or sixty "poor men and women with their hearts burning for war to the very death," was held in January. A little band of "unlearned and ignorant men met . . . determined by the grace of God to shake the whole country out of the sleep of sin." The council was concluded by an all-night of prayer with two hundred present, at which

the addresses and the experiences given abounded in the very clearest expression of the holiness which alone can satisfy the requirements of God, the yearnings of every true heart and the necessities of a sin-ruined world.

4

The new spirit continued to be manifested in new enterprises. The success of the early experiment of putting a woman evangelist in charge of a station was at last to bear full fruit. At 10.35 on the morning of Saturday, 30th March 1878,

Railton saw the first two " Hallelujah Lasses " leave King's Cross for Felling-on-Tyne. "The Cross was before my eyes," wrote one of them afterwards, " and fastening some blue ribbon to a white handkerchief I said I would be ' true blue ' to God and the Mission."

On the Monday morning they telegraphed : " 500 afternoon ; 800 night. Six souls ; lot in pickle. . . ." From that day " in pickle " has been a standing phrase expressing, perhaps a little pungently, the state of being " under conviction " or " pricked to the heart."

The " Hallelujah Lasses " were Rachel and Louise Agar, later Mrs. Ebdon and Mrs. Harry Davis.

When copy for a poster announcing that " Two Lady Preachers " were coming to Felling had been handed to William C. Crow, printer, of Gateshead, by Evangelist Tom Blandy (Sunderland), Crow objected that the term had been used before and would not attract attention. When asked what he would put in its place, he suggested " Two Hallelujah Lasses." At the War Congress (1878) a resolution was adopted thanking Crow for the eminent service he had rendered to the Mission as agent in advance and " general commissioner," and welcoming him to the Council as a representative of the " unoccupied North."

In an address to the Wesleyan Methodist Conference of the United Kingdom in 1880 William Booth said :

I did not invent the term " Hallelujah Lasses." When I first heard of it I was somewhat shocked ; but telegram after telegram brought me word that no buildings would contain the people who came to hear the Hallelujah Lasses. Rough, uncouth fellows liked the term. One had a lassie at home, another went to hear them because he used to call his wife " Lassie " before he was married. My end was gained and I was satisfied.

At Coventry, Evangelists Mrs. Caroline Reynolds and Mrs. Honor Burrell (then widowed) " opened fire." Mr.

Reynolds was with his wife at Coventry, but while Mrs. Reynolds was a fully employed evangelist of The Christian Mission, he held no position in it ; he was, indeed, in poor health and died at an early age. William Booth at the 1878 Conference, when dealing with the question of responsibility for financing stations being shirked by the local authorities, said :

You must not be parties to loading me [*i.e.* the central funds] with a crushing burden of financial responsibility. The question is, how can you make ends meet ? There is Sister Reynolds and her husband, who lived on 21s. a week until I jacketed their treasurer. They had scarcely any furniture. But she would not go into debt to buy any, and after all they were as well off as Brother Dowdle struggling with debt. Now, let everybody understand this, that everything is to be paid before salary ; putting by weekly enough to meet all rents and other current expenses. . . . Whom God sends unto His work God will take care of ; and I will help you all alike as far as it lies in my power.

To open a station at Salisbury, Evangelist (Mrs.) Sarah Sayers (widow) was sent with Evangelist Henry Edmonds as her assistant. Mrs. Sayers was later married to Cornelius Smith (widower), father of Rodney (Gipsy) Smith. Henry Edmonds was not yet 17 years of age ; he had already for a brief period assisted Evangelist Annie Davis at Poplar. It was not unusual at this time for men and women evangelists to be stationed together, though the practice was not long continued.

Commenting in the following issue of the *Christian Mission Magazine* (April 1878) on the number of women evangelists then in office in the Mission, William Booth wrote :

In externals nothing is more remarkable in the recent progress of the Mission than the great advance of our female ministry. It has sometimes been said that female preachers would be the ruin of the Mission. But on the contrary it turns out that the prosperity of the work in every respect just appears most preciously [precisely ?] at the very times when female preachers are being allowed the fullest opportunity.

During the past month sisters have been taking a leading position in the work at no less than nine out of the thirty-six stations. We have at present twenty married evangelists and sixteen of the twenty wives have already taken a great part in the public services.

Before 1877 had come to an end, The Christian Mission was obtaining a large proportion of its leaders from its own converts. How great a relief this must have been was reflected in what William Booth at the next Conference stated, namely, that among the things that hindered and impaired the Mission in its earlier days was that it had had to engage evangelists from outside its ranks who often held notions that were altogether different from those of its leaders, and had secretly sought to alter the Mission, leaving it when they found they could not do this with impunity, and even trying openly to interfere with it.

At the Conference in June, William Booth had been able to say :

There is under our eye and growing up around us at our stations a still further list of able and promising candidates for future service [as evangelists]. It has been often said we must grow our own stuff. . . . *We are doing this;* and I trust now the time is not far distant when we shall be able to act almost exclusively on this rule—to take no one, male or female, who has not been either converted in the Mission or trained in it.

And, nearly a year later, he recorded :

We have already no less than thirty-one persons labouring as evangelists in the Mission whom the work itself has produced—most of them have been converted in the Mission.

To show that " there is nothing like decay in the old branches " he added that from thirteen of the original stations of the Mission, twenty-four prominent workers had been taken into the work as evangelists without there being held one fewer service there.

At a meeting of the committee of The Christian Mission when the opening of the People's Mission Hall was being discussed (1870) a member had said to William Booth :

"You have opened that place opposite Limehouse Church (the penny gaff). You are opening other places, and now this great hall. Where will you get your preachers from ?"

William Booth replied, "We shall get them from the public houses. Men who have felt the fire will be the best men to rescue others, and we shall never fail in getting the right men."

This declaration was, and still is being, literally justified in many glorious instances ; but it was not then, nor at any time, the intention or practice of William Booth to get his preachers exclusively from the public houses. Descendants of men and women saved from drunkenness and other degrading sins are also to be found among present-day officers of The Salvation Army, though memory of the pit whence their forebears were dug may have been almost, if not altogether, lost. But the majority of the leaders of The Christian Mission, and now of The Salvation Army, came from among those who were converted in their youth and consecrated themselves, while still young, to seeking the salvation of others.

CHAPTER EIGHTEEN

LIGHT FROM LETTER-BOOKS

I

LETTER-BOOKS of the headquarters of The Christian Mission covering the 1875–78 period provide much inside information. The books were destroyed in the 1941 blitz, but copies of some of the most important and interesting letters had been made and were saved.

An early suggestion of the military idea, long before it was put into operation, is given in one of the first of these letters (27th November 1875). To an unnamed missioner, Bramwell Booth wrote :

At a meeting of the leaders of the Bethnal Green hall last night I was asked to convey to you a request that you will take the lead of that station, being in every way " captain " so that they may all look up to you for guidance.

Correspondence with Messrs. Truman, Hanbury, Buxton & Co. (January 1876), in which a request was made that the Mission should receive compensation for expenditure incurred for repairs to the Apollo Hall in view of termination of its tenure without notice, confirmed that the Mission had had free use of the building.

An advertisement of hair-dye sent for insertion in the *Christian Mission Magazine* was returned by Railton (18th January 1876) who wrote : " It seems to us so repugnant to the notions of religion adopted by the vast majority of our readers that it could scarcely produce any benefit to the advertiser, and might damage us."

Correspondence with candidates for appointment as evangelists revealed, among other things, that the amount paid to " our female preachers " was 15s. per week (22nd January 1876). Another reply to an applicant—written probably in February 1876—stated :

We have almost abandoned the practice of engaging evangelists temporarily, as we have one stationed at almost all our places now, and we find the constant, regular use of our converts to be more beneficial to them and more conducive to the salvation of others than special services led by comparative strangers.

And :

We scarcely ever entertain an application from anyone over thirty-five, and are less disposed to do so every year because the supply of preachers from amongst the converts of the Mission steadily increases.

A tent—70 × 40 ft.—for use at Leeds was purchased for £55 (17th June 1876).

2

The great majority of the letters were written by Railton ; occasionally one of special importance was signed by William Booth ; there was some correspondence between Railton and William Booth and Bramwell Booth, and between the last-named and " the General."

When an assistant secretary was needed, William Booth wrote (23rd June 1876) to the Rev. Dr. Stacey of Ranmoor College, Sheffield, asking if he knew of a young man, or minister " whose throat had broken down," whom he could recommend :

I am already admirably served by a secretary of the spiritual department [he wrote]. It is the business part of the office for which help is needed.

Railton had a tilt with an evangelist (Garner, 3rd August 1876) on the question of using theatres for preaching :

You say a man of God can get a congregation in a chapel. So he can, but how can a man of God get a chapel to seat as many as a theatre does ? And I remember more than one man of God that didn't get anything like a full place in the White Chapel [Garner had been stationed at Whitechapel]. So long as the devil's dens will hold more than any place we can get elsewhere it is nonsense to talk about it not being the place.

I wonder [he concluded, ironically] if you will ever be found arguing against using unconsecrated places at all. Perhaps we shall have you some day denouncing the preaching of the Gospel in " those wicked streets " !

In the continuation of this letter Railton referred incidentally to his having taken charge, in addition to his other duties, of the Poplar station, in the hope of being able to bring about a revival there :

If we want to reach the masses then it is the largest obtainable place which is the only one we can consistently use, and since we left this simple plan at Poplar and elsewhere and went seeking to make ourselves nice nests and leave the masses to perish, the Lord has just turned His back on us till London has [got] so low that I cannot bear to say more about it.

To James Dowdle (3rd August 1876), Railton wrote :

We have abandoned several small Stations in order to use up all our strength on those we can make something of. Poor Watts has had to go home ill. Mace has resigned in connection with the " split " at [Portsmouth], and so we should have been awkwardly fixed but for having just got a man called Cadman from Rugby.

But Cadman's early eccentricities would seem to have been too much even for Railton, for to William Booth (5th November 1877) he wrote :

If he [Cadman] fails at Whitby I shall be satisfied he is utterly incapable of taking charge of a work and shall be verging upon satisfaction that he is too hard a nut for us to crack, or too peculiar a man to influence others.

Cadman did not fail at Whitby.

Touching the tendency shown even by some of the roughest diamonds among Mission converts to become unduly " respectable " and lose their grip of things, Railton wrote to Bramwell Booth (26th August 1876) :

If it is true that Allen [the one-time drunken navvy who had become an evangelist] objects to noise and put his foot down at once on Lamb's praying band in the theatre, the strange condition of things you reported on is accounted for, also the quietness of the Cardiff lot [Allen had also been stationed at Cardiff].

Bramwell Booth was officially appointed " travelling secretary " by the 1877 Conference. In the same letter Railton writes :

I am told that your pa is proposing to commission you as our traveller, a capital hit in my opinion, the very thing. You can do more by inspecting and organizing and making people work than any amount of preaching would do.

More about the situation at Poplar, and by inference at other Mission stations at this period, is contained in other letters :

I am sick and tired of compromise [Railton wrote to an unnamed missioner on 3rd August 1876]—of keeping up appearances. Though none of my members at Poplar have actually left I doubt whether I should return more than a quarter of them, for I won't return anybody because they have a name to live. I am determined to have the real original Christian Mission or none at all.

To Dowdle, 7th September 1876 :

I have been sadly let in at Poplar. We have allowed the people for two years to learn a different religion from ours, and now to lead them to live for God and souls is almost hopeless. We had, however, got a nice company of folk together who were beginning to go in for God when Mr. Booth's illness and accompanying circumstances cut me off for a fortnight.

Again to Dowdle, 2nd November 1876 :

At Poplar we are beautifully round the corner spiritually. Have now got a new society which, although of course quite raw as yet,

will go on, I trust, unto perfection. We have now broken into
the lines of young chaps and lasses and shall have more rush and
force . . . the old society and congregation are almost gone.
As our life increases they will fade away, I fear, still more. I am
very sorry. God knows I have spared no love or pains over
them ; but they will not have my Jesus and so the publicans and
sinners are getting into their places. I have already a band of
navvies superior to all the old men and we are gaining every day.
We are now feeling the financial pinch of the change from a
comparatively respectable to a poor lot, but never mind. We
shall not want.

In the same month he wrote to William Booth, advocat-
ing the printing of "a plain straightforward and popular
statement of full salvation " :

Never mind the public [he urged]. They have deserted us.
We may not long exist, let us at least leave a clear track behind
us.

To Corbridge at Leicester (10th March 1877) William
Booth, commending the methods he (Corbridge) had
adopted, wrote :

I know the eyes of the entire Mission are upon you, especially on
account of my so prominently endorsing the hallelujah [band]
methods you have adopted . . . I am anxious you should be
able to present us with an ungainsayable schedule that will produce
a profound effect on all our " chapel " people.

Suggestions made in this letter later developed into the
soldiers' meetings and cartridge [1] system of The Salvation
Army.

Humorous touches are not wanting. To an evangelist
Railton wrote (5th May 1877) concerning an assistant being
sent to him :

Brother P. leaves Paddington to-morrow at noon . . . he wears
a city missionary billicock, a little fancy moustache and nothing
more, looking a decided doggy bloke (which the Lord preserve

[1] An envelope into which soldiers (members) place a weekly contribution
towards the upkeep of their corps (station)

him). He shall have a magazine in hand and a bonnet box containing two bonnet shapes for Mrs. C.

Bramwell Booth wrote to his father (11th October 1877) :

Young Smith, the gipsy [later an officer of The Salvation Army and, still later, the well-known revivalist], has been to me to ask if there was any understanding about his clothes. He is a very *gem*. With you for three months he would be equal to a good big station.

From this time onwards a larger proportion of letters about Mission affairs was signed by Bramwell Booth, though Railton's position as the secretary is emphasized by the voluminous " briefs " he continued to supply to William Booth regarding the affairs of places he (William Booth) visited and Mission business generally.

In November 1877 Railton wrote to William Booth about affairs in London, stating that he thought there was much improvement, but expressing a fear that he might have based his judgment on what he had seen on special visits. He gave evidence of possessing wide, even prophetic vision when he added :

But if I could set to and build up a concern in some central spot, say near the Eagle, I cannot see why in the course of years we might not build up a really big concern that would keep a whole houseful of young chaps to be made real soldiers of. . . . There is nothing like piling up people year after year like bricks to make a good organization capable of all sorts of enterprises. Why not try ?

In a long letter to William Booth (November 1877), Railton further emphasized his conviction that above all else something should be done to train evangelists for their work :

The importance of drilling the men we do get daily increases. We are not training one individual in our ideas and ways. . . . The want of greater unity of thought, feeling, and methods will continue to cause great losses with every change no matter how good each man may be.

Can we devise no plan for training folks ? Could we not have a centre in London to which all hopeful young folks could be rallied and where they could be thoroughly looked through and trained ?

There is a superbly central spot—the Eagle—with a splendid artisan neighbourhood E. ; black heathendom W. ; and a stream of the finest young fellows in the Kingdom passing continually. Why not try to form a drill hall there ? . . . We might in the course of years build up a really huge affair that would strike all London.

. . . No college, no book but the Bible, nothing but living teaching—no putting away of anything of the rough natural— only the development of spiritual and natural power and willing to do our way and feel as we do about things.

On the same subject he wrote to Bramwell Booth (6th November 1877) :

You seem upon further reflection to see that the training question demands a solution. But you do not appear, nor does your ma, to understand me. I shall always I trust continue dead against any approach to a college sort of thing which . . . can never produce anything but parsons. We want to train men to be like us.

Railton foreshadowed also a development that was put into operation years later—the Corps Cadet training system, which provides for the training of young Salvationists still in their secular employment for future service as officers (whole time) or local officers (part-time voluntary office-holders in their corps) :

A year's training while in employment and then a year at a London station should turn out men in our mould [he wrote].

Four days later (10th November) he wrote to William Booth again on the same subject. He began by expressing hope that " you will not mention our training scheme in any way definitely to anybody "—he feared opposition ; he had mis-givings lest " Bramwell and even you will have set down the attempt as useless or worse before it has accomplished anything." He saw, if women were to be trained, the need of " the constant and perfect co-operation of a woman." He had been greatly delighted to find

that the Grecian theatre—next door to the Eagle, and one of the most notorious in London—which I had coveted for eventual headquarters on Sundays, instead of holding only 800 has been rebuilt and professes to hold 5,000. Still that shows how far ahead we must look.

The final letter preserved is from Railton to " My dear General " :

Yours is indeed delightful and yet embarrassing from the rush of likely candidates. . . .

The past gives us very little light as to the future because we are bursting out in such a way that another year will find us changed almost beyond recognition. . . . We shall be compelled to do something for all this host of folks [candidates], with whom, if we can only drill and mobilize fast enough, we can overrun the country before Christmas.

CHAPTER NINETEEN

THE SALVATION ARMY: 1878

I

THE Christian Mission was now (1878) an army in all but name ! To its leader the title of General had already been given by his followers, partly because they felt it to be fitting, and partly because " General Superintendent " was too cumbersome for everyday use ; and George Scott Railton was William Booth's self-styled lieutenant. The *Christian Mission Magazine*'s report (June 1878) of the opening of the Limehouse hall had " our worthy general " —without the capital letter.

In October 1877 Elijah Cadman (with Gipsy Smith as his second) had " opened fire " on Whitby with a call for 2,000 men and women to join " The Hallelujah Army," the announcement stating that the attack would " be led by Captain Cadman." [1] Speaking at the " War Congress," 1878, Cadman stated that he had assumed this title in the military sense. He said : " I wrote out a bill—it was just when people were half expecting England to go to war. . . . They thought it must be something wonderful when women as well as men had to fight, and I signed at the foot, 'Captain Cadman,' so that's how I got my title."

A month later William Booth visited Whitby. In Cadman's house he found a poster announcing his coming which designated him, " General of The Hallelujah Army ! " Cadman had hidden this because he feared it might not be approved, but to his delight his enterprise was commended, and he was instructed to send a copy to Railton at headquarters.

[1] Appendix P, The Whitby Posters

Militant Christianity was much in the public mind. In the year (1865) in which William Booth began his campaign in the Whitechapel Tent, the Rev. S. Baring Gould gave to the world his stirring processional hymn, " Onward, Christian Soldiers ! " Fighting hymns were much in use. Moody and Sankey's number one throughout their campaign (London 1875) had been " Hold the fort ! " In the Christian Mission hymn-book were some twenty-five hymns of the type of " Soldiers of Christ, arise ! "

Moreover, war—and rumours of war—had been and were occupying attention. Russia had defeated Turkey, and the British Government had taken a stand with regard to the settlement of the issue which threatened to bring about conflict with the victorious power. The " Jingo " song was being sung, or its tune whistled, everywhere.

The extent of the people's preoccupation with these events and the question whether war was again coming was reflected in the symbolic use the leaders of The Christian Mission made of them. Two articles in its magazine by G. S. Railton had for subjects " Peace or War " and " Terms of Peace " respectively, and another, unsigned but probably from the pen of William Booth, " Rushing into War." Each was given first place in the issue in which it appeared, and all applied appropriate spiritual lessons.

" Captain " Cadman continued—using the local " bell-man " as well as the hoardings—to issue declarations of a warlike character. They reached a climax on Good Friday, 1878, when at the head of a long procession he placed a banner on which was inscribed, " War is declared ! Recruits are wanted ! " Excited men and women, not waiting for a second banner, which bore the words : " The Hallelujah Army, fighting for God ! " jumped to the conclusion that hostilities had broken out and that the recruits called for with such urgency were required for the military forces.

When it was discovered that the " war " announced was not one of actual gun and sword, crowds still came to see who and what were " Captain Cadman " and *his* " war." Cadman's meetings in the " Congress Hall " were regularly attended by 3,000 people ; Whitby's entire population at this time was 20,000. Young Thomas Estill, who also became a leading commissioner of The Salvation Army, was attracted to the services at Whitby by one of Cadman's " war " handbills.

With " Hallelujah bands " and their methods a subject of discussion, it had been an easy, and in the circumstances an obvious, step from " Hallelujah Band " to " Hallelujah Army," but that name did not come into general use.

How the name of The Christian Mission came to be changed is made evident by two " scraps of paper," whose contents also indicate that the alteration was made early in May, 1878; one preserved at International Headquarters ; the other found recently in the cellars of the Clapton Congress Hall.[1]

The first is a printer's proof of the Mission's 1878 report and appeal. The shape and size of the Mission's reports varied from year to year ; the 1878 report was a folder of eight pages, size 4¾ in. by 3 in. The front page was mainly occupied with the statement :

THE CHRISTIAN MISSION

under the superintendence of the Rev. William Booth

is

A VOLUNTEER ARMY

[1] Appendix Q, Date of the Change of Name

THE

Christian Mission,

UNDER THE SUPERINTENDENCE OF THE

REV. WILLIAM BOOTH.

IS A

VOLUNTEER ARMY

RECRUITED from amongst the multitudes who are without God and without hope in the world, devoting their leisure time to all sorts of laborious efforts for the salvation of others from unbelief, drunkenness, vice, and crime.

"I believe that is the only way we shall be able, in the enormous population of this ever-growing country, to maintain the cause of our Lord and Master—to welcome every volunteer who is willing to assist the regular forces; and to arm, so far as we can, the whole population in the cause of Jesus Christ."—ARCHBISHOP OF CANTERBURY.

"The working classes will never be reached but by an agency provided from among themselves."—THE EARL OF SHAFTESBURY.

THE

Christian Mission,

UNDER THE SUPERINTENDENCE OF THE

REV. WILLIAM BOOTH.

IS A

SALVATION ARMY

RECRUITED from amongst the multitudes who are without God and without hope in the world, devoting their leisure time to all sorts of laborious efforts for the salvation of others from unbelief, drunkenness, vice, and crime.

"I believe that is the only way we shall be able, in the enormous population of this ever-growing country, to maintain the cause of our Lord and Master—to welcome every volunteer who is willing to assist the regular forces; and to arm, so far as we can, the whole population in the cause of Jesus Christ."—ARCHBISHOP OF CANTERBURY.

"The working classes will never be reached but by an agency provided from among themselves."—THE EARL OF SHAFTESBURY.

The "printer's proof" and completed title-page of the Report of The Christian Mission, issued in 1878, illustrating how the change of name to The Salvation Army came about (*see* Appendix Q)

Receipts from October 1865.

	£	s	d
Thirteen weeks offerings in the Hall	10	2	9
Private offerings from members		8	9
Offerings from friends	9		7
One hundred Pounds Auckland 0.5.0			
the "Revival" 5.0			
Mr. 2/- friend 6 2.6			
the Rev. Dr. Coffin 1.0.0			
for two Bibles 0.10.0			
Mr. Morris of Cardiff 1.0.0			
Immanuel Husband & Wife 2.0.0			
Mr. Miller of ... 2/- 0.6.0			
Offering in "Revival" 2.12.6			
£8.3.0	8	3	0
	28	14	0
	21	10	0
£	6	11	4

Expenses

In hand towards a Bible Carriage.

Expenses from October 1865.

	£	s	d
Rent of Hall 13 Sabbath nights at 21/-	13	13	0
Sacramental wine 2/6. Deficiency at tea-cart 5/6		8	0
sent to Paris & in offertories		10	
to deserts & baptism Parsonage		4	9
Child stall 21/- Psalms 3/- 2/-		10	
Mother tract Chapel Rupture 5/- Sacramental wine		6	
Mr. Ford for Printing	3		
Cistern & Washhouse	1		
Brother Crooke for Bible stall 25/-		5	6
Anniversary Washhouse	1	5	0
Brother Crooke for Bible stall		5	3
Pr. Offering 2/6	21	0	0
to Carmen for removal 7/6		10	0
to the Stall	21	10	0

William Booth's earliest Statement of Income and Expenditure connected with The Christian Mission, October 1865.   (*See* Appendix I)

Below was a quotation from an utterance by the Arch-bishop of Canterbury (Archibald Campbell Tait) :

I believe that is the only way . . . to maintain the cause of our Lord and Master—to welcome every volunteer who is willing to assist the regular forces ; and to arm, so far as we can, the whole population in the cause of Jesus Christ.

" The second scrap of paper " is the corrected and com-pleted folder. The wording on this is :

THE CHRISTIAN
MISSION

is

A SALVATION
ARMY

The earliest extant references to this change and how it came to be made are in Railton's *Heathen England*. In the first and second editions (1877 and 1878) he had written " We are a corps of volunteers for Christ." In the third edition (1879) this had been changed to " We are an army of soldiers of Christ." In the fifth edition (1880)—and possibly in the fourth (no copy of this is available)—how the change of name was made is described. According to this, Railton had written as copy for the new report (1878) "The Christian Mission is *a volunteer army of converted working people.*"

There is a slight discrepancy here, not an isolated occur-rence in Railton's work as an historian ; the wording of the report issued for the year before (1877) had had " The Christian Mission" is an organization " of converted working people " whereas this phrase did not appear in the printer's proof for 1878.

Railton goes on to say that William Booth objected to the phrase " Volunteer Army." " No," he said, " we are not volunteers, for we feel we *must* do what we do, and we are always on duty." He then, without further word, crossed the room and put his pen through " Volunteer " and above it wrote " Salvation."

The " Volunteers," an auxiliary and part-time citizen army, first constituted in the reign of George III and re-organized in 1863 (later replaced by the Territorials), were at the time receiving much notice—not a little of it derisive.

The scene of the change was, on the authority of Bramwell Booth, William Booth's bedroom, whither Railton and he had been summoned, as was customary early in the morning, to compare notes and receive instructions for the day's work—and out of that conference and the purposeful spirit shared by the three leaders of The Christian Mission, came the inspiration which, by the hand of William Booth, gave the organization a name wholly and unmistakably descriptive of its purposes and character, the appropriateness of which has never been questioned.

2

The new name made its first appearance in the September (1878) issue of the *Christian Mission Magazine* when, under the heading " Our War Congress," reports of the doings of the eighth—and last—Conference of The Christian Mission (Whitechapel, 5th, 6th, and 7th August 1878) were opened with this statement :

The Christian Mission has met in Congress to make War. It has glorified God for the conquests of 1877–78. It has organized a salvation army (*sic*) [" Field Stations of Officers," printed inside the cover of the same issue, has the title " The Salvation Army "] to carry the blood of Christ and the fire of the Holy Ghost into every corner of the world.

Behind this statement were audacity and faith indeed, since the new Army had in the whole of England but fifty stations, manned by eighty-eight evangelists ; and elsewhere —nothing !

Rachel Agar, going into the Whitechapel hall on the morning of the assembly of the War Congress, found William H. Ebdon, her future husband, placing over the platform—at the instruction of Bramwell Booth—a sign on which he had painted in large letters :

SALVATION ARMY

The first session of the Congress (Monday morning, 5th August) had been announced by a single word, " Pentecost." " Assuredly," ran the report, " God broke in upon us with ' the very same power' as was felt in the upper room." William Booth impressed upon all the need for receiving more than ever the power from on high in order that the great work of the past might be far exceeded in the future.

The afternoon was given up to recounting " War Memories," speaking being confined to representatives of new stations, " because we cannot possibly find time for more." Amid great jubilation delegates addressed themselves mainly to the good effects of the change in the government of the Mission, which had by then been in operation for over a year. One of the speakers was " Hallelujah Lass " number one—Rachel Agar—who reported that at Felling they had " had 450 souls " during the 17–18 weeks since she had been appointed to open that station. Congress met in the Spitalfields Wesleyan Chapel, Brick Lane, for the morning and afternoon sessions of the first day ; afterwards in the Whitechapel hall.

Among matters of business dealt with at this War Congress was the question of debt. Some stations had gone deeply into debt for current expenses. William Booth very sternly insisted that in future no liability should be incurred without his having had previous notice of it and having been able to exercise choice in regard to it.

He also repeated that he drew no money from the Mission, but that his support had been provided by " a few gentlemen," adding : " But I have fallen out with some of them through the peculiarities of our work, and when any of these fall through in any way I have to trust in God to fill the gap. I am often very poor."

The public annual meeting in the evening was held in the People's Mission Hall. Prolonged and repeated shouts of thanksgiving greeted the reading of a " Field State " by William Booth which showed increases in every item. The chief of these were that the Mission had 21 more stations than a year earlier ; 57 more evangelists ; 1,331 more members ; 283 more weekly services ; more weekly attendances at meetings by 23,290. A total of 10,762 " anxious inquirers " had been registered, an increase of 6,130.

On the Tuesday morning William Booth spoke on " The Past of the War " and its lessons, turning his attention in the afternoon to " The Future of the War." Dwelling on the difficulty of the task undertaken, he pointed out the necessity for the utmost possible force, and, therefore, for adopting God's plan of organizing a force upon a thoroughly military system, of which the distinguishing features were (1) authority, (2) obedience, (3) the adapted employment of everyone's ability, (4) the training of everyone to the utmost, (5) the combined action of all. He showed that such a system, although almost unknown in the religious world, was manifestly the one best calculated to accomplish their purpose, and asked why it should not be as possible to raise an army of crusaders for the salvation of souls as it once had been to raise armies for the recovery of a sepulchre ?

The holiness meeting, an occasion on which special emphasis was laid, gave many opportunity to bear " the clearest and most irresistible testimony to the power of God . . . to cleanse the heart perfectly from every evil thing, and to keep the life pure and unspotted from the world."

A " musical service " occupied the Wednesday evening :

It was our first [said the report]. We could not be expected to perfect everything at once. . . . We were rather disappointed in the number of instruments, but the fiddlers and concertinists (*sic*) and clarion sounders of the evening showed an example.

One of the " clarion sounders " would be George Leedham, who represented Hammersmith at the War Congress, and of whom Bramwell Booth wrote that he was the first man to play a cornet in a Salvation Army meeting.

3

The change in the system of control of The Christian Mission had been regularly adopted and ratified, but in order that it might have legal effect, the 1875 deed-poll had to be replaced by a document embodying the new constitution.

The minutes of the eighth and last Conference (the War Congress) of The Christian Mission, after setting out formally the membership of that body, briefly summarized the proceedings, recording that The Christian Mission had approved and adopted for itself

the deed declaring the constitution, doctrines, objects, laws, and other incidents of and appertaining to the society association or religious community for some time past called The Christian Mission.[1]

The name " The Salvation Army " does not appear in this document. It would seem to have been regarded, up to the end of 1878, as supplementary to, and explanatory of, " The Christian Mission," rather than as a substitute for it. This

[1] Appendix R, Foundation Deed (1878) of The Salvation Army

view is supported by the wording of the report in which the name was first used, and of the first reference to it. Further, the new name was not legally recorded until 24th June 1880. In this " endorsement," which was not " enrolled " until 20th April 1906, the date of the renaming was given as " on or about the First day of January, One thousand eight hundred and seventy-nine."

A letter-head, bearing date 24th December 1879, has as top line " The Salvation Army " with " called The Christian Mission " following ; " General William Booth " was another line. In this line on the letter-head now referred to, " General " has been ringed and marked with an indication that it should be placed in the more conventional position *after* the name, and the remark " It looks pretentious "—all in the hand of William Booth.

The first step was the completion of an annulment deed. In this William Booth declared : that the annulment was held to be necessary in order to secure " greater freedom for effectuating and furthering the principles of The Christian Mission as recognized and expressed by the Conference at their annual meeting in the year 1877 " ; and that he was acting " by virtue of the power given and reserved to him " by the 1875 deed, " with the concurrence of three-fourths of the members of the said Conference."

This and the new deed-poll (1878) were signed by William Booth and George Scott Railton at the afternoon session of the War Congress in the Whitechapel hall—272 (re-numbered 22) Whitechapel Road—on August 7.

The principal provisions of the 1878 deed-poll are : a renewed assertion that

The Christian Mission should be always thereafter under the oversight, direction, and control of some one person who should be General Superintendent.

That William Booth should continue to be, for the term of his natural life, the General Superintendent of The Christian Mission, unless he should resign.

That William Booth and every General Superintendent who should succeed him should have power to appoint his successor to the office of General Superintendent, making a statement in writing, under seal, as to such successor or the means to be taken for the appointment of a successor.

That the General Superintendent should have power to expend all monies contributed, but should annually publish a balance sheet. That he should have power to acquire or dispose of property and to set up or revoke trusts.

Power to alter the constitution was not retained, consequently the deed-poll (1878) can be varied only by Act of Parliament.

To the annulment deed and to the deed-poll are attached certificates declaring that each " was duly presented to and approved by the persons assembled at a general meeting of The Christian Mission held at 272 Whitechapel Road."

Missioners who were present at this memorable meeting of the 1878 War Congress have stated that it was understood throughout The Christian Mission that there was going to be a change ; indeed, it had already taken place in accordance with the 1877 resolution, and with general approval. Before proceeding to the signing of the new deed-poll (1878), William Booth announced that if any evangelists wished to retire from the service of the Mission because they disliked the change of system, he would do his best to help them into some other sphere of work more suited to their feelings and ideas, but only a very few withdrew. Some who were, admittedly, prejudiced in favour of the old system (notably, on his own statement, John Roberts) nevertheless were so devoted to the Cause that they continued their service under the new conditions and in the end came to see, as Roberts later declared, that " it was better in the interests of the Kingdom of God that The Christian Mission should become The Salvation Army."

Among others present on this occasion were Commissioner William Ridsdel, former Commissioner Thomas B. Coombs, Colonel and Mrs. (Kate Watts) Josiah P. Taylor, Elizabeth Jackson (Mrs. Colonel Phillip Kyle) and Mrs. Salthouse (Honor Fells). Coombs wrote (1935) :

The real and inner meaning of the change was that the Movement was experiencing growing pains . . . it could not wait for committee meetings which often meant long and meaningless speeches, but had to get on with the real work which was in the hands of men and women at the front. It was a radical Salvation urge of " up and at it ! " I do not think there was any serious opposition . . . older men, who came from different Methodist denominations, were accustomed to conferences and voting— and they would be sure to have some remnants of the " old clothing " with them. If there were any of the rank and file who objected, it was from the same cause, and a passing affair. In the main, everybody was for it. The great mass was swallowed up with the work they had in hand.

The process by which The Christian Mission adopted a military form of government and thus prepared itself for transformation into The Salvation Army was truly democratic. That its form of government should be military was decided by the special meeting of the Conference committee (January 1877) ; was ratified by the following Conference (June 1877) and legalized by the War Congress (August 1878), each body exercising the powers it possessed and its inherent freedom of choice.

W. T. Stead well wrote (1891) :

The authority of the General is exercised only by the continually renewed voluntary consent of his soldiers. There is no Mutiny Act in The Salvation Army. There is before every Salvationist the open door through which he can go out whenever he pleases. . . . The Salvation Army is a system of absolutism, carried out to its last development with the hearty assent of its members, every one of whom belongs to the democracy.

Railton wrote with well-founded satisfaction :

We have got an organization managed upon the simple business-like principles of a railway, with all the cohesion and co-operative force of a trades union, formed of people whose devotion, determination, and confidence at least equal that of the Jesuits, and yet all of whom are left to enjoy and use that perfect spiritual freedom and independence which only the Holy Ghost can bestow upon any man.

He added, prophetically, "The generals of the future are being reared in the homes of the rank and file of to-day ! "

Railton's later, considered verdict (1886) on the whole event was :

I do not believe when that Congress ended there was an evangelist or delegate whose heart was not full of joy and satisfaction.

William Booth, at St. James's Hall, London, in 1881, summed up the process that had resulted in the coming into existence of The Salvation Army thus :

We tried, for eleven years, various methods. We tried many plans. . . . Gradually the Movement took more of the military form, and finding, as we looked upon it, some four years ago, that God in His good providence had led us unwittingly, so to speak, to make an army, we called it an army, and seeing that it was an army organized for the deliverance of mankind from sin and the power of the devil, we called it an army of deliver-ance ; an army of salvation—The Salvation Army.

The concluding exercise of the War Congress was an all-night of prayer. In a next-door yard a company of butchers raised a hullabaloo with horns, cans, and cleavers ; some substance burnt near ventilator outlets and in stove pipes set everyone coughing—but these attempts at distraction failed to mar the heavenly influences of the hour. "The great object of the meeting was to address God, and it was in prayer and in receiving answers that the meeting was above all distinguished."

Round the table in the great central square [concluded the report] Satan was fought and conquered, as it were visibly, by scores. . . . Evangelists came there, burdened with the consciousness of past failings and unfaithfulnesses, and were so filled with the power of God that they literally danced for joy. Brethren and sisters, who had hesitated to yield themselves to go forth anywhere to preach Jesus, came and were set free from every doubt and fear, and numbers, whose peculiar besetments and difficulties God alone could read, came and washed and made them white in the blood of the Lamb.

Eminently typical of the spirit of the time was the " Song of The Salvation Army," written to the tune " Ring the bell, watchman," by Captain William J. Pearson when stationed at Bradford (1878) :

Come join our Army, to battle we go,
Jesus will help us to conquer the foe ;
Defending the right and opposing the wrong,
The Salvation Army is marching along !

Chorus   Marching along,
We are marching along,
The Salvation Army is marching along ;
Soldiers of Jesus, be valiant and strong—
The Salvation Army is marching along !

Come join our Army and enter the field,
The sword of the Spirit with strong faith we wield,
Our armour is bright and our weapons are strong,
The Salvation Army is marching along !

Come join our Army, the foe must be driven,
To Jesus, our Captain, the world shall be given ;
If hell should surround us we'll press through the throng,
The Salvation Army is marching along !

Come join our Army and do not delay,
The time for enlisting is passing away ;
The battle is raging, but victory will come,
The Salvation Army is marching along !

APPENDICES

APPENDIX A

SCENE OF THE BEGINNING

BETHNAL GREEN and Whitechapel share honours in the founding of The Salvation Army. The first open-air meeting conducted by William Booth in connection with the Tent Mission was held opposite the Blind Beggar public house, on " the Waste in front of this house which was the halting-place for many years of the Bayswater–Mile End buses." Bethnal Green boundaries at this point are Cambridge Road (west side), Whitechapel Road (north), and Brady Street (east). The " Blind Beggar " stands within this area.

Mile End was at one time " a common near London where pennyroyal grows in great abundance." In the seventeenth century Pepys described it as in the country and a resort of Londoners for fresh air, cakes, and ale. It was so named because Mile End Bars were exactly a mile from Aldgate.

Mile End Waste began at Whitechapel Church (St. Mary's) and reached to Stepney, a distance of over a mile and a half. Near the church it was a narrow wedge, gradually widening as it went eastwards until by Cambridge Road it reached its greatest width northwards.

Along the Mile End Road between the roadway and the pavement there was in the Sixties a wide line of space, much of it used on a week-day by shopkeepers for the exhibition of their wares and capitally adapted for open-air preaching on Sundays. On this " Waste," shows, shooting-ranges, petty dealers, and quack doctors rivalled one another in attracting the attention of passers-by.

In 1865 a toll gate crossed Whitechapel Road from Dog Row (now Cambridge Road) to the east corner of Epping Place

(Sidney Street). Many street names, like these, have been changed. The Act relating to the Road Trust under which the toll gate was set up expired on 31st October 1866. On that evening several thousand persons gathered to celebrate the event. Amid shouting and the letting off of fireworks the gate was removed at midnight, and when day came the site had been paved.

The Blind Beggar public house (situated on the northern side of Whitechapel Road a few doors west of Cambridge Road) was first established in 1673, and was so named after the principal figure of a local legend :

The old ballad of " The Beggar of Bethnal Green " [states Thornbury] written in the reign of Elizabeth (1558–1603) records the popular legend of the concealment under this guise of Henry de Montford, son of the redoubtable Earl of Leicester, who was wounded at Evesham (1265) fighting by his father's side, and was found among the dead by a baron's daughter who sold her jewels to marry him and assumed with him a beggar's attire to preserve his life. Their only child, a daughter, was " Pretty Bessie " of the ballad in Percy.

A variant makes the blinding of Henry de Montford to have taken place in a battle in France.

William Booth did not miss the opportunity this legend gave him. In October 1867 he preached at the Pavilion Theatre on "The Blind Beggar." At least one man who was attracted by the announcement was converted at that meeting. " My mother," he said, " had often told me when a lad about the blind beggar of Bethnal Green. Thinks I, I would like to hear that tale again, I'll go and hear him. But lo and behold, when I got there, it was me that was the blind beggar ! "

The portion of the Waste west of Cambridge Road is now paved, making it easy to suppose the whole Waste consisted only of the enclosed shrubbery to the east of it. Before Whitechapel and Mile End Roads were widened, the Waste was much broader than at present. That localities were described loosely in those days is shown by a contemporaneously printed list of open-air stands then used by The Christian Community which gives one as being in " Mile End Road, opposite the London Hospital."

The " Vine " was another public house in front of which meetings were held by The Christian Mission at a very early date. It stood on the Waste, east of Cambridge Road, facing northwards towards the footpath and shops. In 1885 it was said to be " a quaint half-timbered building that has been apparently standing in the middle of the main thoroughfare for two or three centuries." It was demolished about 1909.

The Friends' (Quakers') Burial Ground, on which the Tent was erected, is nearly an acre in extent. It belongs to the Devonshire House Division, having been acquired in 1687. In 1857 it was closed for interments by Order in Council. It was leased to the Stepney Council in 1897 and is now maintained as a children's recreation ground. On one side is Vallance Street (formerly Baker's Row) and on the other Fulbourne (Thomas) Street ; the latter enters Whitechapel Road opposite the London Hospital.

Appendix B

EARLY WITNESSES

The following persons have given first-hand information with regard to the events of the early days of the Mission, those whose names are marked with an asterisk having been present at William Booth's first meetings (at the Tent or in the open-air on Mile End Waste) in the East End :

THE AGAR FAMILY

*ALFRED. Member of the Gloucester Hall, Philpott Street (Commercial Road), Mission, and a worker at the Tent. Died 31st July 1938, when 95 years of age.

*ELIZABETH (Mrs. Sinclair). As a child attended the Gloucester Hall Mission, and later became a member. Attended meetings at the Tent both before and after William Booth took charge.

*RACHEL (Mrs. Ebdon). " Though only a bit of a girl at the time," remembered being taken by Alfred to a tea-meeting at the Tent. Served over twenty years as an evangelist and officer of The Salvation Army. She and her sister Louise were the first " Hallelujah Lasses." Died January 1940, aged 86.

JOHN. First bandmaster of Whitechapel Corps Band.

LOUISE (Mrs. Harry Davis). An evangelist with Rachel. Remained a Salvationist until her death in 1935, aged 76.

The father had died in 1864 ; Mrs. Agar senior was led to Christ by " Mother " Shepherd in the mid-Seventies at Whitechapel and continued a Salvationist till she died in 1908, aged 84. The family home was St. George's-in-the-East.

*CHAPMAN, Elizabeth. Name was on The Christian Mission's Exhorters' Plan, 1866. A collecting-box given to her by William Booth in the early Seventies is now in the Salvation Army Museum. Died 1928.

*COVENEY, Rev. R. G. (retired Congregational minister). As a boy witnessed the first meetings conducted by William Booth in the open-air on Mile End Waste and was present at the meetings in the New Road Dancing Academy. Later became a member of The Christian Community and an " auxiliary " of The Christian Mission ; his sister was one of the first members of the Mission. Named members of the Community who became missioners, including Alfred Dyer, Frank and Charles Spooner, the Andersons, and Solway ; also E. J. Smith (see below), a close friend whose statements he corroborated. Declared that from the first at least twenty members of the Community assisted in William Booth's meetings.

COXHEAD, Frederick J. Had charge of Millwall station of The Christian Mission 1868. Witnessed John Allen's conversion at Poplar. Had in his possession letters from Charles Owen, the handwriting of which tallied with that in the minute book of the Mission's committee (1868–72). For many years sergeant-major of the Leyton 1 Corps. Died 20th January 1938.

DOWDLE, James. First associated with The Christian Mission in 1867. In 1868 was lay superintendent, in turn, at Poplar and Shoreditch. Was manager of a " Food for the Million " shop at Shoreditch until November 1873, when he was accepted as a full-time evangelist and appointed to Kettering, but after a very short stay he was sent to establish a station at Chatham, following a campaign there by Mrs. Booth. Continued in the work, latterly as a commissioner of The Salvation Army, until his death in 1900.

EDMONDS, Henry. Son of a ship captain-owner of Portland, Maine, U.S.A. First made contact with The Christian Mission at the age of 15 (1876), when at Portsea with his father. Within a year had been accepted by William Booth for work in the Mission, his first appointment being to help in the office at its headquarters in Whitechapel. "There was then," he recorded in his memoirs, "only one clerk employed and the office boy. Mr. Bramwell was at the office only occasionally. Mr. Ballington rarely. Herbert was still at school. Mr. G. Scott Railton seemed to be Mr. Booth's chief helper." Became a colonel in the service of The Salvation Army and had charge of its work in Scotland. Died 1940.

FELLS, Honor (Mrs. Burrell and, latterly, Mrs. Salthouse). Sister to Joseph Fells. Became Mrs. Booth's maid in 1867. In 1869 was married to an outstanding convert of the Mission, named Burrell. Together, about 1874, they took over (by purchase from Mr. Billups after the death of his brother-in-law, Cooper) the " 188 " Whitechapel Road Dining Rooms (see page 196). Burrell died in 1876. Two years later Honor became an evangelist of The Christian Mission. After retirement from active service she settled down at Manchester (which station she had opened) and again married. As Mrs. Salthouse she assisted in local work until, over 90 years of age, she died in December 1938, after a brief illness resulting from a cold contracted when visiting the sick. Visited the East End in 1935 and identified localities and buildings associated with the Mission.

FELLS, Joseph. With his sister Honor, was among the first converts at the New Road Dancing Academy (1865) ; Mrs. Tallack (see below) claimed he was a member and convert of her Bible class. Had charge of one of the five " Food for the Million" shops. On the Whitechapel Circuit Plan for 1872 he was listed as prayer leader, exhorter, and secretary of men's meeting. Fells was an active Salvationist until his death at the age of 75. Married sister of John Eason (see page 170).

*FLAWN, James. Already a mission worker when William Booth took charge at the Tent. Giving an account of what he had done to reach street gamblers and public-house frequenters, he revealed something of his own past. " I once," he wrote, " was a gambler myself. The dominoes and dice and ninepins were my gods, and the public-house parlour and skittle ground were my favourite haunts." Helped in starting relief work that developed into the " Darkest England " scheme. Had charge of catering arrangements at the International Training College for Salvation Army officers at Clapton. Remained a keen Salvationist till his death, over 80 years of age, in 1917.

HARGRAVE, Mrs. Colonel R. (Captain Lizzie Beaty). Her mother, then *Susannah King, was converted at one of the first open-air meetings (opposite the " Blind Beggar ") conducted on Mile End Waste by William Booth in connection with the Tent.

THE JERMYS

JOSEPH, " Dark " Jermy. Member of The Christian Community. In charge at Three Colts Lane (Bethnal Green) station, 1866. Did not remain with the Mission very long, but one of his sisters, Mrs. Payne, was in active service as a Salvationist, latterly at Ipswich, till she died, 17th June 1938, at " Clock House " Salvation Army Eventide Home, Walthamstow, in her 94th year.

JAMES, " Fair " Jermy, cousin to the above. Also member and office-bearer in The Christian Community. Attended meetings of The Christian Mission in the Dancing Academy (1865). Became a member of the Mission (Bethnal Green station) in 1868. Kept an informative journal which he made available. Continued a Salvationist, latterly at the Congress Hall, Clapton, till his death in 1929. His grave is near to that of William Booth in Abney Park Cemetery, Stoke Newington.

*JONES, Mary A. (Mrs. Tallack). Was a worker at the Tent at the time when William Booth went there. Recalled William Booth's having said, on his third day at the Tent, that if it was the Lord's will he would joyfully devote his whole life to East London. Conducted a Bible class at the Dancing Academy ; claimed Joseph Fells was one of her earliest converts (see above).

Continued with the Mission until marriage in 1870. William
Booth had advised against her marrying Mr. Tallack, a Mission
convert, fearing, he said, he would not prove staunch ; happily,
time proved him to be entirely wrong. A Bible, now in possession of a son, is inscribed in the handwriting of William Booth,
as having been presented to Mary A. Jones in 1866 by "a few
Christian friends in token of their appreciation of her self-denying
efforts to promote the glory of God, the Salvation of souls, and
the happiness of the brethren." Supplied a photograph of a group
of early Missioners (in which she appears) but which was too
indistinct for reproduction in this book. See comments thereon
by George T. White (following).

LANE, R. M. Lay-worker and evangelist of The Christian
Mission, 1871 onwards.

MARSHALL, Mrs. Father (Mr. Wells) was member of the
Gloucester Hall Mission and helped in Tent meetings. Had
personal knowledge that relationships between The Christian
Mission and Gloucester Hall were most cordial and that one
helped the other in various ways from time to time.

MONK, Peter. One of the first converts won by William Booth
at the Whitechapel Tent. In his latter days was a soldier of the
Highgate corps of The Salvation Army. In his testimony often
made reference to the association of himself and other workers
with William Booth in the earliest days. His full story is related
by Harold Begbie in his life of William Booth, chapter 22.

ORAM, Mrs. Knowledge of the Mission went back to 1865,
when William Booth conducted services in an East London chapel
(one of the buildings in which short series of meetings were held
on week nights, after the tent had been abandoned in September
1865), when she was converted. With husband assisted in
meetings on Mile End Waste. On one occasion found William
Booth had started an open-air meeting alone before they arrived.

ROBERTS, John (Colonel). Entered service of The Christian
Mission as evangelist from Portsmouth 1877. Died 1935.

REYNOLDS, Caroline (Mrs.). Converted at meeting conducted
by Mrs. Collingridge at Messrs. Owen, Merton and Co.'s
factory, Millwall, when the work carried on there by Charles
Owen was amalgamated with The Christian Mission (August

1867). Her husband Robert was a weaver ; his brother William was employed at the Millwall factory, and his wife and their two sons were converted at the same time as Caroline. One of the sons became a worker with Dr. Barnardo, and the other a Salvation Army officer. Caroline became very prominent in the Mission, was associated with Mrs. Collingridge in the People's Mission Hall porch meetings and other special work and was appointed assistant to Evangelist William J. Pearson at the Whitechapel station in 1876, together with Emma Stride and Jane Woodcock. Continued as a Salvation Army officer and began its work in Ireland. Also held appointments in the women's social work.

RUSSELL, Alfred. Entered The Christian Mission as evangelist from Ninfield, 1875.

*SMITH, E. J. With his friend Mr. Coveney (see above) witnessed the first open-air meeting conducted by William Booth on Mile End Waste. A member of The Christian Community. Supplied much information regarding association of the Community with the Mission and the members who helped in the meetings.

STRIDE, Emma M. E. Appointed January 1876, with other " younger evangelists," for six months to Bromley. Conference minutes for 1876 recorded her acceptance as a preacher on trial. Was one of three women evangelists who assisted Evangelist Pearson at Whitechapel (1876–77). Was present at the 1877 Conference, was then married to a member of the Mission named Brown, but continued in service as an evangelist in her own right. Opened Sunderland station with Evangelist Thomas Blandy as assistant (*Christian Mission Magazine*, March 1878). Later, ill-health compelled her retirement. Eventually went to Australia. In 1940 (then Mrs. Ferguson) supplied identification of delegates included in the 1877 Conference group.

WALKER, Mrs. de Noe. (See Appendix E, under " The Dowager Lady Buxton.")

WHITE, George T. Living at Oshawa, Ont., Canada—21st April 1946 was his 91st birthday. His first contact with the Mission was when it took over in 1866 the Holywell Mount Chapel (New Connexion). George, then between eleven and twelve

years old, was among the seekers at a meeting held by William
Booth in the chapel a year or so later. William Booth himself
led him into the vestry and took such pains to make sure that the
boy understood the way of Salvation that he became soundly
converted. The White family had association with E. H. Rabbits,
having made boots for his shop at Elephant Building, Newington
Butts, for forty years. Mr. Rabbits was specially interested in
the work at Holywell Mount because he was then a member of
the New Connexion and because William Booth was the leader ;
he helped the Mission financially. Detailed and comprehensive
information regarding events, persons, and places connected with
the Mission from 1866 onwards has been supplied by George T.
White in the course of ten years' correspondence, supplemented
by an interview at Oshawa, 21st November 1935.

When a copy of photograph of first missioners was sent to
White, it was identified by him as having been taken in the
garden of his parents' house, Hassard Street, Hackney. He wrote :

The old photo has brought back my childhood days ; I had to
water the old garden in which it was taken and do my home-
lessons before I was free to play. The place at the back of the
picture was our workshop, where bootmaking (hand-sewn) was
done. No meetings were held there, but a great many prayers
ascended, and blessings came down. It was here that Rodney
(Gipsy) Smith, when a lad, asked the Lord to make him a soul-
winner. Certainly William Booth knelt often in the leather
chips.

Mr. White's comments on missioners included in the group
were : John C. Moore. A good business-man (hairbrush manufacturer). He it was who got Mr. Booth to take over the Holywell
Mount Chapel. After the closing of the chapel as a mission station
Mr. Moore did not attend any other, but started holding open-air
services by himself at the corner of Bethnal Green Road in
Shoreditch by the side of the railway. Though not a member of
the Mission, Moore acted as treasurer of the Shoreditch Circuit
until 1879. Mary A. Jones (Mrs. Tallack). Good at praying
and personal dealing, " fishing " it is now called, and at helping
people at the penitent-form. Mr. and Mrs. Collingridge. They
were good and earnest. Mrs. Collingridge was a positive speaker

on Christian perfection. Mrs. Pengally. Was also a "shouter" and could pray and talk well. Emigrated to Canada. James Flawn. Used to visit our home twice a week. Had a business head. With James Dowdle managed the soup-kitchens. Richard Dimaline, the "Happy Ranter." "Praise the Lord!" he would shout, often and loudly. He was a rattling speaker, quick. [Another comment by James Jermy was that "Dimaline was tall and commanding, a ready, fluent speaker, and a match for infidels, critics, or drunkards. Crowds followed him into the theatres. He was given liberty to hold just any kind of meeting he chose."] Totman, husband of the sister whose dress was set on fire at Three Colts Lane. James F. Rapson. The children's man. Secretary to Mr. Booth. My father, George White. He was a shouter. When he retired from work he did "specialling" for The Salvation Army. When he was 79 years of age he conducted a week-end's meetings at Rotherhithe slum corps— spoke at several open-air meetings and three times indoors on the Sunday, and more on the Monday; on the Tuesday he fell ill, had to be taken home in a cab, and on the following Saturday passed away. My mother. She, too, was mighty in prayer. One of my earliest recollections is of Mr. Booth coming to her in a prayer meeting and saying to her, "See that man—he says he is an infidel. Go and speak to him and pray over him." Later this man came out to seek Salvation. When she entered into the fulness of life everlasting she was 96. "Dark" Joseph Jermy. A good all-round man; a singer and a powerful speaker. "Daddy" Williamson. A happy Christian. "Oh, Hallelujah!" he used to shout in a ringing voice. James Dowdle, the converted railway-guard. He was a ready speaker and had good knowledge of the Scriptures. Cook. A quiet old boy, nothing striking about him. When Mr. Booth was at "188" (the Mission's first headquarters) for meals, Mr. Cook, who was cook for the food shop, got them ready—so Mr. Cook was called "Cook, the cook." Not all in the picture were Holywell Mount members. Some were from Three Colts Lane; Totman and wife among them.

Mrs. Payne (see above) corroborated Mr. White's identifications. Mrs. Tallack stated that William Booth was not in the photo because he was away at the time the missioners sat for it. They had had it taken in order that they might give it to him when he returned. That it was taken in the year 1867 is the opinion of Mr. White, based upon his recollection of other events of the time ; this is supported by the presence in the group of James Dowdle, who joined the Mission in that year.

APPENDIX C

MEMBERSHIP OF COMMITTEES

The earliest of the committees whose object was to arrange for the holding of services in the London theatres was the St. James's Hall and Britannia Theatre Committee, of which Samuel Morley was the head. It was formed in 1851 in connection with the Great Exhibition. Next in order was Lord Shaftesbury's United Committee for the Holding of Theatre Services (1859).

From these, more or less directly, sprang the Additional Theatre Services and the East London Special Services Committees. The first was concerned with the whole of London, but it gave special help to and collaborated with the East London Special Services Committee. The latter, in their report for 1862, stated that they were " marshalling their forces and preparing for the resumption of work in theatres engaged by the Additional Services Committee." In October of the same year the two had met and formed a joint committee to provide a central hall for Richard Weaver in East London. There is, however, no further mention of their association, and indeed but little of the Additional Services Committee itself.

The Committee of The Evangelisation Society was formed in 1864.

Inter-relationship between these committees and those of The Christian Mission is shown not only by their more or less close association, but in that some members served on several, and one—George Pearse—on all. Lists are available as follows :

1 ADDITIONAL THEATRE SERVICES FOR THE WORKING CLASSES
   OF LONDON : 1860

H. F. Bowkes	*Secretaries*
Lord Congleton	George Pearse
Captain Fishbourne	T. Shaldam Henry
John H. Gladstone	*Treasurer*
Theodore Howard	Forbes Winslow

In 1861 Captain Fishbourne became treasurer and in 1862
J. F. Elwin took the place of T. Shaldam Henry as a secretary.

2 THE EAST LONDON SPECIAL SERVICES COMMITTEE : 1861

J. F. Elwin	6 Church Row, Hampstead
T. A. Fieldwick	Secretary of British and Foreign Sailors' Society, Mercer Street, Shadwell
W. J. Lewis	5 Old Norfolk Street, New Road, Mile End
J. H. Lydall	23 Southampton Building, W.C.
Messrs. Morgan and Chase	*The Revival*
George Pearse	Stock Exchange
J. B. Wimshurst	52 Broad Street, Ratcliffe
John Stabb	Treasurer, 27 Red Lion Square, W.C.

As far back as 1862 it was recorded (*The Revival*, 19th January)
that "no one is so well qualified to speak of the East End work
as Mr. Stabb." Earlier than this he was associated with others in
promoting the Midnight Meeting Movement (absorbed by the
London Female Preventive and Reformatory Institution, since
January 1946 London Haven for Women and Girls, of which
he continued to be secretary until 1871). At his death in 1897 at
the age of 86 it was recorded that he was "Retired Secretary of
the Monthly Tract Society." In London Directories (1865–68)
he is shown as proprietor of a "Commercial Boarding House,"
24–25 Old Fish Street, Doctors Commons. When Queen
Victoria Street was cut through this district it eliminated the
greater part of Old Fish Street ; what remained was renamed,
and his address became 69–71 Knightrider Street.

Changes noted in 1862 were :
  Treasurer : Henry Thompson, 38 Mincing Lane
  Secretaries : Fieldwick and Wimshurst

To the Committee were added :
  In 1864, John W. Rawling, 52 Broad Street, Ratcliffe
  In 1865, W. Jones Hayden

3 THE EVANGELISATION SOCIETY

George Pearse, J. F. Elwin, Forbes Winslow, Samuel Hanson, and Captain Fishbourne were members of this Society's committee in 1868.

4 THE CHRISTIAN MISSION

Referees and Committees. The formation of a committee was announced early in 1867 by Mr. Frederick Whitaker, of Gray's Inn, with himself as secretary. No other names were given.

The earliest list extant is that printed in the first official report of the Mission (September 1867). Members of this, the central committee, were not necessarily members of the Mission :

Committee :

John Eason	43 Greenwood Road, Dalston
Josiah Harper	125 Upper Street, Islington
C. S. Mitchell	1 Ebenezer Terrace, London Hospital
Edmund Ives	18 Princes Street, Cavendish Square, W.
Charles Owen (Treasurer)	Messrs. Owen, Merton and Co., Millwall

Referees were :

Rev. J. H. Wilson	Secretary of the Congregational Home and Missionary Society
Rev. W. Tyler	New Town Chapel, Mile End
R. C. Morgan	*The Revival*
George Gilbert	Secretary of The Evangelisation Society
Gawin Kirkham	Secretary of The Open-air Mission
G. Hamilton	72 Whitechapel Road, E.

A list published early in 1868 showed the addition to the referees of Samuel Morley, Captain Fishbourne, R.N., and George Pearse. The firm, Messrs. Morgan and Chase, appeared in place of Mr. Morgan only, and George Hamilton was transferred from referees to the committee.

To the committee were added Jabez Skelton, 43 Whitechapel Road ; John Lee Dale, 84 Mile End Road and 25 Stepney Green ; Nathaniel James Powell, Cheapside, and 101 Whitechapel Road ; John McCall, 137 Houndsditch and Walthamstow ; George Gowland, Radcliffe Cross East and Tunstall Lodge, Clapton.

Charles Owen was shown as honorary secretary, and Nathaniel J. Powell and John McCall as joint treasurers.

Powell was a member of a firm of wholesale stationers and account book manufacturers (Messrs. Mead and Powell) of Cheapside and Whitechapel. Was well known throughout East London as a Christian philanthropist. Held office as treasurer for " the first twelve years of Salvation Army history, indeed until the magnitude of the movement rendered anything like honorary treasurership an impossibility."

A list printed in the *East London Evangelist* (December 1868) showed further changes :

To the *committee* had been added John Alfred Merrington, Hamlet Road, Upper Norwood, and W. H. Crispin, Marsh Gate Lane, Stratford and Rickham House, Haverstock Hill.

Nathaniel J. Powell was shown as sole treasurer, McCall having resigned from the committee on account of negotiations proceeding for the purchase by the Mission of the People's Market, his property.

Membership of the committee seems to have continued without further changes until November 1870, when Charles Brewin, of Croydon, joined it. George Hamilton resigned in March 1871. In January 1872 Ivo Cobet and Henry Holme, who had brought about the establishment of the Croydon station, also joined. Charles Owen having failed in business and resigned from the committee in 1873, Robert Paton became honorary secretary. Leicester, C. Dobbin, J. E. Billups, and John Cory were added to the committee in 1874, and its name was changed to " Council."

Referees : Rev. R. Ashton, Secretary of the Congregational Union, was added to the list, and Captain W. E. Smith named as secretary of The Evangelisation Society in place of Mr. Gilbert.

By June 1876 referees had been dropped from the Mission's official records and the council consisted of :

Nathaniel J. Powell	(Treasurer)
Robert Paton	(Hon. Secretary) 43 Highbury Quadrant
John Eason	Dalston Lane, E.
W. H. Crispin	Stratford and Rickham House, Haverstock Hill, N.W.
Edmund Ives	18 Princes Street, W.
Ivo Cobet	2 Clarence Road, Croydon S.
Henry Holme	3 Clarence Road, Croydon S.
John Cory, J.P.	Maindre Hall, near Cardiff
J. E. Billups	Tredegarville, Cardiff
T. Whitwell	Stockton-on-Tees
W. S. Allen, M.P.	Cheadle, Staffs.

No further record is extant beyond a statement that :

Mr. Booth worked in perfect harmony with this council for some years and when, finally, the work had assumed such proportions and so established itself in public favour and confidence as not to require such financial sponsorship, it was dissolved in the most friendly manner.

APPENDIX D

WILLIAM BOOTH'S CALL TO THE EAST END AND HIS PLAN OF WORK

One version of how William Booth was called to East London was that he went to the office of the *Revival* in response to an advertisement for a " supply " for the Tent. No issue of the *Revival* of the period, either on the cover or inside, carried such an advertisement ; nor has any been found in any other contemporary religious periodical. The statement may be an echo of an earlier advertisement (1861) which announced that Messrs. Morgan and Chase had decided to set up a Register of Evangelists, and invited all who desired engagements to send in their names. This advertisement was not repeated, neither did the firm proceed with the register. That such a register already existed under other auspices was no doubt brought to their notice.

Four years later appeared an advertisement similar in character, but this time it was inserted by "The Committee for the Registration of Evangelists" (*The Revival*, 19th January 1865), the secretary being George Gilbert, also secretary to The Evangelisation Society. Earlier, Captain Fishbourne had been the secretary.

In all probability William Booth saw both advertisements. One or the other may have led to his making contact with Morgan and Chase, but this could not have been with particular regard to the Tent Mission. R. C. Morgan when reporting (*The Christian*, September 1878) the opening of the "Salvation Factory," Coventry, included a reference that has a bearing upon this point :

Fourteen years ago William Booth, then a minister and a stranger in London, called at the office of the *Revival* and talked with us of the thoughts that were stirring in his heart. The word of the Lord had come to him—as to Abram of old—bidding him go forth to a place God would show him ; he obeyed and went out, not knowing whither he went. God sent him to the East of London.

The "fourteen years ago" might be taken to place this meeting at about the time of the appearance of the second advertisement, but this was at least six months too early to have any connection with the call for a "supply" at the Tent.

In any case William Booth was already known to the East London Special Services Committee and its members were aware that he was seeking an opening for evangelistic work. When he was in London in June 1865 he again called at the *Revival* office and was then invited, no doubt by the deputation of members of the East London Special Services Committee, to hold a week's services at the Tent.

A suggestion has also been made that William Booth was employed by Messrs. Morgan and Chase in the sense that they financed The East London Christian Mission ; in fact, that it was "a Morgan and Chase enterprise."

Appeals were frequently made by the *Revival* for funds for the East London Special Services Committee, but inquiries at the office of Marshall, Morgan and Scott established that there was no record of the relationship having been closer ; indeed, there was not existing even the shadow of a tradition of anything of the kind. The late Mrs. Morgan declared that she had heard nothing of it, though her husband had frequently described to her all phases of his association with William Booth ; further, that she knew the firm, at that time, had not been in a position, financially, to undertake any such responsibility. B. R. Chase, son of Samuel Chase, was equally emphatic in the same sense.

The Rev. Joseph Pearce claimed—in an article in the *County Express and Dudley Mercury* (19th June 1943)—that as early as during the revival campaign William Booth conducted in the Black Country, in 1863, he was planning an organization on the lines of The Salvation Army. William Booth was then a guest of Mr. Palmer, mines drainage inspector to the New British Iron Company, " a lay preacher of the white-hot brand."

The Palmers (wrote Mr. Pearce) had a spacious garden in which William Booth walked for hours in deepest thought, with head on chest. This happened so frequently that one day Mr. Palmer had the temerity to say, " Excuse me, Mr. Booth, but I cannot help wondering what it is that engages your thoughts so frequently and protractedly as you pace the garden."

Mr. Booth, with face all ashine, replied, " My friend, I am thinking out a plan which, when it is implemented, will mean blessing to the wide, wide world," and then proceeded to outline the said organization.

Mr. Pearce claimed that this organization was The Salvation Army, but such a claim lacks foundation. At Walsall, William Booth in his meetings had made use of notable converts, advertising that they would give their testimonies, and this had been extraordinarily successful in attracting people and gaining further converts. Out of this departure, indeed, came the formation of " The Hallelujah Band," though not under the leadership of

William Booth ; and, while other such bands were formed, the movement did not become permanent.

William Booth, however, was greatly impressed by the success that had accompanied this novel employment of converts, and in planning for his future work he gave the principle prominent place. In the sense that " Saved to save " was the germ idea that later found full development in The Salvation Army, here was its beginning ; but there is ample evidence that not until over ten years later had William Booth any thought of an organization on military lines—and then only when it was forced upon him by circumstances. Indeed, in the course of an address in 1881 he himself made a statement completely disposing of any idea to the contrary :

Fifteen and a half years ago [he said] my own heart was drawn out in sympathy for the masses of the people for whose souls nobody seemed to care, and to deal with whom, and to bring whom into the Gospel net, there seemed to be no particularly successful method . . . and I resolved that, if possible, I would find out whether there was not some plan by which these precious souls could be reached with the tidings of mercy, and The Salvation Army is the outcome of that resolution . . . patiently and determinately persevered in. Beginning, as I did, so to speak, with a clean sheet of paper . . . I have gone on until The Salvation Army has reached its present position.

Often in later years he would say :

People seem to think that I have said, " I will have an army, and captains, and bands of music . . . but these things were not in my mind."

APPENDIX E

EARLY SUPPORTERS

SAMUEL MORLEY
Member of Parliament and philanthropist, a wealthy manufacturer of Nottingham. Treasurer of the Congregational Home Missionary Society. Mr. Morley, after looking into the work of

The Christian Mission in October 1865, gave to it immediate and practical help, the reason for which action becomes apparent when the opinions he held are known. At a gathering of laymen and ministers interested in the nonconformist services being held in London theatres, of the committee responsible for which he was chairman, he said :

He could not help expressing his deep conviction that their churches as such were not touching the masses that were living around them to an extent in any degree commensurate with their means and professions to do good. . . . Many Christians were now disposed to compound with conscience by a money payment instead of both continuing to support agencies and doing such work themselves. Church work and church membership he hoped to be synonymous terms.

Again, when speaking at a gathering of the Norfolk Association for spreading the Gospel, Morley said :

The London Society was increasing the appointment of evangelistic agents . . . but this kind of work was too limited. It was doing the work by proxy. Every Christian should be a missionary, and it should be felt in every church that it was dishonourable to be idle.

In William Booth and The East London Christian Revival Union, he found at last a man and methods after his own heart. A note from Morley to William Booth, dated 20th April 1869, stated :

I will gladly co-operate in any way you can suggest to secure from the Services Committee the arrangement you propose which seems to me to be a very reasonable and suitable one.

What the proposal was does not appear.

When calling on Salvationists to pray for Morley's restoration from illness, William Booth wrote (1886) :

Twenty-one years ago, when we had just commenced to struggle in the East of London, before any of the generous friends who have since gathered around us had heard of the effort, Mr. Samuel Morley sent for us, listened to the statement of our plans and hopes, inquired into our financial methods of support, and at once, not only generously but affectionately, promised to charge himself with a large share of the burden, calling for his cheque-book and giving a substantial earnest of what followed.

Samuel Morley proved a generous and substantial friend, describing himself, when presiding at the Annual Meeting of The Christian Mission in 1874, as a partner in the concern. In later years his co-operation became less regular, but one of his last acts was to make, in 1885, a munificent donation (£2,000) to the women's rescue work of The Salvation Army.

THE CORYS AND THE BILLUPSES

The principal of the friends who were associated with Samuel Morley in provision for William Booth's personal support were the Corys and the Billupses, of Cardiff.

Among the most influential and prominent of the Christian workers who had invited William and Catherine Booth to Cardiff in 1863 were John and Richard Cory, well-known ship and colliery owners who, with rare consistency and increasing liberality, provided financial support for their work then, and later in the days of The Christian Mission and The Salvation Army.

Richard Cory, being a Baptist, differed on some lesser doctrinal questions from the Booths, but minor and theoretical distinctions were not allowed to stand in the way. John Cory was a matter-of-fact, hard-headed, clear-sighted man of business ; he saw the work for himself and judged it by its results ; of criticism of an adverse character he always took a broad, statesmanlike view.

The friendship of Mr. and Mrs. Billups also had its beginnings in the Booths' campaign in Wales in 1863. It was in some respects more personal in character than their association with the Corys, a friendship of warm and unchanging character having sprung up between Mrs. Booth and Mrs. Billups. The Billupses proved themselves unswerving supporters of William Booth in his enterprises alike in the days of perplexity and poverty and at the height of his success.

Their daughter, Mary C. Billups, entered the Booth household in 1868 and became one of the most active workers of The East London Christian Mission.

HENRY REED

Among those associated with The Christian Mission in its early days, apart from William Booth, there was no more striking personage than Henry Reed. When a young man Reed had migrated to Tasmania (then Van Diemen's Land), where he made a fortune in sheep-farming and was led into knowledge of Salvation by two converted convicts. In 1835 he crossed Bass Straits to Melbourne, then a new settlement having only three huts, with the object of devising a plan to save the natives of Australia from the fate threatening those of Tasmania, already nearing extermination. He took part in the first religious service held at Melbourne. When he decided to come home (to England) from Tasmania, to avoid the annoyance of travelling with men who used bad language he bought a ship and chose his own captain and crew !

His great simplicity of spirit, combined with considerable strength of will, sometimes led him to jump to conclusions and act drastically without really understanding what he was doing.

A few days after the opening of the People's Mission Hall, Henry Reed wrote a letter to William Booth (dated 15th April 1870) which was typical of his temperament and outlook. An unexpected increase in the cost of the alterations to the building had led William Booth to ask Reed and other friends to help him meet the debt (£500) thus incurred. In his reply, good Henry Reed protested that thus to go into debt would, unless repented of, be a sin unto death. To his intensely practical mind it appeared that nothing could save the Cause from utter disgrace but the sale, in order to pay its debts, of the Mission's possessions —lock, stock, and barrel—the giving up of all hired buildings, and the dismissal of all paid agents. These measures, he pressed with earnest emphasis, should be put into effect immediately. Reed was perhaps influenced by an underlying feeling of resentment that he should have been rebuffed by William Booth in the matter of the People's Mission Hall scheme, which had been proceeded with contrary to his advice, although there had been a reconciliation.

Later, Reed made a generous settlement upon William Booth (£5,000) to provide for the support of himself and family without his having to draw upon the funds of the Mission. His practical turn of mind was well seen in his providing greatcoats and thick boots for Mission workers.

Reed left Harrogate for Australia in 1873, and in 1880, at the age of 74, passed to his reward from his Tasmanian home. In the course of a warm tribute to his memory, William Booth wrote :

Mr. Reed rendered most generous assistance at the commencement of The Salvation Army, for which I shall be everlastingly grateful. Towards the end of his earthly career his heart came over to me in a still more tender and interesting fashion . . . his earnest prayers went up to heaven on behalf of the Movement in the establishment of which he had been so deeply interested.

And to this, in a preface to Mrs. Reed's life of her husband, he added :

He did not see eye to eye with me in every method employed in those days ; neither did I see eye to eye with him in every plan which he thought ought to be adopted ; but on the main principles and activities of the Salvation War he was one with me in heart and soul !

The Dowager Lady Buxton

The first to send for the funds of the Mission (The Christian Revival Union) an amount reaching three figures was the Dowager Lady Buxton. Lady Buxton (Hannah Gurney), a younger sister of Elizabeth Fry, was married to Sir Thomas Fowell Buxton, Bart. ; born in 1783, she lived until 1872. Early in 1866, at her home in Norfolk, Lady Buxton had received a letter from William Booth appealing for financial help. Before replying, she directed her great-niece, Mrs. de Noe Walker— who later became a Salvationist—who was staying with her, to write to a vicar (unnamed) in East London and inquire what he thought of the work being done by William Booth and his followers. "Any help which you can give," ran the reply, "will be more than well spent; his work is admirable, and I only wish we had a thousand such men."

Lady Buxton at once sent a cheque for £100, and later contributed to the People's Market purchase fund; she and her daughter-in-law, Lady Victoria Buxton, became staunch friends and supporters.

ALBERT L. AND MRS. FREEMAN

Among the friends made by Mrs. Booth during her campaign at Margate (1867) who gave generous financial help to the Mission were Mr. and Mrs. Freeman. One of their first gifts was £25 towards the purchase, as a hall for The Christian Mission, of a Unitarian Chapel at Stratford (1868). Freeman was a successful American merchant who had been in business in China (Shanghai), but had retired to England in the early Sixties on account of the precarious condition of Mrs. Freeman's health; but shortly after they both made contact with the Booths, Freeman himself died (1871). Mrs. Freeman, a thorough believer in the self-sacrifice and separation from the world which Mrs. Booth advocated, continued the reliable and generous friendship that her husband and she had begun together. Her daughter (a ward in Chancery) and Henry Edmonds were married in 1886, when Edmonds was in charge of the work of The Salvation Army in Scotland.

In 1905 William Booth wrote to Mrs. Freeman:

"It must be some little satisfaction to you to know you were able to have a hand in getting this great Movement on its feet."

RICHARD COPE MORGAN

Co-founder, with Samuel Chase, and editor of *The Revival* (now *The Christian*). With his partner he gave full backing in *The Revival* to William Booth in the formative days of The Christian Mission, which he continued in *The Christian*, and warmly approved the step that eventually brought The Salvation

Army into full being. He was not always pleased with everything said and done, but was invariably kindly, if candid, in his objections. In particular he saw what he considered to be danger in the teaching of The Salvation Army on the doctrine of holiness of heart and life, but to the end showed his regard for the organization and its leaders by practical and generous help. He frequently attended, spoke at, and himself reported special meetings of The Christian Mission and The Salvation Army.

LORD SHAFTESBURY

In its earliest days, Lord Shaftesbury was friendly to the Mission, and at his invitation William and Mrs. Booth took part in conferences called by him in 1872, which had in view the amalgamation of the various undenominational organizations at work in the Metropolis, but which proved abortive. An entry in a diary in which William Booth noted engagements would seem to be connected with this : " Thursday, 19th December 1872. Meeting at Freeman's (36 Albion Street, Hyde Park), of the Evangelistic Union."

Later, however, his lordship became bitterly antagonistic. On more than one occasion Mrs. Booth sought a personal interview in order to hear and answer his objections, but he persistently refused either to examine the work for himself or to give its leaders an opportunity to meet those whose criticisms had biased him against it.

APPENDIX F

DOCTRINES

Articles of Faith from Christian Revival Society document :

1 We believe that the Scriptures of the Old and New Testament were given by inspiration of God, and are the only rule of Christian faith and practice.
2 We believe that there is only one living and true God ; the Father, the Son, and the Holy Ghost—three persons in one

God—equal in power and glory ; and the only proper object of religious worship.

3 We believe that in the person of Jesus Christ the Divine and human natures are united, so that He is truly and properly God, and truly and properly man.

4 We believe that all mankind, in consequence of the disobedience of Adam, are sinners, destitute of holiness, and justly exposed to the penalty of the Divine Law.

5 We believe that the Lord Jesus Christ has, by His suffering and death, made an atonement for the whole world, so that whosoever will may be saved.

6 We believe that repentance towards God, faith in our Lord Jesus Christ, and regeneration by the Holy Spirit are necessary to Salvation.

7 We believe in the immortality of the soul—in the resurrection of the body—in the general judgment at the end of the world —in the eternal happiness of the righteous—and in the endless punishment of the wicked.

The constitution presented to and adopted by the first Conference of The Christian Mission (1870) contained a revision of the doctrines of The Christian Revival Society. This was identical with the doctrines set forth in the 1878 Foundation Deed (Appendix R), with two minor exceptions. The concluding clause of No. 2, " and who is the only proper object of religious worship," was transferred thereto from the end of No. 3 ; and No. 8 was made to read, " by grace through faith " in place of " through grace by faith."

A statement of the rules of The Christian Mission (Appendix N), adopted by the 1875 Conference, set out the doctrines with the differences from the 1878 Deed already noted, and one other : " everlasting " was substituted for " endless " in No. 11, " endless " being restored in 1878.

Conference references to doctrines other than those elsewhere noted were :

1873. Resolved that no person shall be allowed to teach in The Christian Mission the doctrine of Final Perseverance apart from perseverance in holiness, or that the moral law was abolished, and that if any person after having been cautioned by the Superintendent continued to propagate this doctrine, they should not be allowed further to preach or speak in the Mission. Moved by Bramwell Booth. Seconded by Dowdle.

1876 Resolved that the following definitions of the doctrines numbered 9 and 10 in our list of Doctrines be printed and issued to all our members.

That is to say—

We believe that after conversion there remain in the heart of a believer inclinations to evil or roots of bitterness, which, unless overpowered by Divine Grace, produce actual sin, but that these evil tendencies can be entirely taken away by the Spirit of God, and the whole heart thus cleansed from everything contrary to the will of God, or entirely sanctified, will then produce the fruits of the Spirit only. And we believe that persons thus entirely sanctified may by the power of God be kept unblameable and unreprovable before Him. Moved by Railton. Seconded by Garner.

APPENDIX G

PLEDGES

Bond of Agreement from the Christian Revival Society document :

1   We engage from henceforth to strive earnestly to depart from all iniquity, and to aim at the highest degree of personal devotedness to God.

2   We agree to set our hearts upon the salvation of souls, and to put forth constant personal effort to secure the conversion of sinners.

3   We engage, so far as we have opportunity, to attend the meetings held by the Society, both indoors and in the open-air, and to co-operate to the utmost of our ability in every effort put forth by the Society to bring souls to Christ.

4   We will strive to cultivate a spirit of brotherly affection towards the members of the Society, and to manifest this by

seeking, as far as we have opportunity, each other's temporal and spiritual welfare.

5 We will contribute according to our ability weekly offerings to assist the Society in its operations.

Appendix H

PROGRAMME OF THE EAST LONDON CHRISTIAN MISSION
(From the Mission's first official Report, September 1867)

Sunday 8   Breakfast meeting, charge 3d. During breakfast conversation on the previous week's labour; after that an address on some religious topic and general conversation on the same.

    11   Preaching in the hall and in the open-air.

    3   Breaking of bread or experience meeting, and service in the open-air.

    $4\frac{1}{2}$*   Tea for workers and friends, 3d. each. From 70 to 90 attend. After tea, prayer for the evening's work.

    6   Brethren branch out for open-air meetings.

    7   Service for young people and preaching in the theatre.

Every day of the week there was a midday prayer meeting, the time for this being given as $12\frac{1}{2}$ to $1\frac{1}{2}$ p.m.

Every night but Saturday there was preaching in the hall at 8 o'clock. Wednesday evening's preaching was specially for " believers."

Each day too had its programme of additional events special to it.

Monday 2 to 5   Mothers' meeting.

    $6\frac{1}{2}$ Open-air service.

    7   Meeting of brethren and sisters engaged in district visitation.

* This seems to have been the usual way to set out half-hours

Tuesday	6½	Writing, reading, and arithmetic classes.
	7	Believers' meeting ; open-air meeting.
	8	Bible-class for young people.
Wednesday	7	Singing class ; open-air service.
	8	Drunkards' Rescue Society.
Thursday	7	Believers' meeting ; open-air service.
Friday	5	Tea and conference with helpers.
	8	Bible-class for workers.
Saturday	7 to 9	Savings bank.
	8	Prayer meeting.

In addition to these public efforts, the sick and the poor in the neighbourhood are visited, 120 tickets for meat and bread are given away weekly, and we purpose establishing a soup-kitchen, sick-club, girls' sewing-class, and other meetings.

Appendix I

BALANCE SHEETS OF THE CHRISTIAN MISSION

Technically these are not " Balance Sheets," but Statements of Income and Expenditure. Later, with the adoption of double entry book-keeping, complete balance sheets were issued. There has been no break in the issue of such statements and balance sheets from 1867 to the present day ; the stock accusation of early criticism that none such were published was entirely without foundation.

The manuscript statement reproduced, facing page 229, covering the last quarters of 1865, would suggest that account of all income and expenditure was kept from the very first days of the Mission.

The first " balance sheets " publicly issued were for 1867–68. Each was printed in the Mission's magazine, as well as being otherwise distributed. They are reprinted here. The 1868 statement covered nine months only, so that the accounts of the Mission might be brought into line with the customary closing of the financial year in September.

BALANCE SHEET FOR 1867

GENERAL SPIRITUAL WORK

Dr.		£	s.	d.		£	s.	d.	Cr.
Total offerings for the year . . .		1,559	10	0	Expenditure	1,333	17	1	
					Balance	225	12	11	
		1,559	10	0		1,559	10	0	

DESTITUTE SAINTS' FUND

	£	s.	d.		£	s.	d.
Total offerings received	136	7	6	Bread, meat, and money given out .	137	6	8
Balance	19	2					
	137	6	8		137	6	8

GENERAL POOR FUND

	£	s.	d.		£	s.	d.
Total offerings received	350	18	10	Bread, meat, money, etc.. . . .	458	12	5
Balance	107	13	7				
	458	12	5		458	12	5

POPLAR MISSION HALL BUILDING FUND

	£	s.	d.		£	s.	d.
Total offerings received . . .	55	15	1	At Bankers	55	15	1

Audited and found correct. Wm. C. BOARDMAN, Accountant, Dorset House, The Grove, Stratford, E.

BALANCE SHEET FOR NINE MONTHS FROM 1st JANUARY TO 30TH SEPTEMBER 1868

General Spiritual Work

	£	s.	d.
Balance from 1867	225	12	11
Offerings in nine months . .	1,156	5	3½
„ Purchase of Stratford Unitarian Chapel . .	131	16	6
„ Purchase of Bible carriage and stock . .	33	9	1
„ Sales in shops and Bible carriage	42	3	5¾
„ Towards formation of Nursing Fund . .	10	0	0
„ Towards fitting up Limehouse Gaff . .	30	15	0
„ Evangelisation Society .	316	3	8
	1,946	5	11¼

	£	s.	d.
General working expenses of theatres, halls, and other stations . .	801	15	0¼
Salaries of evangelists, Bible women, etc. . .	476	5	11
Purchase and fitting up Stratford Chapel	279	8	6
Repairs and alterations of Shoreditch Hall . .	93	16	10
Do.—Hackney Road . .	19	10	0
New Bible carriage and stock for it and shop . .	50	17	4¼
Printing and posting bills, stationery, advertisements, postage, etc. . .	121	8	0
Travelling and petty cash . .	10	18	0
Part payment on account of Limehouse Gaff . .	59	8	0
Balance in hand . .	32	18	3¾
	1,946	5	11¼

DESTITUTE SAINTS' FUND

	£	s.	d.		£	s.	d.
Offerings in nine months . . .	168	11	6	Amount overpaid in 1867 . . .		19	2
Amount paid beyond receipts	17	3	8½	Bread, meat, money, etc., given out	184	16	0½
	185	15	2½		185	15	2½

GENERAL POOR FUND

	£	s.	d.		£	s.	d.
				Amount overpaid in 1867 . . .	107	13	7
				Bread, meat, money, etc. . . .	210	15	2½
				Balance in hand . . .	9	3	9½
Offerings in nine months . . .	327	12	4		327	12	4

WHITECHAPEL NEW HALL FUND

	£	s.	d.		£	s.	d.
Offerings . . .	252	14	11½	Amount in hand	252	14	11½

POPLAR NEW HALL FUND

	£	s.	d.		£	s.	d.
Amount in hand from 1867 . . .	55	15	1	Amount in hand . . .	87	4	1
Offerings in nine months . . .	31	9	0				
	87	4	1		87	4	1

TOTALS FOR TWENTY-ONE MONTHS—JANUARY 1867 TO 30TH SEPTEMBER 1868

	£	s.	d.		£	s.	d.
Receipts . . .	4,603	12	2½	Total expenditure . . .	4,238	14	11½

Audited and found correct. J. BEDDOW, Public Accountant, 2 Gresham Buildings, Guildhall, E.C.

The support of Mr. Booth is not included in the above sheet, that having been provided expressly for by a few Christian friends. The Committee invite any who are in sympathy to unite with them therein.

EXTRACTS FROM THE MINUTES OF THE SHOREDITCH CIRCUIT ELDERS' MEETING

At a meeting of the above held on 25th August 1868 the under-signed were appointed members of the committee :

Mr. Thomas Rouse, J. C. Moore, P. Monk, Longmore, White, Hipple, Rowe, Crosier.

General Stewards $\begin{cases} \textit{Treasurer}, \text{ J. C. Moore} \\ \textit{Secretary}, \text{ P. Monk} \end{cases}$

Hall Stewards $\begin{cases} \text{Thomas Rowe} \\ \text{Walter Crosier} \end{cases}$

The following rules were agreed to :
The treasurer steward to receive all monies and pay them over on each Tuesday evening at Elders' Meeting. The secretary steward to keep a record of all monies received and paid.
The hall stewards to take measures for promoting order in hall and theatre, to see to placing people in seats, also the cleanliness, lighting, and comfort of the place.
The hall stewards to see that all announcements from the pulpit are properly made, the sacrament observed, and the services advertised.
Arranged that Brother Rouse apply to the Tract Society for tracts.
Agreed that a temperance committee be formed, that Brother Crosier be secretary and Brother Rouse [altered to Rowe] and Brother Monk be members of committee.

[Appears to have been countersigned by Charles Owen, Hon. Secretary of the Mission's central committee.]

September 29, 1868. Chairman C. H. Owen. Bros. Moore, Crosier, Monk.

Bro. Moore is requested to have the skylight repaired. Bro. Crosier to see to the gas and meter.
Bro. Crosier to have the bills changed at once.

[The following entry is ruled through : " No open-air meeting after 8 o'clock, by order of the Secretary." See facsimile reproduction, facing page 100.]

The brothers are ["requested" is crossed out and "invited" written over it in Owen's handwriting] to attend upon the people and conduct them to their seats.

Meetings progressing favourably. Many souls earnestly seeking for Salvation.

September 30, 1869. Brother Dowdell [*sic*], Superintendent.

It was proposed and agreed to let the shop at 5s. per week, gas for same to be 1s. per week. One week's notice to be given on either side ; the room to be let at 3s. per week, a week's notice either side.

It was also proposed and carried unanimously that the Hall should be washed once a week and swept every night, 2s. a week allowed for same. 1s. 6d. per week to be paid to doorkeeper and Brother [no name inserted] requested to enquire into his character.

February 6, 1870. Sister Collingridge, Superintendent.

Proposed by Sister Collingridge and agreed to :

That a Drunkards' Rescue Society be formed at once, also a Sick and Visiting Society and Tract Distributing Society.

It being announced that the chapel-keeper wanted an increase of wages, the matter was referred to Mr. Booth.

Suggested by Brother Cress that we should be careful in speaking to the people.

February 16, 1870. Sister Collingridge in the chair.

Proposed by Sister Collingridge and agreed to that a Sick and Visiting Society be formed, the brethren to take different districts and to confine their visits principally to members of the chapel.

Brothers Moore and Price to take the Curtain Road and Gardens.

Brothers Monk and Harrison the Spitalfields district.

Brothers Cress and Lane the Kingsland district.

All that is given away to come through the Elders' Meeting.

The reports to be sent in weekly. The names and addresses of the people to be left at the hall.

November 4, 1870.

Present : Chairman Bro. Allen, Bro. Moore, Bro. Longmore, Bro. Bannocks, Bro. Barber, Bro. Price, Bro. Gabriel.

Proposed by Bro. Allen that two Elders be chosen for the Whitechapel Conference to be held on 15th November.

Proposed by Bro. Moore, that Bro. Longmore, seconded by Bro. Price [*sic*]. Proposed by Bro. Longmore that Bro. Moore be chosen, seconded by Bro. Allen for the coming Conference. Agreed to.

Mission Hall, Hare Street, Jan. 6, 1871.

Proposed by Bro. Moore, seconded by Bro. Price, that Bro. Barber be paid 10s. out of the General Fund for building a copper in the above hall for the use of the Mission.

The meeting was opened and closed with prayer.

    Chairman, Arthur Beable
    Secretary,   Alf. Bannocks

Mission Hall, Hare Street. March 10, 1871.

Proposed by Bro. Bannocks, seconded by Bro. Moore. That in consequence of this branch of the Mission being so in debt that the moiety allowed for hall cleaning be discontinued. Carried.

The Minutes of the last meeting read and confirmed. The meeting opened and closed with prayer.

At Bro. Barber's house, Dec. 15, 1871. Bro. Beable in the chair.

Proposed by Bro Richardson, seconded by Bro. King, that No. 18 Hare Street be given up and the whole of the things be removed to the Apollo Hall, notice be given to the landlord on Saturday, December 16, 1871. Carried.

Leader's Meeting. May 23, 1872. Bro. Beable in the chair.

Resolved : That Bro. Moore take the chair at the Temperance Meeting at the Apollo Hall for six weeks from this date and that Bro. Edwards lead the singing also act as Secretary to obtain subscriptions for the Temperance Society.

The meeting commenced and ended with prayer.

At Bro. Dowdle's, July 11, 1872. Bro. Moore in the chair.

Resolved : 1st. That a vote of censure be passed upon Bro.

Wardle for his continued disappointments at Shoreditch and that a letter be sent to him of the same. Moved by King, seconded by Edwards.

2nd. That the Temperance Meeting at our hall be placed on the plan and supplied by speakers.

Moved by Bro. Dowdle, seconded Bro. Moore, that three speakers be planned each Friday night and that the first named be the leader for that night, and should any good speaker be seen in the hall during the meeting that the said leader for the said night should be at liberty to ask the said speaker to address the said meeting, as a good number of our own brethren will be continually talking before our friends who attend our meetings regularly and like a good change for the benefit of the meetings generally, also the work of God at large.

The meeting commenced and ended with prayer.

At Bro. Dowdle's, Nov. 7, 1872. Bro. Beable in the chair.

Resolved : 1st. That Bro. Beable be requested to see Mr. Booth and ask if he thinks it would be best for us to repair the ceiling of the Apollo Hall or for him first to see Mr. Fraser at the Brewers, or does he know of any person or persons who are likely to help us in buying the said hall.

2nd. That the Quarterly Festival be removed to 1st December and that Miss Billups preach in the morning, Mr. Booth or Mr. Tyler afternoon, and Mrs. Booth evening. Also that Mr. Powell be solicited to take the chair on Monday 2nd, and the following speakers be published : Mrs. Booth, Beable, Wardle, Dowdle, Eason, Moore, Patter[?], White, and Jacks.

At Bro. Dowdle's, May 22, 1873. Bro. Beable in the chair.

An account was given by the Hall Treasurer that we are 17s. in arrears which could be paid by our festival.

Resolved that the Tea Meeting be held on Whitsun Tuesday instead of Monday as per plan.

That Mrs. Dowdle provide for the tea.

That Bro. Dowdle [then in charge of the Shoreditch "Food for the Million" shop] be requested to provide the cake for our Tea at the same price as we paid Mr. Willets—5½d. per lb.

That we ask Bro. Booth to take the chair on Whitsun Tuesday, and should he fail then Bro. Beable.

That the following speakers be published. Messrs. Booth, Railton, Beable, Dowdle, and Moore, or in the absence of Mr. Booth, Messrs. Beable, Railton, Dowdle, Eason, Moore, White, Putter[?], and Thomas.

At Bro. Dowdle's, August 13, 1873. J. C. Moore in chair.

Resolved that Bro. Cornish be Hall Secretary in place of our dear departed Bro. Barber.

That Bro. Edwards' kindly offer be accepted to make tables and trestles by the assistance of Bro. Shaw by Saturday week.

That we have a Tea and public meeting on Monday, 25th August, '73. 100 large bills, 100 large tickets, and that Bro. Corbridge get them. Tea 6d. at 5½.

That Sister Dowdle provide for tea, also cake, as before—that Bros. Gable and Edwards see to the copper and tables.

That the following speakers be published, Bro. Corbridge in the chair—Bros. Bugget, Dowdle, Moore, Jack, and White.

Bro. Corbridge came to the above meeting, when the chairman proposed they should all rise in respect and confidence of their future superintendent for the Shoreditch Circuit.

July 30, 1874. The Rev. W. Booth in chair.

After some conversation and complaints from some present the meeting was adjourned.

Sept. 18, 1874. W. J. Pearson, Chairman.

Proposed by Bro. Gable, seconded by Bro. Cornish, that Bro. Moore's resignation of all his offices be accepted as regards Shoreditch Station. Carried unanimously.

Appendix K

MEMBERSHIP OF THE FIRST CONFERENCE, 1870

The *Conference Journal* gives the membership of the first Conference as follows :

William Booth in the chair. Present : Brothers Maxon (Mackson), Rapson, Lamb, Ritchie, Davis, Hamilton, Hare, Beable,

Corbridge, Allen, Flawn, Rodgers, Jacks, Moore, Longmore, Eason, Wales, Williams, Heigho, Martin, White, Knott, Ferris, Skilton, Barber, Tidman, Brewin, and Mitchell, and Sisters Booth, Short, Diaper, Collingridge, Mathieson, and Tidman. Maxon was secretary and Rapson assistant secretary.

In *Twenty-one Years Salvation Army* (1886), chapter 5, Railton stated that the smallest Conference was composed of eleven members. The basis of this statement would appear to be that Conference of 1871 having directed that eleven of its members who were members of the 1870 Conference should attest the minutes of that occasion, eleven signatures, in addition to that of William Booth, appear thereon in the *Conference Journal*, and this was mistaken for the full membership.

Appendix L

RULES OF THE CHRISTIAN MISSION, 1870

Table of Contents

Doctrines (see Appendix F)

Rules

10 Poor Stewards (in each case two stewards, one acting as treasurer and the other as secretary)

11 Exhorters' Society (charged with planning appointments of exhorters and prayer leaders)

12 Female Preachers (to be eligible for employment as preachers and class leaders and for any office, to speak and vote at all official meetings)

13 Local Preachers

14 Evangelists (elders' meetings to engage)

15 The Itinerant Preachers (engaged at the will of the General Superintendent)

16 Preachers' Meetings (to have the oversight of and be responsible for doctrinal views, pulpit capabilities, and official conduct of all on the plan)

17 Children's Mission

18 Societies and Branch Stations

19 Circuits and their Superintendents (two or more societies grouped together)

20 Quarterly Meetings (composed of the preachers and members of elders' meetings of circuit)

21 Circuit Stewards (treasurer and secretary)

22 Annual Conference

23 The Conference Committee (composed of the General Superintendent, Secretary of Conference, and five members of the Mission to conduct business during the year)

24 Open-air Services (one or more to precede every indoor public service)

25 Public Services

26 Prayer Meetings (one or more to be held at every station every week, and at the close of preaching services)

27 Bible Classes

28 Meeting for promoting Holiness (to be held weekly, on Friday evenings for preference. Detailed instructions as to how meetings are to be conducted and with regard to dealing with penitents)

29 Watchnights

30 Quarterly Fast (members to abstain from food so far as

consistent with health. At large stations services to be continued without intermission)

31 Baptisms (mode left to members. Discussion of the subject strictly forbidden. Not to be imposed upon any having conscientious scruples against it. No baptism by immersion at any station—if desired—to be administered elsewhere)

32 Marriages

33 Lovefeasts (a public lovefeast to be held at least once a quarter)

34 The Lord's Supper (once a month unless two-thirds of the members of a society desire it oftener. Confined to holders of members' tickets or notes of admission. Unfermented wine only to be used)

35 Temperance Societies and Meetings (all meetings to be conducted throughout in a Christian spirit)

36 Bands of Hope

37 Societies seeking union with the Mission

38 Mission Property (see Appendix O)

APPENDIX M

CONDITIONS OF MEMBERSHIP, 1870

Section V of the First Constitution of The Christian Mission, 1870

Members

1 All persons shall be eligible for membership who believe on the Son of God to the salvation of their souls, and shall give evidence thereof by their walk and conversation.

2 All our members shall, if possible, meet in a believers' meeting commonly called a class meeting, in order that they may be counselled and watched over, and that a record may be kept of their residences, so that, in case of absence through sickness or otherwise, they may be visited and cared for.

3 All candidates for membership attending the believers'

meetings shall meet in class not less than eight clear weeks ; and if at the end of that time the leader shall be satisfied of their suitableness for membership, he shall propose their names at the elders' meeting, and if no objection shall be made they shall become members, and receive tickets at the following quarterly visitation ; but if objection be made on account of known immorality, or not complying with the directions laid down in the rules, the matter shall be investigated, if necessary, and they shall be refused membership, continued on trial, or dealt with as shall seem most fitting to such meeting.

4 Persons desirous to be members, but unable to attend a believers' meeting, shall signify the same to the superintendent of the station, or to one of the leaders, who shall bring their names before the elders' meeting, which shall cause inquiries to be made respecting their fitness for membership. If such inquiries shall prove satisfactory, their names and addresses shall be entered in a book kept for the purpose, and they shall receive tickets accordingly. If it be found at the end of eight weeks, by the elders' meeting, that their walk is consistent, they shall receive tickets of full membership, which shall be taken to their place of residence by the superintendent of the station, when inquiries shall be made as to their spiritual progress, suitable counsel given, and prayer offered. If in particular cases this plan be inconvenient, their tickets shall be handed to them in such manner as the elders' meeting may approve.

5 Members removing from one class to another shall explain the reason to their leader previous to their doing so.

6 Each member shall contribute, when convenient, not less than one penny per week, and sixpence per quarter, and as much more as he or she can afford towards the support of the preachers employed in the Mission. Those meeting in class shall give their weekly offering to the leader at the close of each meeting ; but those who do not attend the weekly believers' meeting shall be provided with collecting boxes in which they shall store their weekly offerings, and such offerings shall be collected quarterly.

7   All our members shall be urged to abstain from the use of all intoxicating drinks, except in cases of absolute sickness, and also from smoking, and all other evil and offensive habits.

8   No person shall be received or continued as a member who shall keep a public house or brewery, or be engaged in the demoralizing traffic or sale of intoxicating drinks ; or who shall frequent any public house or dram-shop, except on business ; or who shall sell obscene books or pictures, fortune-telling books or ballads, or any other publications of irreligious tendency, or who shall exhibit bills for theatres, concerts, or balls in their windows or premises.

9   Our members shall not sell or read the *London Journal*, *Family Herald*, or any other publication of similar character.

10 Our members shall not follow the costly and foolish fashions of the world in dress or otherwise ; on the contrary they shall be patterns of modesty and simplicity, as directed in the word of God. 1 Tim. ii. 9, 10 : "In like manner also, that women adorn themselves in modest apparel, with shame-facedness and sobriety ; not with broidered hair, or gold, or pearls, or costly array ; but (which becometh women professing godliness) with good works." 1 Peter iii. 3, 4 : " Whose adorning let it not be that outward adorning of plaiting the hair, and of wearing of gold, or of putting on of apparel ; but let it be the hidden man of the heart, in that which is not corruptible, even the ornament of a meek and quiet spirit, which is in the sight of God of great price."

11 Any members guilty of falsehood, slander, backbiting, habitual frivolous or foolish jesting, drunkenness, divisive or quarrelsome conduct, of wearing fashionable and unbecoming dress, of propagating any doctrine or opinion which is calculated to hinder the work of God and divide the Society, or for the breach of any other of our rules, shall for the first offence be reproved ; for the second, be suspended from membership for such time as the elders' meeting shall think proper ; and for the third, shall be expelled as directed by rule. Should the offence, however, be flagrant or notorious, then, upon due evidence being given before the elders'

meeting, they shall be put out of the Society immediately, and shall only be received back again on proof of repentance satisfactory to the elders' meeting.

12 Should any member consider himself injured by another, he shall conform to our Lord's direction, " If thy brother shall trespass against thee, go and tell him his fault between thee and him alone. If he shall hear thee, thou hast gained thy brother ; but if he will not hear thee, then take with thee one or two more, that in the mouth of two or three witnesses every word may be established ; and if he shall neglect to hear them, tell it unto the church [society, congregation, or assembly] : but if he neglect to hear the church, let him be unto thee as a heathen man and a publican "—Matt. xviii. 15-17. And in the last case the elders' meeting shall deal with the offender according to the rule respecting the expulsion of members.

13 If a member transgress any of these rules, or be overtaken in a fault, his leader, on ascertaining this, shall endeavour to restore him by faithful but affectionate reproof and counsel, and report the case to the elders' meeting. But should the case be grossly immoral, or of public rumour, then it shall be dealt with as to Rule 11 ; but the preacher or leader shall give the offender three days' notice, in writing, specifying the nature of the charge, the name of the person preferring it, and the time and place of trial. Or, should an aggrieved member demand an investigation of his case, he shall give notice thereof, in writing, to the preacher, or leader, who shall fix the time and place for the purpose, and notify the same to the aggrieved person at least three days before the meeting ; at which meeting evidence shall be heard on both sides, and the matter shall be decided by the elders' meeting.

14 Should a member feel himself aggrieved by the decision of the elders' meeting, he may appeal to the next quarterly meeting, upon giving one week's notice to the superintendent and the elders' meeting ; which meeting shall take the necessary steps to furnish the quarterly meeting with the evidence laid before it. The appellant shall have the right of being present with any witnesses, at both the elders' and the quarterly meetings.

15 Should a member be of opinion that the decision of the quarterly meeting has not been a righteous one, he may appeal to the General Superintendent, who shall advise with the Conference committee, examine the evidence, and give a final decision.

16 A person shall not necessarily be disqualified for membership by differing with us on minor questions of doctrine, unless such difference, in the judgment of the elders' meeting, is likely to hinder the usefulness and mar the peace of the Society.

17 Persons belonging to other churches seeking membership with us shall be admitted on presentation of their note of transfer, if such can be obtained.

18 All our members shall be especially careful of each other's reputation, watch lovingly over each other's welfare, and promote it so far as lies in their power :

1 By praying for each other.

2 By sympathy and practical help in the time of poverty, affliction, bereavement, or any other kind of tribulation.

3 By never allowing evil to be spoken of them unrebuked, by anyone, in their absence.

Appendix N

RULES OF THE CHRISTIAN MISSION, 1875

At the 1874 Conference it was resolved :

That Bros. W. B. Booth, Anthony, and Hitchcock and Sister Billups be a committee to prepare a concise statement of the Rules of The Christian Mission touching members for general circulation among our people, and a revised edition of the Rules to be published as soon as possible.

This statement was presented to the 1875 Conference, adopted, and printed. Conditions of membership were thus set out :

1 Anyone can become a member of the Mission who is turned from darkness to light, and from the power of Satan unto God, and who lives consistently with such a change.

2 Each member's name shall be recorded in the roll of a believers' meeting which he attends once a week, unless unavoidably prevented.

3 Members who cannot attend the believers' meeting shall be visited by the evangelist of the district.

4 Each member shall contribute according as God shall enable him to the funds of the Mission.

5 All members are entreated to abstain from the use of intoxicating liquors or tobacco.

6 No one can be a member of the Mission who deals in intoxicating drink, who frequents a public house or dram-shop except on business, who sells obscene books or pictures, fortune-telling books or ballads, or any other publications of an irreligious tendency, who exhibits bills for theatres, concerts, or balls, or who does not dress with Christian simplicity.

No person would be disqualified for membership on account of minor differences in doctrine provided such did not cause dissension in the Society.

Rules regarding procedure at Conference and Conference committee meetings ; the programme of the activities of the Mission ; appointment of officers (a treasurer and secretary for every station were essential) and of evangelists ; and doctrines (Appendix F) were dealt with in other sections.

APPENDIX O

MISSION PROPERTY

The 1870 Constitution of The Christian Mission (Section 38) provided :

1 All the property, freehold and leasehold, bought or erected wholly or partially with money contributed by the Mission,

or given to the Mission, shall be the property of the general Mission, and settled on trust accordingly.

2 A trust deed shall be prepared which shall serve as a model deed for all places belonging to the Mission.

(Such trust deed will provide that, when the income appropriated to the support of the building shall not be equal to the expenditure, and the trustees are satisfied they will be involved in difficulties, they shall have power to sell the property ; provided always, that in such a case the property shall first be offered to the Conference. But should the Conference decline to become the purchaser or to relieve them of their liabilities, then the trustees shall have power to sell to any other parties, provided further, that, should the purchase money exceed the liabilities, the balance shall be paid over to the treasurer for the benefit of the Mission.)

3 Twelve persons shall be selected in the first instance by the General Superintendent, who shall hold in trust for the purposes of the Mission all the property of the Mission. As vacancies occur in this number by death, removal to reside in foreign parts, bankruptcy, or mental incapacity from affliction, or resignation, such vacancies shall be filled by the Conference.

4 All the premises rented for the purposes of the Mission shall be held for the Mission ; and when possible, several persons whose names shall be approved by the superintendent of the circuit shall be associated together in the tenancy of any places held for the Mission.

5 In none of our places of worship shall any sittings be let or set apart for any person or persons for pecuniary consideration.

6 None of our places of worship shall be used or let for penny readings, secular concerts, political meetings, or any meetings of a similar character.

7 On all occasions where any service of sacred song is held in any of our premises, it shall be interspersed with prayer and exhortation ; but in no case shall any unconverted person be engaged to publicly take part in such service.

At the 1873 Conference it was resolved :

That in every case where property is rented for services, the person or persons in whose names the place is taken shall sign a document to the effect that they hold the said property only on trust for the Mission.

This Conference also accepted a provisional trust deed and ordered that all property of the Mission should be immediately settled accordingly, but the terms of this deed were not recorded.

The 1875 Conference also considered a model deed and after it had been read over resolved :

That the Conveyance of Land at North Woolwich marked B which has been read throughout to this Conference be now approved, and that the same serves as a deed of reference for the settlement of Mission halls on trusts for the benefit of The Christian Mission.

[This deed, unfortunately, was destroyed when The Salvation Army's International Headquarters was burnt down in 1941.]

For the provision made for the General Superintendent to be sole trustee, see Appendix R, Foundation Deed of The Salvation Army, 1878.

THE WHITBY POSTERS

WAR ! WAR ! IN WHITBY

2,000

MEN AND WOMEN

Wanted at once to join the Hallelujah Army,
That is making an attack on the Devil's Kingdom
every Sunday in

ST. HILDA'S HALL at 11 a.m., 3 and 6.30 p.m.

And every week night in the Old Town Hall at 7.30

To be led by CAPTAIN CADMAN from London
Evangelist of The Christian Mission

MR. BOOTH THE GENERAL

of the

HALLELUJAH ARMY

is coming to

WHITBY

TO REVIEW THE TROOPS

GREAT BATTLES

WILL BE FOUGHT

Appendix Q

DATE OF THE CHANGE OF NAME

By comparing the contents of the printer's proof and the completed report and appeal of The Christian Mission (1878), it is possible to arrive at a conclusion as to when the name " The Salvation Army " was hit upon.

The leaflet contains a list of the stations of the Mission. In the completed copy this occupies two pages ; from the proof one of the pages is missing. Comparing, however, the portion of the list in the proof with the same portion in the completed copy it is found :

1 St. Leonards, which appears on the proof, is absent from the completed leaflet.
   At the 1878 Conference (August) William Booth reported, " We have relinquished some small stations during the year," and named St. Leonards as one of them.

2 The following stations, which appear in both lists, were reported in the *Christian Mission Magazine* for June 1878 as opened on the dates appended :
   North Shields, 22nd April ; Spennymoor, 28th April ; South Shields, 29th April ; Rotherham, Bishop Auckland, Dowlais, specific dates not given, but evidently during April.

3 Barnsley is reported in the *Christian Mission Magazine* for July 1878 as having been opened on 26th May. It is crowded in at the end of the list in the completed leaflet.

4 In the same issue of the magazine, Blaydon-on-Tyne is reported as having been opened on 19th May, but it is not shown in the list of stations.

From this information it would appear that William Booth made the historic alteration that gave The Salvation Army its name, at the latest, early in the month of May 1878. The reason why Barnsley appears and not Blaydon is probably that the arrangements for the opening of the first were completed earlier than for the second.

In *Captain Ted* (1880), Railton stated incidentally that the name, Salvation Army, had been taken months before the War Congress (August 1878).

Appendix R

THE FOUNDATION DEED OF
THE SALVATION ARMY, 1878

INLAND
REVENUE
STAMP
10S.

TO ALL TO WHOM THESE PRESENTS SHALL COME I William Booth of 3 Gore Road Victoria Park Road Hackney in the county of Middlesex Minister of the Gospel the founder and General Superintendent for the time being of The Christian Mission Send Greeting.

Whereas in the year 1865 the said William Booth commenced preaching the Gospel in a tent erected in the Friends Burial Ground Thomas Street in the parish of Whitechapel in the County of Middlesex and in other places in the same neighbourhood.

And whereas a number of people were formed into a Community or Society by the said William Booth for the purpose of enjoying religious fellowship and in order to continue and multiply such efforts as had been made in the tent to bring under the Gospel those who were not in the habit of attending any place of worship by preaching in the open air in Tents Theatres Music Halls and other places and by holding other religious services or meetings.

And whereas at the first the said Society was known by the name of the East London Revival Society and afterwards as the East London Christian Mission.

And whereas other Societies were afterwards added in different parts of London and a Society was also formed at Croydon.

And whereas the name of these united Societies was then altered to that of " The Christian Mission."

And whereas divers halls or Meeting-houses School-rooms

Vestries lands buildings and appurtenances situate lying and being in various parts of Her Majesty's dominions and elsewhere have been or are intended to be and hereafter may be given and conveyed to certain persons in such gifts and conveyances named and to be named upon trusts for the purposes therein and herein mentioned or any of them and generally for promoting the objects of the said Christian Mission under the direction of the General Superintendent.

And whereas in order to render valid and effectual such trusts to remove doubts and prevent litigation in the interpretation thereof or as to the terms used therein to ascertain what is the name or title and what are and what shall be for ever the doctrines of the said Christian Mission and also in order to preserve the system of the said Christian Mission generally by means of a General Superintendent it has been deemed expedient to make and execute these presents.

Now these presents witness that for the purposes aforesaid I the said William Booth Do hereby declare :—

Firstly : That the name style and title by which the said religious community or mission hereinbefore described hath during the last nine years been called known and recognised is " The Christian Mission."

Secondly : That the religious doctrines professed believed and taught by the Members of the said Christian Mission are and shall for ever be as follows :—

1 We believe that the Scriptures of the Old and New Testaments were given by inspiration of God and that they only constitute the Divine rule of Christian faith and practice.

2 We believe there is only one God who is infinitely perfect the Creator Preserver and Governor of all things and who is the only proper object of religious worship.

3 We believe that there are three persons in the Godhead the Father the Son and the Holy Ghost undivided in essence and co-equal in power and glory.

4 We believe that in the person of Jesus Christ the Divine and human natures are united so that He is truly and properly God and truly and properly man.

5 We believe that our first parents were created in a state of innocency but by their disobedience they lost their purity and happiness and that in consequence of their fall all men have become sinners totally depraved and as such are justly exposed to the wrath of God.

6 We believe that the Lord Jesus Christ has by His suffering and death made an atonement for the whole world so that whosoever will may be saved.

7 We believe that repentance towards God faith in our Lord Jesus Christ and regeneration by the Holy Spirit are necessary to salvation.

8 We believe that we are justified by grace through faith in our Lord Jesus Christ and that he that believeth hath the witness in himself.

9 We believe that continuance in a state of salvation depends upon continued obedient faith in Christ.

10 We believe that it is the privilege of all believers to be " wholly sanctified " and that " their whole spirit and soul and body " may " be preserved blameless unto the coming of our Lord Jesus Christ " (1 Thess. v. 23).

11 We believe in the immortality of the soul in the resurrection of the body in the general judgment at the end of the world in the eternal happiness of the righteous and in the endless punishment of the wicked.

Thirdly : That the said Christian Mission is and shall be always hereafter under the oversight direction and control of some one person who shall be the General Superintendent thereof whose duty it shall be to determine and enforce the discipline and laws and superintend the operations of the said Christian Mission and to conserve the same to and for the objects and purposes for which it was first originated.

The General Superintendent shall have power to expend on behalf of The Christian Mission all monies contributed for the general purposes of the said Christian Mission or for any of the special objects or operations thereof but he shall annually publish a Balance Sheet (duly audited) of all such receipts and expenditure.

The General Superintendent shall have power to acquire by

gift purchase or otherwise any Hall or Meeting-house School-room Vestry land building and appurtenances and any seats fittings furniture or other property whatsoever which may in his judgment be required for the purposes of the said Christian Mission and to build upon such land or alter or pull down any such buildings and to hire on lease or otherwise any land or buildings and to lend give away let sell or otherwise dispose of any such property land or buildings as he may deem necessary in the interests of the said Christian Mission wherein all Trustees shall render him every assistance and he may in all such cases as he shall deem it expedient so to do nominate and appoint Trustees or a Trustee of any part or parts respectively of such property and direct the conveyance or transfer thereof to such Trustees or Trustee with power for the General Superintendent to declare the trusts thereof and from time to time if it shall seem expedient to him so to do to revoke any such trusts or the appointment of such Trustees or Trustee and upon such revocation the same property shall be conveyed or transferred to such person or persons and upon such trusts as he may direct but only for the benefit of the said Christian Mission.

Fourthly : That the said William Booth shall continue to be for the term of his natural life the General Superintendent of The Christian Mission unless he shall resign such office.

Fifthly : That the said William Booth and every General Super-intendent who shall succeed him shall have power to appoint his successor to the Office of General Superintendent and all the rights powers and authorities of the Office shall vest in the person so appointed upon the decease of the said William Booth or other General Superintendent appointing him or at such other period as may be named in the document appointing him.

Sixthly : That it shall be the duty of every General Superintendent to make in writing as soon as conveniently may be after his appointment a statement as to his Successor or as to the means which are to be taken for the appointment of a Successor at the decease of the General Superintendent or upon his ceasing to perform the duties of the office such statement to be signed by the General Superintendent and delivered in a sealed envelope to the Solicitor for the time being of The Christian Mission but such statement may be altered at will by the General Superintendent at any time during his continuance in office upon a new statement being signed by him and delivered as before mentioned to such Solicitor as aforesaid.

In witness whereof I the said William Booth hath [*sic*] hereunto subscribed my name and affixed my Seal this seventh day of August in the year of Redemption One thousand eight hundred and seventy-eight.

Signed Sealed and Delivered }
by the said William Booth }   WILLIAM BOOTH   *Seal*
in the presence of }

THOS. WHITTINGTON
   3 Bishopsgate Street Without, Solr.
J. E. BILLUPS

This Deed was duly presented to and approved by the persons assembled at a General Meeting of the Christian Mission held at 272 Whitechapel Road in the county of Middlesex.

And we the undersigned William Booth and George Scott Railton do hereby in the name of The Christian Mission set our hands hereto in ratification of and for perpetuating testimony of this Deed.

Dated this same 7th day of August 1878.

Witnesses to both signatures   General Superintendent
   THOS. WHITTINGTON   WILLIAM BOOTH
   J. E. BILLUPS

                G. S. RAILTON
                Secretary of The Christian Mission

Enrolled in the High Court of Justice (Chancery   *Seal of the*
Division) the 13th day of August in the year of our   *Enrolment Office in*
Lord 1878 (being first duly stamped) according to   *Chancery*
the tenor of the statutes made for that purpose.

72 P   GEO. THOS. JENKINS,
                        C. R. W.

BE IT REMEMBERED and entered as of Record that Whereas the Society called and known previously to the end of the year One thousand eight hundred and seventy-eight as "The Christian Mission" was on or about the first day of January One thousand eight hundred and seventy-nine with a view to the more beneficially extending of its operations renamed and has been since that time and is now usually known as "The Salvation Army."

Now I William Booth the General of The Salvation Army (and also the General Superintendent of The Christian Mission) do hereby by virtue of all and every powers and authority in me vested declare that the said Society formerly known and in the within written Deed described as The Christian Mission is now and is intended to be hereafter called and known or described for all public purposes of its operations as " The Salvation Army " and that the expression " The Christian Mission " in the within Deed contained shall be taken to mean " The Salvation Army " and that everything in the within Deed contained relating or referring to The Christian Mission shall be taken as relating or referring to " The Salvation Army."

In witness whereof I have hereto set my hand this twenty-fourth day of June One thousand eight hundred and eighty.

WILLIAM BOOTH

Witness, THOS. WHITTINGTON

Enrolled in the Central Office of the Supreme Court of Judicature the twentieth day of April in the year of our Lord 1906.

42 P Fos. 4. 4/-

Seal of the Supreme Court of Judicature, Central Office, Enrolment Department

APPENDIX S

RELIEF OF DISTRESS IN EAST LONDON

Round the administration of relief in East London raged a considerable storm. The *Saturday Review* (25th January 1868) attacked with great bitterness The East London Mission and Relief Society which was using, the *Review* declared, the considerable sum of money the public had subscribed in response to its appeals to " tempt the poor to worship by the bait of a breakfast and coal ticket " : in short, they were spending the money in furthering the interests of their own and other missions rather than that of the poor.

The *Saturday Review*, on the one hand, attacked the clergy of the East End for alleged failure to keep account of the funds administered by them, while, on the other hand, the *Church Review* (29th May 1869) protested that the East London Relief Society " with its propaganda of tracts and teas and blankets " had " ignored the clergy and filled the pawnshops."

Joining in the fray later came the *Christian* (22nd November 1877) with an attack on the Charity Organisation Society for " assuming to itself the office of inquisitor-general of benevolent agencies " and saying it " did not know any society which has done so little good and so much mischief during its brief term of life."

The irony of the whole controversy was that the agency that got the most abuse from the secular press—The Christian Mission —was one that had taken the greatest pains to avoid indiscriminate charity, with the exception of assisting in the provision of a few free breakfasts paid for by certain charitable individuals ; that had been most exact in accounting for the spending of money entrusted to it (see Appendix I : Balance Sheets) ; and that, while not neglecting the spiritual needs of the people, had in no way made attendance at meetings, or profession of religion, conditions of receiving help. Furthermore, a strict line was drawn by the Mission between funds contributed specifically for the helping of its members, many of whom were in direst need, and money given for general relief.

William Booth's abhorrence of the use of " coal and blanket " methods of trying to secure converts was well known to all who had close contact with him. " No compulsion will for a moment be allowed with respect to religion," he stated in *In Darkest England and the Way Out* (1890), and one of the fundamental conditions of admission to any institution of his scheme was : " No benefit will be conferred upon any individual except under extraordinary circumstances without some return being made in labour." His conclusions, he stated, were based upon his experience since his first attempts to reach the starving and hungry crowds. It would seem that his recognition of the danger of the Mission's drifting into the use of such methods led to the cessation of attempts at general relief which, after all, were too small to make much difference to the situation, until he was able some ten years later to resume them upon a larger scale and under conditions that had nothing in common with " coal and blanket " proselytism.

Speaking at Penzance (June 1882), William Booth declared :
Free teas, petticoats and blankets made many hypocrites ; no money was given—not even to those who had just been saved, except in very exceptional circumstances, though the Soldiers seemed to love and help each other, and God most surely helped the converted who relied on His help.

And at Oldham, later in the same year, he made the significant statement that he had found out that though they might bribe people to come and hear the Gospel by a "free tea, supper or breakfast, gruel, etc.," in fact when a working man got a ticket he gave it to his wife, and his wife gave it to the children, and the children as soon as they had eaten the " stuff " went off.

BIBLIOGRAPHY

Official Records of The Christian Mission

First Report, 1867 ; How to Reach the Masses with the Gospel, 1872 ; Plan for Whitechapel Circuit, 1872 ; The Masses Reached, 1873 ; Annual Reports, 1877 and 1878.
The Conference Journal, 1870–1878. Minutes of : The Christian Mission Committee (Council), 1868–1874 ; The Conference Committee, 1875–1877 ; Shoreditch Circuit Elders' Meeting, September 1869–October 1871.
Letter-books, 1875–1878.

Periodicals of The Christian Mission and The Salvation Army

The East London Evangelist (monthly), October 1868–December 1869. *The Christian Mission Magazine* (monthly), 1870–1878. *The Salvationist* (monthly), 1879.
The War Cry, No. 1, 27th December 1879 (weekly ; twice weekly from 12th October 1882 to 13th February 1886).
"Fifty Years of Fighting. Events in the Life of Commissioner Ridsdel." By Arthur Copping. Serial in the *War Cry*, 23rd June–25th August 1923.
All the World (monthly), January 1894, June and August 1897, February 1912.

Books of The Christian Mission and The Salvation Army

Heathen England and What to do for it, by George Railton (1st edition 1877 ; 2nd, 1878 ; 3rd, 1879 ; 5th, 1880)
Behind the Pigeon Shop, by George S. Railton (1878)
Mother Moore, by George Railton (1880)
The Salvation Navvy. The Life of John Allen, by Commissioner Railton (1880)

Twenty-one Years Salvation Army, by George S. Railton (1886)
In Darkest England and the Way Out, by General Booth (1890)
General Booth, by W. T. Stead (Isbister, 1891)
Catherine Booth, by F. de L. Booth-Tucker (1892)
Three Coronations (Life of Staff Captain Minnie Stabb), by Mildred Duff. No. vii of " The Warriors' Library " (1903)
Commissioner Dowdle: the Saved Railway Guard, by George Scott Railton
General Booth, by George S. Railton (Hodder and Stoughton, 1912)
General William Booth, by Harold Begbie (Macmillan, 1919)
Commissioner Railton, by Eileen Douglas and Mildred Duff (1920)
Echoes and Memories, by Bramwell Booth (Hodder and Stoughton, 1925)
Catherine Booth och Salvationismen, by Dr. Laura Petri (Lund, 1925)
The Happy Warrior, Life Story of Commissioner Cadman, by Humphrey Wallis (1928)
These Fifty Years, by Bramwell Booth, C. H. (Cassell, 1929)
Marianne Pawson, the " Zulu Queen," by Ruth Tracy (1944)

RELIGIOUS PERIODICALS

The Methodist New Connexion Magazine June 1855
The Revival 1859–1869. Name changed to *The Christian* 1870–1878
The Nonconformist 1860–1868
The Baptist Almanac 1863
The Wesleyan Times 1865
The Methodist Recorder 3rd November 1865
The Christian Advocate and Review No. 59, January 1866
The Christian Times 1866–1868
The Christian World 1866–1868
The British Friend 1868
The Christian Year Book 1868 (Jackson, Walford and Hodder)
The Church Review 1869

RECORDS OF RELIGIOUS ORGANIZATIONS

The Methodist New Connexion General Rules, 1823

Minutes of the New Connexion Conference : Nottingham, 1857 ; Hull, 1858 ; Liverpool, 1861 ; Dudley, 1862

Minutes of the Primitive Methodist Conference, Sheffield, 1862

Minutes of the Wesleyan Methodist Conference, Camborne, 1862

Minutes of the Trustees (Society of Friends) owning the White-chapel Burial Ground, 18th July 1864, *et seq.* to September 1865

Membership Rolls of the London District of the Society of Friends, 1864

History of The Christian Community and Reports of Anniversary Meetings, 1865 and 1866

The Open Air Mission, Annual Report, 1866, and *Life of Gawin Kirkham*, by Frank Cockrem (Morgan and Scott, 1894)

The Evangelisation Society ; " Objects and Principles," and Minutes of Meetings of the Committee, 1867–1869

The Story of The Evangelisation Society, by the honorary secretary, John Wood (1907)

BIOGRAPHIES AND OTHER BOOKS

Henry Reed : Incidents in an Eventful Life, and *The Dunorlan Tracts* (1873) ; and *Henry Reed : an Eventful Life devoted to God and Man*, by Margaret S. E. Reed (Morgan and Scott, 1907)

Life of Reginald Radcliffe (Morgan and Scott, 1875)

A Collection of Sermons by Rowland Hill, by Edward W. Broome (1881)

Man's Partnership with Divine Providence, the 38th Fernley Lecture, by the Rev. John Telford, B.A. (Robert Culley, 1908)

Richard Cope Morgan : His Life and Times, by George E. Morgan (Morgan and Scott, 1909)

God: the Invisible King, by H. G. Wells (Cassell, 1917)

Freeman of Shanghai, by F. de Lautour Tucker (Marshall Bros., 1923)

NEWSPAPERS

Hansard 24th February 1860
The Times 2nd July 1864
The British Standard 28th September 1866
The Pall Mall Gazette 12th, 13th, 15th, and 16th January 1866
The Lancet 3rd February 1866
The East London Observer 1866–1868 and 17th March 1877
The Saturday Review 1868
The Morning Advertiser 1869
The Eastern Post 4th July 1869

HISTORICAL, ETC.

Pamphlet on Whitechapel, by George Goodwin, Editor of *The Builder*, *circa* 1865
London Directories 1865–1875
Report of Medical Officer of the Privy Council on the Cholera Epidemic in East of London (31st March 1867)
The Charity Organisation Society.   Reports of the District Committees and of the Council, London, 1877
" History of Bethnal Green " (*Eastern Argus*, 1877)
Old and New London, by Walter Thornbury (Cassell, Petter and Galpin, 1879–1885)
London at a Glance (1885)
London Past and Present, by Henry B. Wheatley (John Murray, 1891)
London Burial Grounds, by Mrs. Basil Holmes (1896)
" East London Antiquities," by C. G. Smithers (*East London Advertiser*, 1902)
The Co-Partnership Herald (The Commercial Gas Co., Stepney)
Alcohol and the Nation, by George B. Wilson (Nicholson and Watson, 1940)

INDEX

PRINTED IN GREAT BRITAIN AT
THE PRESS OF THE PUBLISHERS